D1388902

THE
CROWDING
SYNDROME

Other books by the author:

The Invisible Scar
Born Female

Caroline Bird

THE CROWDING SYNDROME

Learning to Live with
Too Much and Too Many

DAVID McKAY COMPANY, INC.
New York

THE CROWDING SYNDROME

COPYRIGHT © 1972 BY CAROLINE BIRD

LIBRARY OF CONGRESS CATALOG CARD NUMBER: 75-188260

MANUFACTURED IN THE UNITED STATES OF AMERICA

To my son Johnny
and all his friends

Acknowledgments

My first debt is to Helene Mandelbaum, whose creative editing made a book out of a loose mass of data and insights. Without obtruding views of her own, she asked questions which compelled me to arrive at slightly different conclusions than either of us expected. She made me think better.

Magazine editors encouraged me by letting me do articles on various aspects of my subject. They are: *Glamour*, July 1969, "The Search for Privacy"; *Personnel*, September-October 1969, "Talent Squeeze in Middle Management"; *New York*, March 16, 1970, "What New York Can Learn from the World's Largest City"; *Think*, May-June 1970, "The GNP—A Beast to Be Bridled?" My study, "The Communications Explosion in the President's Office" was distributed to members of The Presidents Association of the American Management Association in September-October 1969.

In 1969 I felt I had to lay eyes on Japan to see how another culture coped with crowding. David Riesman and Reuel Denney put me in touch with Japanese sociologists. Dero Saunders, managing editor of *Forbes*, gave me assignments to explore the economy of Japan which helped to get me there and put me in touch with helpful business figures. The Society of Magazine Writers Charitable Trust helped with a cash grant for out-of-pocket travel.

People who not only listened to me while I was developing the concept but actually read part or all of some of the drafts include John and Carol Barach, Barbara Currier, Reuel Denney, Stephen Dunwell, Clay Felker, Peter French, Howard Greenwald, Patricia Haskell, Faye Henle, James Grier Miller, Richard Meier, Harry Runyan, Diarmuid Russell, Alvin Toffler, Ray Vogel, and information specialists at the Bell Laboratories. Leslie Koempel made detailed suggestions on the final draft. Many specialists generously checked facts for me, among them Myra Barrer, James Brain, Robert Carpenter, Stanley Ferguson, Jeh Johnson, Sanders A. Kahn, and Herman Miller.

Special thanks go to Helen Runyan who let me hole up incommunicado at The Captain's House in Chatham on Cape Cod for a month of brooding and writing in September 1970, and to The MacDowell Colony in Peterborough, New Hampshire, where I spent another month of serious writing in 1971. The book could not have been written without the help of many reference librarians, especially Joan Murphy, Frances Goudy, and Marguerite B. Hubbard of the Vassar College Library and those of the Adriance Library in Poughkeepsie who procured endless photocopies of scholarly papers from the New York State Library in Albany.

Esther Vail cheerfully and faithfully typed the many drafts. Beth Ashenburg, Sherry Daniels, Marge Godfrey, Gail Justin, Silvia Merino, and Sandra Harris checked facts and did library research.

Finally, I owe a great deal to the patience and moral support of my husband, Tom Mahoney, who in addition to his usual flow of relevant information, contributed instant sympathy at the moments when it was needed most.

Foreword

The decade of the 1960s, which began with high hopes, ended in doubt and confusion. The war in Vietnam was the focal point of American political unrest, but it was not the only cause of our national uncertainty. We learned from that war that the United States cannot control the shape of societies a half a world away, however powerful we may be. At home we learned that abundance, technological genius and organizational skills are no guarantee against poverty, massive breakdowns in electric power systems, communications and transportation, and serious threats to life from the waste products of our crowded society.

Malthusian pessimism and revolutionary rhetoric have been natural by-products of the crisis of abundance that Caroline Bird describes in such vivid detail. Ms. Bird does not accept the argument that only rigid, mechanical limitations on population growth and social organization can save us from destruction. She invites us to explore solutions to the problems abundance has brought us. She is not persuaded that we will fail, and asks us to examine with her a number of possible new approaches to the dilemma of breakdowns which accompany growth, and poverty which accompanies plenty. She offers the information needed to understand our paradoxes and the refreshingly hopeful idea that we can develop new national policies to provide sensible use of our resources and talents.

Foreword

Ms. Bird reminds us that history provides frequent instances of "overload" followed by breakdown, in which a restructuring of the social and economic systems has usually resulted in preventing seemingly inevitable disaster and chaos. Slowdowns, as she points out, have the virtue of giving us time to examine new ways of dealing with expanding populations, environmental pollution, overburdened equipment and facilities, and wasted resources.

Such problems cannot be overcome by insisting that the *status quo* be maintained. Neither can they be resolved by ignoring our capacity to adapt ourselves and our institutions to new circumstances. In the final analysis, *The Crowding Syndrome* is an argument for the vitality of democratic institutions and their ability, given an educated electorate and committed leadership, to overcome the most frightful threats to humanity.

Within these pages you will not find comfort nor a prescription for a twentieth-century utopia. You will find a view of the wrongs of the abundant society as we know it, and the basic resource of human nature that can be applied to right these wrongs through voluntary movements and legislative action. This is, in short, no lament for a lost world, but a challenge to a free society to make the most of its creative and humanitarian capacities.

Edmund S. Muskie
Washington, D.C.

Contents

THE
CROWDING
SYNDROME

Chapter I

Breakdown!

The house lights in the central power control room flickered before the instruments registered trouble. The telephone rang, and the man monitoring the dials stopped long enough to answer it. "I don't know myself," he said.

As he hung up, the lights all over the city went out.

With the lights went subway service, commuter trains, television stations, movie screens, theater stages, gasoline pumps, furnaces, air conditioners, elevators, refrigerators, food freezers, milking machines, factory lines, printing presses, electrically operated garage doors, and all the computers.

About the only things left working were automobiles, battery-operated radio receivers, telephones and broadcasting stations with their own power.

People and things were stuck wherever they happened to be—in the air, in skyscraper elevators, in subway trains, in tunnels, on bridges. But there was no panic, less crime than usual, and more human courtesy and resourcefulness.

74-05522

A doctor delivered the second of twins by flashlight. A famous pianist gave his concert in the dark. When the runway vanished beneath him, a pilot landed his 80 passengers by the light of the moon. Following planes found other airports. A hospital rescued its blood supply from the warming cooler and put it outside in the cool fall night. To save his tropical snakes, a zookeeper brought in portable propane gas heaters.

This is not science fiction. It all happened on the night of November 9, 1965, when, at 5:15 P.M. electric power suddenly and mysteriously failed for 30 million people, most of them living in the densely populated, affluent New York-Boston megalopolis. Reaching out to each other in the dark, strangers talked about the Chinese atom bomb, the hot line, the chances of sabotage. Word quickly spread through transistor radio sets that it was not a civil defense drill or a trick pulled off by demonstrators, but a simple power failure. Most people shrugged, expecting the lights to go on momentarily. But in New York City they did not go on until morning, and it was weeks before everything was running smoothly.

The Consolidated Edison plants which supply electricity to New York City are part of the Northeast Power Grid. This is a network of lines and plants that enables individual utility companies to help each other, to pool their power, and sometimes to substitute cheap hydroelectric power from Niagara Falls for the power that is produced more expensively by steam generators. The grid is in two connected parts—New Jersey-Pennsylvania-Maryland, and Ontario-New York-New England. These or parts of either can be disconnected by human decision or by automatic safety devices which are supposed to make a massive power failure impossible.

It took six days of feverish investigation to find out how the "impossible" had happened, and the explanation was not reassuring. Engineers warned that the same thing could, and unless drastic action was taken, most probably would, happen again. "Cascading" overload had finally broken the system. What had happened was this:

At the peak of the New York rush hour, when power systems as far north as Canada were sending electricity toward Manhattan, a relay in the Sir Adam Beck Station No. 2, an obscure installation in Ontario four miles west of Niagara Falls, conked out. Investigation revealed that the relay, a telephone-sized automatic control device to regulate current, was improperly set.

When it failed, surges of power rushed from one power system into another, knocking them out in domino fashion. The flow of power southward was reversed and became a massive drain. This pulled out all of New York City's generators before the man at the Energy Control Center of Con Edison could push the buttons that would have cut New York out of the grid. All his conditioning had been to save the grid, so he didn't cut out until too late. Other controllers had reacted the same way. Rescuer after rescuer had gone down with the victim.

Automatic switches safely disconnected the New Jersey-Pennsylvania-Maryland part of the grid in the crisis. Circuit breakers protected the state of Maine, Staten Island, and part of Brooklyn. The Stony Brook, New York, area was saved by an alert supervisor who pulled a switch. But at the height of the blackout all the rest of the vast Ontario-New York-New England area was without power. Men and machines had been defeated by overload.

● *Overloaded Traffic*

Seven weeks later, on New Year's Day 1966, New Yorkers had another object lesson in overload. The subway and bus workers went out on strike. The paralysis cost business

$100 million a day. Hospitals ran short of blood because donors couldn't get to collection centers. But the most impressive phenomenon of the tie-up was the monumental traffic jam produced by thousands of workers struggling to get into Manhattan by commuter train or private car. Passengers brushed by conductors to overload Long Island trains headed for the city, and in the evening, the line of passengers waiting to board homebound commuter trains at Grand Central Station was 6000 people long. Bridges and streets were jammed with cars. So many people tried to walk that the sidewalks were overloaded, too.

The strike was a reminder that Manhattan is becoming dependent on workers who live increasingly farther away, and who come into town on inadequate transportation facilities. During the strike, thousands of commuters insisted on using their own cars. There is only one off-street parking place in Manhattan for every 50 cars coming into it, so parking places were grimly hunted and fiercely contested, occasionally by drivers who got out of their cars and assailed each other with their fists. There weren't enough policemen to tag illegally parked cars; some people simply put garbage cans over fire hydrants when that was the only space. There weren't enough clerks to track down people who ignored tickets that the police *did* hand out. Streets were so jammed with parked cars and stalled traffic that fire trucks and ambulances couldn't get through. In desperation, police tried to tow away illegally parked cars, but there weren't enough tow trucks for the job.

• *Overloaded Garbagemen*

In February, 1968, two years later, a sanitation strike piled New York sidewalks and alleys with more than 100,000 tons of uncollected garbage and gave New Yorkers a whiff

4

of the garbage overload. Thirteen percent of the land area of New York City had once been dump, but city planners now estimate that by 1978, the city will run completely out of space in which to put the garbage. There aren't many feasible alternatives. There are legal and ecological objections to dumping in the open sea. Industrial wastes carried by New Jersey rivers have already created a vast dead area in the Atlantic just outside the harbor. City incinerators are violating the clean air laws.

"See those gray hairs?" the Superintendent of Fresh Kills, Staten Island, the city's last dump, told a reporter. "Every one's a barge that took too long to unload. No one realizes the pressure here. If we break down, it backs up into the city."

- *Overloaded Stockmarket*

During 1968, the New York Stock Exchange also came close to breakdown although officials realized this only later. On April 1, 1968, 17.7 million shares were traded, surpassing for the first time the ominous record of October 29, 1929, the worst day of the Great Crash. But unlike that unhappy day, trading continued high the next day and the day after to an all-time record of more than 21 million shares on June 13.

Brokers weren't prepared to handle the business. They had never bothered to modernize the clerical procedures for exchanging stock certificates. Transferring a share of stock takes more than 80 clerical steps, many of them mirror-image duplicates of the same step on the other side of the transaction. Errors mounted. Stock certificates worth more than 3 billion dollars were not delivered to their buyers within the time prescribed by Exchange rules.

Dozens of suggestions were made on how to reform,

automate, and simplify the system, but all took money and time. While waiting, Wall Street tried to trim down business to its real capacity. In January 1968, the New York Stock Exchange started closing at 2 instead of 3:30 P.M. In June, it started closing a whole day every week and ordered 35 member firms whose records were snarled to stop soliciting new business until they cleaned up the mess.

Self-regulation did not really help. By December 1968, $4 billion in securities were undelivered—more than the capital of all the firms on the Big Board, and a dangerously big wad of negotiable paper for any system to misplace, let alone one which lives by the faith that a man's word is his bond. The confusion was very tempting to the underworld. During that year the Mafia infiltrated the backroom of Hayden Stone & Co., and engineered the transfer of a million dollars worth of IBM stock certificates to a bankrupt Pennsylvania insurance company. Securities worth $500 million were stolen from overworked and careless brokers in the next two years.

When recession set in, the cure was worse than the disease. The volume fell as the market declined, so that brokerage fees dropped significantly while the costs of modernizing the paperwork continued to rise. Small brokers merged. Some quit. Hayden Stone paid a record fine of $150,000 for violating procedural rules and reorganized.

The overload did not lead to a market crash. But it was the straw that precipitated a near breakdown for the telephone system.

• *Overloaded Phones*

Wall Street is the heaviest and least predictable user of the telephone. During the rising market of the late 1960s, demand for service on Wall Street rose more than four times as fast as the company or the Stock Exchange expected. It takes 18 months to build a new telephone exchange, and the company was as reluctant as the brokers to invest in capacity for a demand that might disappear as abruptly as it had come. By the time the stock market was in frank overload, exchanges were operating at peak load, which meant that the dial tone went dead when there was a flurry of calls in response to an event such as the assassination of Martin Luther King, or a storm that knocked out the electricity.

Such a catastrophe was unwittingly provided by the Stock Exchange itself. When hours were cut to limit trading volume, brokers all over the country competed to get their orders to the floor before the close. When exchanges went dead, some brokers tried to route calls via London. The Dow Jones Company set up a special private wire to keep banks alerted to changes in the prime interest rate.

Telephone breakdown was especially unnerving because the phone had always been "there." Psychoanalysts say that phone calls in dreams symbolize communication with God. If so, God became progressively more inaccessible and often proved dead, absent-minded, uncaring, and even fiendish. Instead of the reassuring ("God is there") dial tone, the instrument sometimes gave off ominous bongs and crackles, snatches of fairy-faint conversation, or metallic announcements appropriate to an authority figure in a Kafka novel. A New York woman was billed for three calls to Ireland she did not make and then picked up her phone and heard violin music.

The phone company patiently explained that peak capacity overloaded not only the circuits, but the operators and mechanics who keep them open. The people who had to deal with these breakdowns in the heavily impacted central cities took longer to train, and didn't stay as long as the middle-class boys and girls who had built the Bell System's reputation for superhuman reliability and courtesy.

● *Overloaded Air*

Meanwhile, air travel lost its glamour the same way and on the same timetable. In 1965, the Federal Aviation Administration predicted that airlines would be carrying 130 million paying passengers in 1975, but this traffic arrived much sooner. To their surprise, and the delight of their stockholders, the airlines carried 146 million revenue passengers in 1968.

It was hard on the passengers. The jet age arrived piecemeal. Computers handled the new volume of reservations with enticing speed and ease, but once hooked, the customers had to wait in line for everything else. Ground services and airport roads hadn't grown as fast as the planes. Traffic around the Miami airport was once so badly snarled that air traffic controllers couldn't get through it to work their shifts. Waiting for luggage, waiting to get on and off planes, waiting for information, made the trip seem longer than going by car or train, even when it wasn't. About all the airlines could do to mitigate the impact of hurry-up-and-wait on the human nervous system was to play soothing music. Under the best of circumstances, more than half the travel time between cities 250 miles apart or less was spent on the ground.

The bigger the traffic, the worse the traffic pattern. Most of the new business involved the half dozen big metropolitan airports, and more of it than ever before was rush hour travel. Chicago (most planes), and New York (most passengers), were soon operating routinely at peak capacity under emergency rules. A real emergency, however slight, could back up as many as 80 planes waiting to take off on

8

the runway at Kennedy, or keep 15 planes circling, waiting to land. Trivial emergencies rippled out, delaying subsequent flights of the aircraft they affected. Stewardesses might roll out reserves of liquor, and pilots extinguish the no smoking sign to make the wait easier, but when the gas runs low, a stacked plane has to make for whatever airport can take it. And when Kennedy runs late, Kennedy-bound planes wait on the runways at Los Angeles and Tel Aviv.

The weakest link in the network were the air traffic controllers responsible for policing the sky jams over New York. During the summer of 1968 this small group of underpaid and overworked civil servants balked at the speed-up which left their nerves jumping from "bloodrushers" (near collisions) and insisted on going back to a strict interpretation of safety rules. Traffic had grown so much heavier than the capacity of the New York airports that the slowdown resulted in a breakdown of vacation travel schedules.

The "Big Sleep-In" the following winter was more dramatic. When 17 inches of snow closed Kennedy in February, 1969, 6000 passengers and employees were trapped for three days in a facility designed to pass many times that number through it for stays of only an hour or two. Waiting rooms filled up. Restaurants ran out of food, and hungry passengers broke into an employee cafeteria. Restrooms ran out of toilet paper. Three men seized a helicopter some others had chartered and forced it to take them to Manhattan. Airlines tried to ease the tension by showing movies in grounded planes. Meanwhile, passengers all over the country had to wait until Kennedy dug itself out.

● *Overloaded Mail*

In March 1970, the mail stopped. Overloaded and underpaid postal workers simply dropped their sacks, holding up wedding invitations, eviction notices, medical prescriptions, job offers, draft notices, census forms, love letters, passports, and most painful of all, checks. Not since the Bank Holiday of 1933 had so much money been frozen in transit, and those who recalled the earlier crisis observed how much more of the 1970 necessities of life depended on money changing hands. President Nixon didn't fool around. He called out the National Guard and when the postal workers were promised a raise, they came back to their sacks.

For people on a lot of mailing lists, the strike was a liberation from the overload of junk mail which littered their offices and their lives. The post office was struggling to deliver 400 pieces of mail a year for every man, woman, and child in the country, about twice the mail per capita delivered in the previous decade. Mailboxes—and wastebaskets —grew bigger, and deliveries grew slower until a spot check showed that only two out of three first-class letters were reaching their destinations in the continental United States within one day, the time the Post Office sets as normal.

The mail breakdown was like the others: creeping overloads, leaving the system with no margin for predictable emergencies; a breakdown at the weakest link dramatically unraveling the whole network. The weakest link was New York City, where the traffic was heaviest and the rise in the cost of living hardest on nationally-set postal service paychecks.

• *Overloaded New York City*

Overloaded New York City services of every kind reached the breaking point in the late 1960s. The public schools struggled merely to keep open. Representative James H. Scheuer reported that 102,000 New York City children were dangerously overcrowded at school and 20,000 couldn't be taught a full school day. At Junior High School 231 in Queens, classes were held in the teachers' lounge and the assistant principal worked in a dressing room. In the fall of 1968, the teachers struck, leaving a million children out of school for 36 days. By December attendance had fallen to a record low of 75 percent, pupils protested lengthening the school day to make up for the time lost on strike, and there weren't enough truant officers to enforce the school attendance law.

The police were in the same boat as the schools. The national crime rate doubled during the decade but the highest crime rate of any city was in New York. In 1968 it took a violent turn: crimes against persons began to rise faster than crimes against property, which are mostly automobile theft. The rise overwhelmed the institutions responsible for public safety.

Spot checks showed that many of the rapes, felonious assaults, and robberies committed in the city never came to the attention of police at all. Those which did seldom resulted in punishment for the perpetrators. Charges were not pressed because there wasn't space to hold those arraigned, prosecuting attorneys didn't have time to bring more cases, and when Federal money was provided to hire more prosecutors, attorneys couldn't be found to fill a quarter of the newly created posts. New York court calendars were so overloaded that magistrates let muggers off with a $10 fine if they pleaded guilty. At the Brooklyn Criminal Court, a man waiting to be arraigned on a narcotics charge simply walked out, unnoticed in the hubbub, when the policeman who had brought him in stepped out of the courtroom to fill out commitment papers.

Prisons were so overloaded that work could be provided for only half the inmates of the City reformatory on Riker's Island. The rest had to be kept quiet watching tele-

11

vision. Judges tried to parole as many of those convicted as possible, but at times there weren't enough probation officers in New York City to determine the eligibility of a criminal for parole within the time the law allowed. Prisons speeded up the release of prisoners to make room for new arrivals even though they knew that more than half would come back again to serve time for new crimes.

Since the upsurge of crime, New York City residents have begun to take their safety into their own hands. There is a brisk demand for police dogs. Girls carry tear gas to throw in the faces of muggers and apartment dwellers install outsize bolts on their doors. Residents living in private houses on Manhattan subscribe to burglar alarm services. Apartment houses, stores, and merchants hire private guards. In its final report to the President of the United States, the National Commission on the Causes and Prevention of Violence said that the trends it had studied added up to a frightening picture of a future "fortress city" in which slum neighborhoods would be "places of terror, perhaps entirely out of police control during night time hours"; slum schools, libraries, and playgrounds would operate with police guards during the day, and middle-class people would be afraid to venture out of their high-rise apartment buildings and privately guarded residential compounds.

Public workers in New York City demand—and sometimes strike for protection against assault. Bullet-proof partitions were installed to separate cabbies from their fares. After a series of holdups, bus drivers no longer have to make change, and accept only exact fare. Firemen have been stoned so frequently on their way to fires (does the siren itself attract attack?) that serious consideration has been given to equipping them with body armor, and the areas where firemen stand on engines is now roofed over with steel. The Commission warned that precautions of this kind

12

could multiply until "private automobiles, taxicabs, and commercial vehicles will be routinely equipped with unbreakable glass, light armor, and other security features. Armed guards will 'ride shotgun' on all forms of public transportation."

New Yorkers fear not only that they might be hit over the head any minute, but that they couldn't get a doctor if they *were* hit. New York City has the highest ratio of doctors to patients in the country, but they are all so busy that even well-to-do people have given up trying to get their personal physicians in an emergency, and struggle to the nearest hospital. Outpatient clinics cope with the new traffic by limiting treatment to first aid. The doctor on duty will sew you up if you come in bleeding, but getting the stitches out is your problem.

In order to get into a good, voluntary hospital, you have to be the patient of a doctor on the staff, and he might have to lie about your condition. (One New York physician confessed that he was relieved when a patient had a heart attack in the hospital because it proved that he had been justified in insisting that the patient was sick enough to be admitted.) Voluntary hospitals stretch their beds by putting private patients in wards, borrowing beds from one service to another, performing surgery six days a week instead of five, and keeping rooms in use even when they are being painted.

Public hospitals have always been grim places for the poor. During the 1960s, overcrowding and understaffing made New York's hospitals progressively more depressing in spite of the fact that they housed some of the most sophisticated medical practice in the world. In 1965, John Lindsay called New York City public hospitals "an unmitigated disgrace." At Bellevue, where corridors have been lined with beds for years, mental patients were sleeping on the floor with their belongings beside them in shopping bags. There were no registered nurses on many wards, and patients sent directly to them after operations sometimes died for lack of attention. Lindsay tightened the reorganized hospital administration, but some of the improvements created new problems. Expensive new patient-monitoring equipment stood idle for lack of personnel. Convalescent children were kept in bed at Metropolitan Hospital because a research project had taken over their play space. Ulcer patients occupied beds for weeks while their doctors waited for X-rays. By 1969, the best that Eileen McCaul, associate director of the New York State Nurses Association could say was that the rate of deterioration of the public hospitals had "slowed."

Other New York City health services, on the contrary, have been admittedly getting worse faster. Venereal diseases, long controllable by antibiotics, have risen to epidemic proportions. Cases of gonorrhea quadrupled. In 1970 the syphilis rate interrupted its twenty-year slide and rose instead, and there were fewer VD clinics and school examinations to deal with the threat. At a time when health services are being cut back, VD clinics are suddenly needed again.

The blackout was noteworthy because it was the first, but since 1965, breakdowns of all sorts have become commonplace in New York. It is worth a spot on the morning news any day when "all subways and commuter trains are running on time." And John Lindsay wasn't thinking only of riots and student protests when he commented in 1970, that New York was suffering from a "spiritual, and perhaps even a physical breakdown."

There are reasons why things always look worse in New York, even when they are not. The breakdown of network systems—air travel, phone, mail, electric power—starts

14

at the hub and spreads from there until the whole system is down. Other systems, such as crime prevention, schooling, health care, refuse disposal, and traffic control are simply more visible when they break down in New York. New York is big, its troubles are reasonably well reported by news services, and they interest people in other places who enjoy reading about how much better off they are at home in Podunk away from the exciting city.

But it isn't fair to say, as Americans have been saying for a hundred years, that New York's troubles are unique, and that things are fine "once you got west of the Hudson, into the heartland."

• *West and East of the Hudson*

People everywhere have begun to complain of breakdowns, at home, at work, and at school. According to the U.S. Office of Education, there were 1.3 million more schoolchildren in 1969 than "pupil stations" to accommodate them, and some of the children were being taught in buses or tied up boats. Students in the new state university systems have had to sit on windowsills or listen to lectures by closed-circuit television from an adjoining room.

So many pleasure boats are afloat that traffic is almost as bad on water as on land. Skiers have to pay so much attention to avoiding each other on the slopes that they can not feel wild and free. So many take to the national parks that the camp grounds no longer offer escape from the overpowering sights, sounds, and smells of impacted human flesh.

Garbage ("solid waste" as the technicians call it) is piling up everywhere. In 1969, half the communities in the United States with populations of 2500 or more weren't doing what the Federal Solid Wastes Program could regard as "even a minimally acceptable job" of solid waste collection and disposal. When canneries in Oakland, California, ran out of space to bury their wastes, they had to tow them out to sea. When the barge crews struck, the canneries didn't know what to do with the stuff. In San Jose, a program for fermenting cannery wastes and feeding it to cattle had to be abandoned because the wastes contained too much DDT from sprays that had been used on produce.

What to do with the junk can be a hotter problem for small communities than for big ones, since dumps are more visible when they are closer to residential areas. Old cars devastate the hinterlands. In Schoharie County, New York, there is one rotting junker for every four people. Junked cars are becoming a problem even in tidy Sweden.

Overloaded telephone exchanges have silenced dial tones in Florida, Los Angeles, the scientific research enclave around Cambridge, Massachusetts, and the downtown sections of cities as far off the beaten track as Denver, Colorado. Phone systems abroad have always been worse than ours in the United States, with long waits for new phones, but in Great Britain service is now deteriorating further while the Post Office-operated phone system is slowly reducing the backlog of new subscribers. According to an independent survey made by *Which?*, the British magazine of the Consumer Association, a quarter of the long distance calls reach wrong numbers.

Europe's mail, traditionally faster and more frequent than our own, has begun to fall to our standard. According to one student of philatelic history, letters flown out of the siege of Paris in 1870 by balloon reached their destinations faster than some letters postmarked in Paris a hundred years later. Russians complain that the Soviet mails are slower now than in the days of Tolstoy.

Traffic is worse in Europe's medieval cities than on Manhattan, where millions of dollars have been spent since World War II on highways that move large numbers of cars in and out of the downtown area. Cars back up 100 miles on roads leading out of London on weekends. Parking lots encroach on the Champs-Elysées in Paris, and strike an anachronistic note on Rome's Piazza Colonna. It is hard even to walk along Picadilly in London in the tourist season, and the sidewalks in Siena, Italy, are one-way to avoid pedestrian collision.

European cities are so cramped that they run out of space sooner and sometimes more dramatically than in America. A flu epidemic that doubled the death rate of Berlin in the winter of 1969 precipitated a "funeral crisis" that piled up occupied coffins awaiting the location of grave space. In the United States, we have a cemetery shortage too, but it is less acute because we have more land.

• *Everything's Coming Apart*

We've been able to reach the moon, but nothing on earth seems to work right any more. You can't be sure of getting anything repaired, moved, or delivered, and hospital authorities admit that a high percentage of diagnostic tests simply are wrong.

The simplest relationships are coming unstuck.

No one knows how many retail sales are lost because the merchandise doesn't seem to be worth the struggle to get the attention of an unenthusiastic clerk. It is harder and harder to get the time of day out of business organizations. Voices on the other end of the telephone are dim, and clerks often take phones off the hook or let phones ring rather than bother to answer them. Banks have begun to discourage depositors from calling up for their balances by charging them for this elementary information. If you need to get the time of a train, you have to keep dialing the station until you catch one of the lines just as someone is hanging up. As a result, heavily called numbers answer with recordings of the train schedule, the movie being shown, the hours of the store, or whatever it is that *most* of the calls are about, and there is no way of getting anything else.

Citizens band radio is so jammed in some places that SOS calls can't get through. In 1965, the communications officer of the Third Coast Guard District around New York reported that due to jammed bands, the pilot of a helicopter lost radio contact with a boat to which it was trying to lower a pump and had to dangle it over the deck in hopes that the crew would understand what had happened and catch it.

Left hands don't know what right hands are supposed to be doing. Big companies have trouble keeping track of their people. Unbeknownst to each other, two salesmen for the same firm frequently descend on the same prospect the same week. Service departments contradict the promises made by salesmen, and a department advertising for stenographers once found itself interviewing stenographers being laid off by another department in the same organization. Computers are being installed to handle overloads, but they sometimes dun customers for bills already paid, keep sending books and other merchandise already refused, and are maddeningly deaf to the pleas of their victims. The blizzard of print has overwhelmed librarians. During the last decade, scientific researchers have developed a rule of thumb: if it costs less than $100,000, it's cheaper to do the research over than hunt in the library to see whether it has been done before.

No cautionary tale on left and right hands is as bad as what actually happened in San Francisco Bay on May 16, 1969. On that day, two repair crews happened to be pursuing jobs in different parts of the *Guittaro*, a new U.S. Nuclear submarine which was divided into two watertight compartments so that if one was flooded the other would keep it afloat. Oblivious to each other, the two crews let water in at the same time and in five minutes sent her straight to the bottom at dockside. Even in the long and distinguished annals of military stupidity rarely has a Navy succeeded in absentmindedly sinking one of its own ships before it puts out to sea.

● *Crowds*

The simplest things can no longer be taken for granted. Air, water, and empty space are no longer free, and there are more and more restrictions on the personal freedom of individuals to move about as they please. ("No Standing," "Do Not Enter," "Keep Moving," "Line Forms At Right," "Subway Exit Closed Saturdays and Sundays.")

Crowds have become a problem. Authorities weren't prepared for the size of the well-behaved gatherings in the 1960s, let alone riots and demonstrations. So many mourners jammed the route of the late Robert Kennedy's funeral train, that two persons were pushed off the platform at Elizabeth, New Jersey, and killed by a train coming in the opposite direction. The thousands of young music lovers who gather at rock festivals sometimes surprise police by their good humor but there are so many of them that the ticket-selling apparatus breaks down, and promoters do not take in enough money to pay the performers. City authorities have begun to plan public toilet facilities for demonstrations and parades, the way Moscow administrators have been doing for a generation.

Museums have traditionally been quiet havens for the well-behaved, but now their guards, insurance protection, staffs, and even the exhibits and buildings themselves can't stand up to the traffic. The first day the new Whitney Museum in New York was open on a Sunday, the tramp of thousands of visitors set a chrome-and-glass sculpture teetering ominously on its plexiglass stand and shattered a man-high slate sculpture by Noguchi, presciently named "Humpty Dumpty."

• *New Crimes*

Dense concentrations of strangers provide unprecedented opportunities for madmen and extortionists. The makers and reporters of real and imaginary bombs appear. And neither the law of piracy nor traditional police techniques have ever anticipated that a man could buy an airline ticket to Miami and get himself transported to Havana by sticking up the pilot and coincidentally threatening the lives of everyone on board.

Smart crooks have found ways to take advantage of breakdowns. When public garbage disposal broke down in Westchester County, the Mafia smelled an opportunity for racketeering in the private carting services that had sprung up to take care of restaurants, and made them pay, as it were, through the nose. They systematically filch credit cards distributed by mass mailings. Airline tickets, honored by all lines and distributed in blank to thousands of travel agencies are as negotiable—and as poorly protected—as the stock certificates that the Mafia regularly was stealing from the backrooms of brokerage houses on Wall Street.

Petty, unorganized crime has become an intolerable menace in impacted cities. Small boys have always yearned to heave stones at windows, but by 1971 so many train windows were being shattered that the Metropolitan Transportation Authority began patrolling its tracks around New York City by helicopter. The rise may have something to do with the failure of city crowds to intervene in crimes occurring before their eyes. In the big cities, neither policemen, guards, nor neighbors seem to pay attention to meddlesome boys and adult psychopaths in the street.

Breakdown!

Vandalism—wanton, profitless destruction of public property for the hell of it—has become an uncontrollable problem for public schools, libraries, museums, and public places of every sort. Graffiti blossom everywhere. The fire alarm rate is one of the statistics sociologists use to measure the deterioration of a neighborhood. In 1970, the New York City Fire Department was answering three times as many alarms—real and false—as they had in 1960.

In 1971, coin-box vandals made one out of every 10 pay phones in Manhattan inoperable on a given day. A systematic stuffer could make $25 a day by putting things in the coin boxes to trap the genuine dimes of customers and then returning to reap the harvest. Stuffing is also a form of psychological warfare. In one neighborhood, small boys kept customers from retrieving their dimes by putting raw eggs into the phones. Nuisance calls from psychopaths whispering obscenities have become so big a problem that the phone company has had to install a special detective service to protect their subscribers.

- *Anomaly*

More and more things simply don't make sense. Women's magazines keep printing recipes that begin "have your butcher do so and so" and selling the issues to women for whom the "butcher" is a faceless packager in the backroom of a supermarket. College freshmen know more facts, as evidenced by machine scorable true-false tests, but they can't write a simple grammatical paragraph because compositions that have to be corrected by a teacher have disappeared from the curriculum of many overloaded high schools. Police are supposed to deter crime, but in the big cities police per capita and crimes per capita rise together. Antibiotics have not wiped out venereal disease. Adoption

21

of the contraceptive pill coincided with a dramatic rise in the rate of illegitimate births. In New York City the percentage of housing units abandoned by their owners rises with the shortage of livable and rentable space.

Direct action demonstrating public anger has become the political style since the late 1960s. Protests are organized not only against the war in Vietnam and the oppression of blacks, and college authorities, but against landlords, supermarkets, and public works which would require the condemnation of land for badly needed generating plants, transmission lines, thruways, aqueducts, airports, and public housing projects. In New York, ghetto dwellers protested against the Sanitation Department by throwing garbage in the street.

Comparisons are difficult to make, but it does seem to reporters and social scientists that more people are reacting with disproportionate violence to what was formerly tolerated as petty annoyance. Around Grand Central Station in New York, to take a minor example, taxicabs are more frequently contested by two parties entering simultaneously from opposite doors.

Individuals have begun to fight back on their own. A Wall Street banker wouldn't pay his telephone bill until service improved, and a court wouldn't let the company take his phone out. Merchants sued the Newark police for failing to protect their property in a riot, and neighbors sued the farmer who invited the Woodstock Music Festival for the nuisances created by the half million young people who attended.

• *The Right Questions*

How, when, and why did the Soaring Sixties bring on the Surging Seventies? Americans started the Sixties full of hope, with one of the most attractive men ever to be President of the United States. We sustained rising prosperity for more years on end than any previous boom had lasted. Yet even before the boom ended, just before the end of the decade, it was clear that in the words of the Old Testament prophets, "all we like sheep had gone astray."

Midway through the 1960s, I began to feel that it wouldn't last. I found myself making symbols out of everyday experiences. Traffic jams in supermarket parking lots. The rising dirt and declining service in our New York apartment house. The clearly insane price-earnings ratio of IBM stock. All seemed to be symptoms of some unnamed disease.

The common principle behind the symptoms seemed to be overload, the way quantity changes quality. Too many people. Too many things. Too much talk. Too little space and time for it all. During the 1960s my husband and I bought a house in the country and got used to spreading out so quickly that we now wonder how we ever had managed to squeeze into the New York apartment on a full-time basis. I felt sure that the next generation would have to cut back on big families, and that they ought to cut back on all the things we buy (why, for heaven's sake, frozen pop-up waffles, electric toothbrushes?). I felt sure that we ought to stop littering mailboxes and our ears with half-attended verbiage that pursued us in print or came streaming out of boxes.

Along with many other people, I advocated cutting back until the ecology drive of 1970 whipped up what sounded like an excessive concern for clean water, clear air, quiet, and nature. Some of the enthusiastic supporters of the movement to save the environment sounded as if they preferred trees to people.

The new interest in ecology looked like a red herring to detract attention from the problems of the ghetto. I became uncomfortably aware that I was personally running away from the problems of New York City instead of staying there and doing something about them, and I was increasingly uneasy about the cliches that were passed around as explanations for the decline in amenities of everyday life. Cutting back—on people, things, talk—began to sound like an elitist remedy to protect the comforts of the rich, the privileged and the educated.

Family planning leaders joke about one famous rich man who became interested in the cause of population control because he began to have more trouble every year finding enough space at increasingly crowded marinas in which to dock his yacht.

Too many people for what? For whom? How much is too much? No one seems to have made a serious effort to find out. There are no good estimates of the number of people the earth can support, let alone how many we ought to have. There is surprisingly little data on how many people can be jammed together in small quarters. Economists airily assume that there is no end to the process of getting rich. Nobody knows how much more knowledge can be discovered and circulated.

Attempts to answer these ultimate questions dissolve in a shower of "ifs." What's more, you can't keep the ideal number of people, things, or ideas separate, because you very quickly discover that they affect each other. Each stimulates the others. The more I thought about quantitative overloads, the more I suspected that I had been looking at the problem backward. The solution really isn't to reduce the number of yachts, but to find bold new ways of accommodating all the people who want to enjoy the water.

Chapter II

Too Many People

What will life be like when there are twice as many human beings on earth as there are today?

You may live to see it. According to the United Nations, there were 3.6 billion people in the world in 1970 and if they continue to increase at the rate of nearly two percent annually, there will be 7 billion in the year 2006. Of all the generations of human beings that have existed since man emerged, those of us now alive are the first to see the human race double within our own lifetime.

Historians piecing together the past think that in the time of Christ the population of the whole world was 250 million, little more than the population of the Soviet Union alone in 1970.

1650 years after the birth of Christ, these 250 million had doubled to half a billion, and they were spreading out from Europe into the New World.

The next doubling came much sooner. Two hundred years later, the human race had 1.1 billion souls, and the mechanical reaper had made it possible to produce enough food to feed them all. Eighty years later, in 1930, there were two billion people on earth. In 1970, 3.6 billion.

The doublings come faster as the numbers grow bigger. Everyone now alive who lives a Biblical three-score years and ten will experience a doubling of the world population. For older people, the doubling will take most of their lives. For the young, it will come sooner, and if the current rate of increase continues, the next generation will survive *two* doublings. After that, and no further in the future than the birth of my grandfather is in the past, there will be ten times as many people on earth as there are in 1972.

There is no dearth of ideas of how to feed and house such inconceivable numbers. They could be nourished on manufactured products, on seaweed processed to resemble the steaks of olden times; on dogs, cats, rats, bugs, grass, algae, and ultimately on each other. The last prospect is not an idle joke. In 1966, no less an authority than Nobel Laureate Albert Szent-Györgyi of the Marine Biological Laboratory at Woods Hole, Massachusetts, warned a Senate committee that mass cannibalism would be inevitable if the human population kept growing.

Cannibalism makes sense to biologists. The total "biomass" of all living things is limited by the world supply of raw materials for life which circulate from plants to animals to man and back again. According to N. J. Berrill, a Canadian zoologist, the limiting ingredient is the element phosphorus which in small quantities is essential to all forms of life. Little fish incorporate the phosphorus in algae and are eaten by big fish, but when a man catches and eats the big fish, he carries the phosphorus he does not excrete to his grave in his bones. As men multiply by eating up all the fish and other animals and plants faster than they can grow, they would have to reprocess their own sewage and dead into food to recapture phosphorus. Eventually births would outnumber deaths so fast that the living would be tempted to tap the only remaining source—living human flesh.

In an overpopulated world, people couldn't be housed as they are today, but one vision of the future suggests that 50 billion people could live underground in a continuous belt circling the globe.

One's first thought is that human beings wouldn't stand for life under any of these circumstances. But people get used to very severe conditions. In *Man Adapting*, René Dubos, the historian of science, warns that the danger is that human beings may adapt too well. They are so plastic that they might learn to put up with conditions that at first seem degrading if not physically impossible. Life could become so regimented and restricted that we wouldn't think it worth living.

The quality of life has already begun to deteriorate because of overpopulation, according to a team of Yale sociologists, Lincoln and Alice Day. They cite "increasing restrictions on individual behavior, greater centralization in Government, higher taxes, heightened competition for educational and recreational facilities, greater friction between people living in closer contact, shortages and declining quality in social services, enervating delays in getting places, and a steady loss in time, beauty, solitude, and tranquillity."

Those who predict disaster unless population growth is stopped, list the essentials of civilized life that an excess of people overloads:

1. _Natural Resources_. We have too many people for our resources of land, air, water, fuel, wilderness, and power. We are using up materials so fast and in such volume that we can't absorb the wastes of our consumption. Overpopulation causes pollution, crowding, and eventually starvation.

2. *Service Systems*. We have too many people for our water, sewer, phone, transportation, police, fire, and sanitation systems. We can't even service the cars and washing machines we buy. We don't have enough roads or hospitals or doctors or schools to take care of all our people. In 1967, Professor Joseph J. Spengler of Duke University, a past president of the American Economic Association, estimated that $10 to $20 million worth of new construction of various kinds was needed to add each thousand people to the population of the United States, and we weren't beginning to spend anywhere near that much.

3. *Balance of Nature*. Nature cuts back any species which outgrows its environment, and this will happen to man. Man has no predator, but he is an animal dependent on the web of plant and animal life he is destroying. Ecologists say that man is a latter-day Noah who is kicking all the other animals out of the ark.

4. *Human Nature*. Man is a hunter and more recently a farmer. There is a limit to how well he can learn to live in cities. Crime, suicide, neurosis, rioting, drug abuse, family disorganization, and breakdowns result when too many people try to live too close together.

For those who see all of these dangers, there is only one solution: stopping population growth.

• *The Birth Control Movement*

As a problem, too many people is something new. A big and growing population used to be cause for congratulations. As recently as 1959, McCann-Erickson, the ebullient New York advertising agency, promised its clients 45 million more consumers during the "Big Sixties." The estimates were wrong. By 1970, we had added only 25 million, but in those ten years our view of growth had changed drastically and even this modest increase looked like "people pollution." To Neil Armstrong, the first man on the moon, the earth was "an oasis of life in space that must be protected from its own population."

Today, all our problems are blamed on too many people: too many pupils for the schools, too many teen-agers for the colleges, too many golfers for the links, too many passengers for the airlines, too many patients for the hospitals, too many corpses for the cemeteries.

The number of people in a country has always been a topic of general interest and prognostication, but like the weather, most people thought that nothing could be done about it. There were exceptions. Military-minded leaders, including Hitler and Mussolini, occasionally tried to swell the supply of soldiers for their successors by bonuses and awards for mothers, with special honor, of course, to those with the forethought to bear sons. On the other side, there had long been a modest private movement to promote birth control. Even before Margaret Sanger, feminists had exhorted the poor to improve their individual standing of living by limiting their families, as the middle classes had long been doing.

However the idea that birth control is a function of government is very new. It seems to have originated as a policy Americans recommended to the teeming Asians as a condition for feeding them. When the population of India began to soar after World War I, American relief workers began to wonder whether their aid was only bringing more people into the world to live in the misery from which they had hoped to extricate the original population. Kenneth Boulding, the economist, in his book *The Image*, called this possibility the "utterly dismal theorem" to dramatize what modern science could do to the "dismal theorem" of Thomas Malthus, the eighteenth-century English parson who had warned that population always tends to outrun the food supply.

Private organizations had long been urging the Indian

government to promote birth control, but the United States government was reluctant to make official policy on this delicate subject. As late as 1959, President Eisenhower declared that birth control and population were emphatically "none of the government's business."

During the 1960s, Americans rapidly overcame their squeamishness. President Kennedy worried in public that the rising populations in underdeveloped countries were cancelling out the effects of the economic aid we were sending to them. In 1963, Planned Parenthood, the voluntary association that had fought the battle of birth control for American women, added "and World Population" to its name. In 1965 President Johnson promised to "seek new ways to use our knowledge to help deal with the explosion in world population and the growing scarcity of world resources." The next year, the United Nations declared that it was a basic human right of individuals "to decide the number and spacing of children."

What was good for the Asians, wasn't necessarily bad for Americans. During the 1950s, when the birth rate was high, moralists like Margaret Mead began questioning whether we had a right to exhort the Asians to stop having so many babies when we kept on having them at a rate which was then about as high as theirs. Soon everybody who was anybody was saying the same thing. The Methodist Church, the Department of Health, Education, and Welfare, the National Academy of Sciences, the United Nations, and the American Association for the Advancement of Science were among the establishment organizations which publicly pondered whether individuals should limit the size of their families in the interest not of their own health and comfort, but of the nation's. And as often happens, this high-minded concern attracted the support of others whose motives were more immediate, such as taxpayers who were appalled at the steadily growing expense of new schools, and at the escalating costs of welfare which were partly due to the increased proportion of children on the rolls.

In 1966, President Johnson warned Congress that "fifty years from now our population will reach that of today's India." In July 1969, President Nixon made population an official policy concern by asking for a national commission to study the impact of our domestic population growth.

Naturalists who were familiar with the dynamics of animal populations, talked about the danger of an overgrowth of the animal, man. In September 1969, ecologists joined feminists who were interested in the liberation of women, to urge a deliberate policy of population control at hearings in the House of Representatives on "Effects of Population Growth on Natural Resources and the Environment" chaired by Wisconsin Congressman Henry Reuss. The next month, conservation and birth control activists joined forces again at a national Conference on Conservation and Voluntary Sterilization sponsored by the Association for Voluntary Sterilization (AVS), a eugenics organization committed to slowing the growth of the population in the United States.

"Zero Population Growth" became one of the major youth crusades of 1970. In January, Johnny Carson invited Professor Paul Ehrlich, a 37-year-old biologist from Stanford University to tell the audience of *The Tonight Show* about "The Population Bomb" against which he had warned in a paperback book of that name. Ehrlich preached a new brand of doom: earth was a fragile spaceship, overloaded with people who were rapidly making the planet incapable of supporting civilization. He urged immediate and drastic population control to cut down on the "death control" inevitable when the species man fouled his home.

Thousands of viewers wrote in, most of them enthusiastically. College groups took up the cause. On Earth Day, April 22, students sported "Stop at Two" buttons provided by the AVS. Ehrlich let it be known that he had undergone a vasectomy after fathering one child. Young couples all over the country talked of having one child and adopting the second.

The movement helped to build a quiet Congressional majority for the appropriation of Federal money to supply poor women with birth control. It secured respectful attention in state legislatures for abortion reform and by the fall of 1971, 16 states had done something to make abortions easier to obtain.

Today, most self respecting communities have a chapter of Zero Population Growth, devoted to warning of the dangers of too many people.

• *Voluntary or Compulsory?*

Those who favor stopping population growth don't always agree about what can be done to achieve it. Two schools of thought have appeared, one advocating voluntary control and the other compulsory control.

Voluntarists think that universal birth control will solve the problem: the population will decline, they say, if every child is wanted and planned. This is the old liberal birth control position and it is now the establishment position taken by the past two administrations with remarkably little opposition from the Roman Catholic Church. The growth of a consensus that supports the right of a woman *not* to have an unwanted child has made abortion reform easier than leaders in the birth control movement ever thought possible.

The compulsorists aren't willing to leave it to individual choice; they want to prevent conception by force. They are impressed by the fact that the children overpopulating the United States are not the unwanted babies of the poor, but the far greater number of wanted children of middle-class parents. They argue that the population will continue to grow as long as families are allowed to have as many children as they wish, because even those who see the danger of overpopulation can argue that one child more or less is not worth the personal sacrifice for themselves.

In a brilliant essay, "The Tragedy of the Commons," Garrett Hardin, Professor of Biology at the University of California, Santa Barbara, likened the situation to the dilemma of a community of farmers who pasture their herds on a common. Each sees the danger of overgrazing the common pasture, but he also sees that he has more to gain than to lose by adding animals of his own to the common. An appeal to conscience would make the population problem worse, Hardin added, because "non-cooperators would outbreed cooperators." He suggested that we celebrate the bicentennial of the Declaration of Independence by making 1976 a year of "pregnant pause" during which no baby would be conceived.

Those who believe in compulsory birth control are almost all biologists, zoologists, physicists, and hard scientists who are not accustomed to dealing with social problems. Their training makes them underestimate the influence of culture and they put their reliance on mechanical or chemical devices without regard for individual rights. Suggestions being circulated in the scientific community reverse the usual contraceptive pattern. Instead of requiring people to do something to avoid conception, the compulsory schemes would require couples to do something special in order to conceive.

Scientists have come up with some extraordinary ideas. Richard Schreiber, Professor of Plant Cytology at the University of New Hampshire, is designing a contagious virus that would travel around the world like a flu epidemic, sterilizing rich and poor alike in every country. The virus would interfere with the synthesis of a hormone required in the female reproductive cycle, and Schreiber has said he wouldn't let it loose until he had deposited a vaccine against it with the United Nations.

Dr. Melvin M. Ketchel, Professor of Physiology at Tufts Medical School, is looking for a fertility control agent that could be delivered automatically through water; in a staple food such as salt; by aerosol through the air; or by contagion like Dr. Schreiber's virus, at dosage levels the government could vary depending on the birth rate desired. The Ketchel plan preserves individual choice. If you want a baby, you can take steps to counteract the sterilant everyone is getting; if you don't, you use regular birth control to be sure. The rest of the population is subject to the chance of getting pregnant at the rate at which the anti-fertility chemical is being distributed. That way, the Government does not determine which individual shall be permitted to conceive —just the percentage.

Deciding who shall be permitted to conceive is a thorny political problem. One way to give everyone an equal chance would be to add a sterilant to the water supply or a staple food and distribute the antidote by lottery. Luckily, none of the compounds has yet been invented, and all of these schemes present formidable technical difficulties. Water supplies don't reach the majority of people who get water from wells and a contagious virus might wipe out domestic animals. But repugnant as these measures sound, they are morally more defensible than bills proposed in several state legislatures for compulsory sterilization of a welfare mother of two or three children.

However, even the most militant compulsorists don't expect chemical controls now. They frankly say that they are talking about them to shock people into seeing the danger. Tactically, they join forces with a growing middle group who could be called the persuaders.

The persuaders propose discouraging big families by withdrawing the subsidies and favor given them in tax laws, welfare allotments, admission to housing projects, scholarships, school tuitions, discounts for travel, and preferences for fathers in employment. The persuaders are usually social scientists supported by conservationists, feminists, and some political conservatives who fear that welfare expenses are going to get out of hand. Their spokesmen have been two husband-and-wife teams in sociology, Kingsley and Judith Blake Davis now at the University of California at Berkeley, and Lincoln and Alice Day at Yale.

They advocate a policy that would counteract the influences that make women feel that they have to have children. Judith Blake Davis told the Reuss Committee how traditional policies favor childbearers: "We penalize homosexuals of both sexes, we insist that women must bear unwanted children by depriving them of ready access to abortion, we bind individuals into marriages that they do not wish to maintain, we force single and childless individuals to pay for the education of other people's children, we make people with small families support the schooling of those who have larger ones, and we offer women few viable options to full-time careers as wives and mothers except jobs that are, on the average, of low status and low pay."

The Women's Liberation Movement is also drawing attention to the many economic, social, and psychic carrots-and-sticks which promote big families. Long-term proposals to change these range from actually paying women *not* to have babies, or paying for sterilization, as has been tried in India; a "responsibility" prize for women of childbearing age who do not conceive during five years of marriage; higher welfare payments to welfare mothers who refrain from becoming pregnant again; a direct tax on children, diapers, baby food, or toys, with safeguards against penalizing the innocent children rather than the parents; financing of education by a special income tax on big, rich families.

As an immediate goal, the Davises and the Days suggest removing the hidden subsidies for large families that are now written into laws in the United States. Bills limiting tax deductions for children were introduced in Congress during 1970. Under a new law that became effective in 1971, a single person may take the deduction offered to heads of households—small potatoes, perhaps, but a beginning. Another victory was a Supreme Court decision permitting a state to set an absolute limit on welfare payments to large families.

Ultimately, say the Days and the Davises, we've got to give women something to replace the satisfaction they now get from motherhood, and they freely concede that this means restructuring the family and abolishing the present division of labor between the sexes. Richard L. Meier, Professor of Environmental Design at Berkeley, has suggested that while we're restructuring society, we might create attractive new social roles for women who don't have children. Professor Spengler, the economist from Duke University, suggests a marriage tax that would go into an insurance fund which would pay off heavily if the couple bore no children. Finally, medical technology might help by providing couples who wished a child of each sex a sure way of getting a boy and a girl on only two tries.

• *How Many Is Too Many?*

Regardless of the method used, the population controllers are united in their goal: fewer births, and a lower population than they fear we will have if they do not intervene. Those who fear overpopulation have one thing in common: they like things the way they are and see a rising population as a threat to their political, economic, and/or social advantages. But how many is too many? And how many is right?

It is diverting to collect the population size that various social critics consider ideal. Desmond Morris, the author of *The Human Zoo*, thinks a fitting ecological balance between trees, animals, and man could be maintained in the United States if we got down to 10 million, the population of 1820. Stewart Udall, former Secretary of the Interior, favors 100 million, the population of 1915. In the interests of "solitude and breathing space," Paul Ehrlich, the population control activist, wants to get rid of 50 million Americans, or back to the population of 1950. Ehrlich is younger than Udall. It is tempting to check the numbers they propose against the population of the United States the year those selling them were born.

Each of these ideal sizes is, of course, based on a different value. How many people the world should have depends on what is most important to you. Frequently, people who talk about restricting population growth do not disclose or even realize that they have an axe to grind. It's convenient to classify the criteria that may influence these population goals under the old-fashioned headings: political, economic, social, and religious.

Political Values. Back between the world wars, when Hitler and Mussolini were urging big families for the greater glory of their nations, Gunnar and Alva Myrdal were suggesting that the Swedes also increase their numbers. Although their rationale was economic, and their real motives social equity, the elaborate program of family benefits was

37

approved by the government in part at least, with an eye on Sweden's expansionist neighbors.

In 1972, population levels no longer figure prominently in military calculations. The technology of war has become so elaborate that even the richest belligerents cannot afford to keep large armies in the field. Since the atomic bomb, military manpower is not critical anywhere. Numbers are disregarded even where they seem to count, as in Southeast Asia. No one is suggesting that Americans have more babies in order to match the apparently inexhaustible human resources of the Vietcong. The notion is so unthinkable that we forget how recently our grandfathers worried about being overwhelmed by hordes of Asiatic people—"the yellow peril."

No one now feels that a country has to compete in numbers in order to command respect. Statements made by Philip M. Hauser, the demographer, illustrate the shift in emphasis during the last quarter century. In 1945, right after World War II, he warned that "the continuing rapid rate of increase of the already large population masses of the Orient will necessarily make the population of the United States a smaller and smaller proportion of the total population of the world" with unpredictable results on "the position of the U.S. as a world power." Twenty-three years later, when Professor Hauser was installed as the President of the American Sociological Association, he said that rising domestic population was the "paramount problem of the United States." He was no longer worried about the effect of numbers on the position of the United States as a world power.

Other countries are also having second thoughts about the value of sheer numbers.

In the 1970s, conservative politicians in France and Japan were urging women to have more babies to increase the supply of labor (particularly cheap street-cleaning type labor), but the masses invited to bear the children were notably unenthusiastic. French women booed Defense Minister Michel Debré for the suggestion.

Recently there has been more concern about another political consideration: the effect of population size on government. Many people now believe that New York City is out of control because it is "just too big" to govern. To many, the right size for any group—a school class, a guided tour, a city, a country, even the world—is the size which is easiest to govern, or more accurately, is governable by democratic means. In the 1970s, the complaint "too big" is leveled at big universities, at business organizations too big to respond to the complaints of customers, and to the presidency of the United States. Both President Nixon and President Johnson have been criticized for being "out of touch" with popular sentiment.

The bigger the city or nation, the smaller the minority that could—and usually does rule it. Historians cite the small size of ancient Greek city-states as a key to the institutions which they developed, and they are, of course, right. A 1969 study of Vermont town meetings found that the smaller towns are more democratic because more of their citizens speak up in meetings. The implication, of course, was that participation made the small towns "better."

The ancients favored limiting city size to the number within the sound of one man's voice. Plato thought a city should have no more than 5000 households, because he wanted to get all the household heads into one stadium at a time; if you'd given Plato a radio, he might have opted for a bigger city.

Economic Values. Some ideal population sizes are based on economic criteria. The capitalists favor a size of city or

39

country or work group which gets the most production out of a given quantity of capital. Marxists, on the other hand, say that size doesn't matter because all wealth is created by labor.

It is the capitalist view that usually colors the American concept of the right numbers of people that make an economic system operate most efficiently.

To eighteenth-century, country-living Thomas R. Malthus, the most important capital was land, and the most dramatic feature of land capital is that there's just so much of it. People increase, but land doesn't. In 1798 he wrote a law about it. "Population, when unchecked, increases in a geometrical ratio. Subsistence increases only in an arithmetic ratio. A slight acquaintance with numbers will show the immensity of the first power in comparison with the second." If population was everywhere unchecked, Malthus concluded, it would rise to the number who could survive on the land available, and that would always be more than the number who could be well nourished on it.

So long as food is the main product, and land the main capital, the rule of Malthus works like a charm. It works beautifully for animals. Spill sugar, and ants multiply just enough to devour it. It seems to work this way in India and other underdeveloped countries, where slight improvements in the standard of living have been reliably followed by big increases in population. It used to work in the United States too. During the early nineteenth century, when the United States didn't have enough people to cultivate its newly available land, we had one of the highest recorded birth rates of history and we imported people, sometimes forcibly, in addition. Our population grew toward the numbers that could exploit the land under the agricultural methods of the time.

Then the industrial revolution came along and dramatized the fact that capital was not the fixed quantity of land alone, but factories, machines, and inventions as well. To socialist Karl Marx, it was obvious that all of these factors of production were really products of human labor. Orthodox Marxists say there's no such thing as overpopulation because "every mouth comes into the world with a pair of hands."

But capitalists continued to think of capital as something separate and fixed, which under prevailing industrial conditions created a measurable demand for labor and hence people. Adam Smith, the pioneer capitalist, had discovered that wealth increased when workers specialized, and he thought that a rising population would spur competition between people and that workers would be encouraged to specialize in order to make the available capital more productive.

In the Depression of the 1930s, modern capitalists favored a rising population because it would increase the number of consumers of industrial production as well as the labor supply. Humanists though they were, both Myrdal and John Maynard Keynes subscribed to an economic theory that valued people because they "put capital to work."

Until recently, labor was needed to make capital assets fully productive. Now, in the mid-twentieth century, increased numbers of people are no longer necessary, and from the capitalist viewpoint, population control makes sense. Those who control or own capital can get rich with fewer employees, and the people who are not needed have to be supported by increasingly steep welfare expenditures. The "extra" people are an economic drag, and there are those who think that steps should be taken to prevent them from being born. Zero Population Growth is supported by conservatives some of whom subscribe, often unconsciously, to this deeply anti-human value.

41

Social Criteria. As a social unit, the ideal size for a class, a firm, a club, a city, a country, or for that matter, the world, is the size which makes possible the biggest sum total of human satisfaction. For purposes of measuring it, we might invent the "hubisat," a standard unit of human satisfaction experienced by one human. The city with the highest per capita hubisat would be one in which living conditions are most pleasant. For a firm, it would be the size which makes it a "good place to work." Hubisats would equalize the contribution to satisfaction of pay, sociability, and achievement.

A foundation executive who visits many colleges once remarked that Dartmouth was the "wrong size" for a college: too big for students to recognize most of the people they met while walking from one building to another, but not big enough to attract the outstanding scholars who go to Harvard, often at no greater reward, simply to be with more of their colleagues.

For a grade-school class the best size would be the size which facilitates learning for all members. Whatever the best social size for a class, it might be smaller than the best "political size" or the number that the teacher could comfortably control. The ideal social size would probably be smaller than the economic size favored by a cost-conscious taxpayer association surveying the school system.

We don't know much about these social criteria, except that they are figuring more prominently all the time in the choices young people make about colleges, employers, and places to live. At every level they seem to call for smaller numbers than the economic or political ideals. They may be surfacing now because economic considerations are less urgent: you don't have to live in a big city to get a job you can live on, and relations with co-workers could be more important than salary in some cases. But social con-

42

siderations may also be emerging because people sense that the old economic limitations no longer protect them from groups that could be uncomfortably big.

Religious Criteria. Religions have traditionally urged the faithful to propagate for the glory of God, however uncomfortable big families may be for the faithful, but the "higher" considerations are now for reducing human numbers. Some of the "friends of the earth" have made a pantheistic religion out of the balance of nature. In this view, the duty of man is to occupy the ecological niche of some point in natural history, usually a past time when his numbers were fewer. "Maybe what's good for us isn't good for the squirrels," a student speculated at one of the talk-ins preceding Earth Day 1970. "Who are we to lord it over the earth?" Richard Bower, one of the founders of Zero Population Growth suggests mass suicide to put humanity in its rightful place in the natural order.

The interesting thing about all these considerations— political, economic, social, and religious—is that they all prescribe fewer people at every level than we now have or are about to get in the United States.

Some specialists can think of ways to accommodate many more people in the United States, but none of them suggest that the country would be better off with increased numbers. Many experts think we are about the right size now. Ansley Coale of Princeton, a demographer who seems less alarmed than most by rising population, would like to see the United States stop at 290 million. Max Ways, *Fortune*'s resident economist, thinks the 1970 U.S. population is about right. But you can't think very far ahead about the United States alone.

Taking the planet as a whole, it is obvious that there is a limit to the number of people it can hold. That means that population growth will have to slow down. If it doesn't, it is only a matter of time before our descendents will be squeezed to death. In 1960, three statistically-minded electrical engineers at the University of Illinois calculated that if the world population kept growing as fast as it had been growing in the past 2000 years, Doomsday would be November 13, 2026, a date within the lifetime of the living. They figured that on that particular Friday the 13th, human numbers would approach infinity. The exercise is a useful reminder that population projections are merely pointers showing where we are headed at a particular moment in time, not where we are going to get.

- ● *What Will Stop It?*

Population growth has to slow down eventually, of course. Something will happen to prevent present rates of population growth from continuing until we have standing room only. The important questions are: when will it stop and what will stop it without compulsory measures suggested by those who foresee imminent disaster?

How far will the world's population rise from the 1970 level of 3.6 billion before it heads down? Estimates vary widely. The British economist Colin Clark thinks that the earth could support 157 billion people at a subsistence level. Most estimates are much lower. John B. Calhoun, a psychologist at the National Institute of Mental Health at Rockville, Maryland, thinks that the human population will peak at nine billion. The Population Division of the United Nations thinks the world might reach a peak of 15 billion people. A Committee of the National Academy of Sciences thinks we'll start leveling off much sooner—when we reach 10 billion, which is three billion more than its chairman personally thinks can be supported at a moderately affluent Western standard of living. That's much less than the 30 billion the same group thinks could be supported only at a level of chronic malnutrition, even with the help of all the known improvements and the new ones we're likely to invent along the way. Herman Kahn, in his projections of the future made at the Hudson Institute also figures on a world population stabilized "somewhere between ten and 50 billion" in the next few centuries.

What will stop growth first? The usual answer is that the critical limitation might very well be in natural resources. Will shortages of food, minerals, fuel, and other natural resources kill people off or prevent births or both?

A lot of people think both to be true. In 1967, for instance, William and Paul Paddock, an agronomist and a retired diplomat, wrote a book called *Famine-1975.* In his 1970 book, *Population, Resources, Environment,* Paul Ehrlich estimated that 10 to 20 million people were *already* dying of starvation every year with more to come in the very near future.

However, specialists in world agriculture are not so sure Asians would starve to death, even without the promised "Green Revolution" that it is hoped will drastically increase crop yield. Gross malnutrition is easy to find almost everywhere in the world, but lethal starvation is hard to define. Ehrlich's millions of deaths by starvation were, in his definition, "any deaths that would not have occurred if the individual had been properly nourished regardless of the ultimate agent." But there is nothing to back up the assumption that such deaths will increase faster than births. In 1969, the Food and Agriculture Organization of the United Nations expected actual food supply in the underdeveloped nations to increase 2.7 percent a year, a shade above their expected increase of 2.6 percent in population. The crisis was not that Asian nutrition was getting worse, but that it wasn't getting any better.

Each specialist tends to see the limitation in some other field than his own. Nutritionists and biologists worry about the depletion of metals and paper, while those best acquainted with the resource in question can think of ways around the shortage. Something new always seems to appear when we seem to be approaching a limit. In 1900, when the country depended on horsepower for transportation, the limit to the supportable population of the United States was the pasturage available for horses.

We've learned a lot more since then. Physics teaches that matter and energy, though finite, are interchangeable. This means that with enough energy we could remake the crust of the earth to our needs. Cheap energy makes it economic, for instance, to extract minerals from ores too low-grade to be worth mining. It may be nip-and-tuck for a dozen years, but even the pessimists think we'll invent our way round the energy limitation in time. The geologist, Preston E. Cloud, Jr., a Malthusian on resources, puts it this way: "Unless we find a lot more uranium, or pay a lot more money for it, or get a functioning complete breeder reactor or contained nuclear fusion within 10 or 15 years, the energy picture will be far from bright. There is good reason to hope that the breeder will come, and after it contained fusion, if the U235 and helium hold out—but there is no room for complacency." Most scientists are more optimistic about the timetable.

When one limitation of matter-energy is overcome, scientists can point to another usually so far distant that it hasn't been considered seriously before. Malthus couldn't see beyond the limitation of arable land. Our grandfathers couldn't see beyond the limitation of fossil fuels. So it is hard for us to think seriously what will stop us materially once we get continuous fusion power from atomic energy.

Physicists with sharp pencils have provided an interesting theoretical answer. Some suggest that the limitation will be our ability to get rid of the heat generated by the production of energy. According to one calculation, when kilowatt production gets close to 5 percent of the total power received from the sun, the earth's climate will change. The polar icecaps will melt, raising the sea level 300 feet to inundate New York, London, Tokyo, and the many population centers of the world which have grown up around seaports. Large-scale combustion of any kind could have unpredictable effects on the thin layer of oxygen which supports all life.

Fire, flood, suffocation. These are the unexpectedly apocalyptic limits to human use of the earth's finite matter-energy base. Millions or billions of people could burn up, drown, or smother to death, but this is not what laymen have in mind when they assume that the population of the world will be limited by the earth's natural resources. Like the phosphorus for which human beings might ultimately eat each other, some metals are becoming scarce. However, the shortages are expressing themselves in higher prices which automatically stimulate substitutions, conservation, and new research. Supply and demand "solve" material shortages so smoothly that scarcities seldom become public issues.

Not supply, but the disposal of the waste products of consumption has emerged as the most expected limitation, and the problem is not technical. Air and water can be cleared of pollutants. Junk cars can be reprocessed. City dumps can be mined and the mounting garbage sorted, recovered, composted, compacted into building materials, used as landfill, or burned for fuel. Paper, metals, rubber, and textiles are already being reclaimed, bottles are being reused, and water is being recycled. More sophisticated technologies to handle waste are waiting in the wings, ready to go as soon as they become "economically feasible."

The problem is not economic either. In spite of protestations of ignorance, we know enough about what waste is costing, all told, to establish that the recycling and reclaiming and reuse are worth the price.

A growing army of environmental and ecological specialists know exactly what is wrong and say so on the frequent occasions their advice is publicly solicited. The issue is not technical, nor economic, but political. Who is to pay for the cost of disposing of waste products for which no one now is responsible?

If poisons discharged into the environment are going to limit the human population, then man is indeed a self-limiting species, limited not by predators or the four horsemen of the apocalypse (fire, flood, pestilence and war) but by the failure of his unique human ability to analyze a problem and organize to solve it.

● *Are Numbers the Issue?*

The indictment "too many" is formidable and even plausible, but the case is hard to prove. It's just as easy to show that large populations can be less crowded, less wasteful, less disruptive of the balance of nature, and have more humane environments in which to live than small ones. The bigger the better is almost a rule of history.

Ecologists now believe that only a few thousand nomads made the Holy Land a desert by overgrazing it in Biblical times. In Israel, a few million modern Jews are restoring the land.

London is now mercifully less polluted than it was

48

when it was a small fraction of its present size in Shake-speare's day. Like other cities of its time, London had a death rate so much higher than its birth rate that it maintained its population only by recruiting immigrants from the country, where pollution was less noxious. It is only with the advance of sanitation systems that cities have become hygienically safe for millions.

The values endangered by bigness vary widely, and often they are sneakily implied rather than stated. The University of California at Berkeley is widely faulted for being "too big," but its graduates are quite as well educated by any standard as the alumni of intimate little liberal arts colleges where students are in no danger of being "folded, stapled, or mutilated." By what unspecified yardstick is the University of California too big?

Yardsticks slide, too. Although A.T.& T. is now widely regarded as too big for anyone to manage, it still provides better service per dollar invested and access to more other phone subscribers than smaller phone systems.

We expect the crime rate of New York to be high because the city is so big, but Tokyo and London have lower crime rates although their population is about the same. Hong Kong, Paris, and Brussels average out more inhabitants per square mile than New York City, but their crime rates are lower. In the United States it is not New York City, with its eight million inhabitants, that has the foulest air, but little Steubenville, Ohio, population 34,000.

There is no universal or necessary connection between the size of a country, city, company, college, family, or other human group, and its wealth, growth, greatness, or form of government. India is big and poor; the United States, big and rich; Guatemala small and poor; Switzerland small and rich. The biggest companies don't necessarily return the most profit per investor's dollar, nor do the small-

49

est. Crowding is supposed to have made the Germans war-like, but it hasn't had that effect on the East Indians. India is big and democratic; China big and totalitarian; New Zealand is small and democratic, and Uruguay small and autocratic. Small college towns often have more cultural resources than big business-oriented cities.

• *Why "Cut" Won't Work*

The population alarmists don't see that slowing growth is not only impractical, but won't necessarily bring back the golden age they mourn. Why? They aren't all hired by tax-payer associations to cut the costs of schooling and welfare. Most of them, as a matter of fact, are well-intentioned public-spirited intellectuals who wish to see an improvement in the quality of life.

Overpopulation is a most plausible evil on several counts. First, it comports with those deep feelings or "instincts" we call common sense. We may indeed inherit from our territorial animal ancestors a vestigial sense of discomfort when we find ourselves in a group that is larger than seems "right." The "right size," of course, is the size the group was when you first became aware of it, and population growth means that that size is apt to be getting bigger.

If you are middle-aged—say fortyish—there are now four people for every three in the country twenty years ago, when you began fending for yourself. If you are really old, and can remember what life was like before World War II, you are sharing the land with almost twice as many people as you had to contend with when you started contending on your own thirty years ago. You lament the passing of the open fields in which you played, but your children think it's

50

natural for one yard to abut on another. It is easy to blame these visible differences for many of today's problems.

But the most important reason why the fallacies are hard to see is that the population alarmists confuse numbers with a lot of things that don't necessarily depend on numbers at all.

Everyone's favorite example of overpopulation is India. The population alarmists have created the impression that cutting the population of India—or even cutting its rate of increase—would automatically leave more to go around and so improve the standard of living of those remaining. They imply that India is poor *because* her population has increased so dramatically in the past twenty years. This just isn't so. Indian vital statistics are admittedly inaccurate, but such as they are, they show that the Gross National Product per capita has reliably risen a hair's breadth ahead of the annual population increase. What the more careful population alarmists are saying is that the Indians would be richer in the future if they would only act like us and invest their rising wealth in factories instead of in babies. We are distressed not because they are worse off than when they were fewer, but because they aren't as much better off as they would be if they adopted our priorities.

The misery of Calcutta might not be relieved by cutting the population of India, but it produces an emotional impact that bolsters the case for population control. Still, numbers do make a difference, and since we are going to have a big population in the United States as well as India, it is worth looking into the difference that numbers really make.

Chapter III

Living With Numbers

There are many ways in which the population of the United States makes it a different country in which to live than Sweden, for example, which has a smaller population but resembles the United States in so many of its economic and cultural institutions. More simply still, there are ways in which every family of six differs from every family of three, but the differences are hard to see from the inside.

Some of the important consequences of population size are built right into the numbers themselves.

• *Exploding Minorities*

The most obvious—and least recognized consequences of high numbers are purely arithmetical. The larger the total population, the harder it is to dismiss as freakish any small percentage of cases, because even a small percentage comprises a large number of human beings. The range is wider than in a small population. And, all other things being equal, it's harder to change a lot of people or things than it is to change a few.

Big numbers magnify the accidents, minorities, anomalies, and trivia which go unnoticed when the population is smaller.

Floods and fires now affect more people because there are more people around for them to affect. Oil spillage from tankers attracts attention because there are more people living along the shores to notice it.

Accidents, disease, unemployment, and other hazards of life are declining risks in the United States. Rates are generally down, but they affect so many more people that it doesn't seem that way. Human beings are not rates. In the West, at least, they are irreplaceable individuals, each one of whom quite possibly has a unique and immortal soul. This means that the bigger the population, the less margin for error.

Side effects of drugs are a good example. The contraceptive pill is one of the safest and most effective drugs ever marketed. It fails only one percent of the time. But in a population the size of the United States, that one percent failure can result in 250,000 unwanted human beings.

Or take automobile accidents. We are glad to learn that the odds against getting killed while driving into town are better than they used to be, but there is so much more driving that cars kill more human beings nearly every year. In 1969 and 1970, cars killed more Americans than the war in Vietnam. Car makers are under pressure to add safety devices.

Unemployment is more serious for a big population. In 1970, for instance, we had four million people out of work, just about the same number as in the Depression year 1930. Business was actually doing a much better job of employing those willing and able to work. Percentagewise, only 4.9

percent were unemployed in 1970, compared with 8.7 percent in 1930, when the labor force was little more than half as big. But four million people are four million people, and it is no comfort to any of them that their misfortune is more exceptional than it was in 1950 or 1930. On the contrary, their very rarity raises an ugly question: if just about everyone else can get a job, why can't I?

The discomfort of being statistically exceptional helps to explain the increasing bitterness of black women heads of family, who now constitute a substantial number of the citizens officially designated as poor.

All conventional economic wisdom is based on the premise that most people are poor. The economic and social structure is a pyramid, with the higher the fewer. After World War II, something new happened on this planet. In the United States, in Scandinavia, and now in other industrial countries such as Japan, the pyramid no longer described the distribution of wealth. In these countries, most people were not and did not regard themselves as poor. Poverty became not the common lot of most people, but a special problem. For the first time it became necessary to establish an official definition of poverty. Under the U.S. Census definition of poverty, which in 1971 was almost $4,000 a year per family, depending on its makeup and location, the poor declined from 22 percent of the population in 1960 to 13 percent in 1970. The decline was enough to cut the absolute numbers of poor people by 14 million, but during those ten years, the absolute number of black women left with children to support increased substantially. Black women heading families don't have to be statisticians to feel that they are just about the only people in the United States who aren't better off than they used to be.

Increasing numbers magnify dissent even more dramatically. The news is full of extremist attacks on the establishment from the right and the left. It looks as if the country is indeed more "polarized" than it used to be, but it may only be that there are many more people well-enough informed and self-confident enough to protest.

In 1969, most of the noise on college campuses came from radicals frankly aiming to overthrow the American power structure by force. *Time* magazine estimated them to be two percent of the student body, about what they had always been. But in the quiet 1950s, two percent scattered over 2500 campuses seldom added up to enough radicals on any one campus to keep a movement going. All studies of campus outbreaks show that bigger schools, regardless of their complexity or type, had more incidents of violence. And in 1970, two percent of the student body of the United States amounted to 100,000, quite enough to wage a guerrilla war if they all got together.

In human affairs, as in physics, there seems to be a critical mass beyond which explosion occurs. M. Herbert Danzger, a sociologist at Lehman College in New York City, studied race riots of the late 1960s to see what differentiated cites that had outbreaks from those that did not. He suspected that cities with fewer than 5000 blacks didn't erupt into violence, even when they were so small that blacks predominated. It may take a community of 5000 to become conscious of itself and confident enough of its identity to undertake mass action. It may take 5000 to provide the exceptional individuals who can lead a protest movement. But the most likely explanation is that a community of 5000 can support the division of labor or function essential to organized activity. With 5000 there are enough young people to mount street demonstrations, enough people with clerical skills to keep lists and mimeograph circulars, enough people who can and will distribute circulars, enough people who can and will rally workers by telephone.

• *More Class Distinction*

The more people, the more chance that some exceptional individual will be born. A boy has to be taller and better to make the basketball team of a big college than a small one. It is harder for young people to get into good colleges than it was for their parents, since the increase in applicants means that admissions standards can be higher. It's harder to stand out among many than among few, and sometimes the limitations are mechanical. Perhaps because there is a limit to the number who can be listed between the covers of one book, the percentage of Americans deemed eminent enough to get into *Who's Who in America* has declined to a mere three out of every 10,000 for the 1970–1971 edition.

Since "exceptional" includes both ends of the spectrum, there are as many very short boys as very tall ones in big colleges. And because they are brought together within encounter range of each other, the differences are apparent to all. Even if big groups try to be democratic, these visible differences widen the gap between extremes of talent, privilege, experience, wealth, beauty, or any other difference between individuals that matter to them.

• *Harder to Change*

A big system is slower to move and harder to change than a small one. The reason is statistical. When a large number of people have to move, as in a crowd, the pace slows to that of the slowest individual.

Change is bound to be slow when a large number of

units of anything is involved. Consider, for instance, reforming the automobile traffic system. In the United States we now have 109 million motor vehicles and almost as many licensed drivers. Changing either component would take years. The U.S. car population is too big for experiment. It would make more sense to try a new air pollution control system out on the car population of Australia.

Most of the time, of course, stability is a good thing. Big companies weather recessions that put small ones out of business. Famines wipe out small primitive tribes; China and India have enough people so some always survive. However, resistance to change can be a critical failing when an organization has to respond fast or lose out, as is the case for political parties or cosmetic manufacturers. The garment industry, which lives on fashion, comprises a large number of small enterprises that move fast.

A big population means that all the groupings of interest and objective have more people in them, too. Bigger countries tend to have bigger cities as well as more of them. Their universities and their business enterprises involve more people, and so does every administrative arm of government.

Big organizations require more division of labor, more finely divided specialization. The bigger they are, the more energy goes into overhead or staff services not directly chargeable to any one product. It takes more time and money just to keep the show together. That is why it costs a big company, such as General Electric, more to service their home appliances than it costs when the work is done by a neighborhood repair service.

The most important thing about big mobilizations of effort is not so much that many individuals aren't accustomed to being mobilized in such large numbers, or even that the cost of what they accomplish may be higher than it is when the same work is done by a smaller group. The important thing is that big mobilizations are essential to serve big populations. The hard fact is that even if the population growth slows down, the already existing large numbers will continue to require large mobilizations of effort to support them.

• *Growing Pains*

In order to think clearly about the effects of large numbers, it is necessary to make some clear distinctions:

Size and growth are different. The population of Latin America is small but growing fast, while Russia's is big and growing slowly. New York and Los Angeles are both big, but Los Angeles is growing while New York is standing still or even losing population.

There is a very real difference between bigness and the uncomfortable process of getting big. Growing pains hurt, but as every adult knows, they are a separate set of hurts from those encountered in maturity.

Americans may be especially confused, because we are traditional boomers, promoting growth, while deploring the personal price individuals must pay when they move from a small town to a big city, a small firm to a big one, from poverty to affluence, or even from ignorance to "sophistication."

And although we speak of "growth" and "size" as interchangeable evils, they are not the same. Field studies show, for instance, that fast-growing little communities have higher rates of hospitalized depressive disorders and suicides than slower-growing big ones. At a conference on contemporary violence, Karl Menninger, the psychiatrist, observed that civilization may have made man less aggressive, but in his opinion, the improvement had been more than offset by the tensions generated by an "ever-growing population."

What, specifically, generates these tensions? Growing populations are heavily weighted with young people, and with newcomers, whether by natural increase or immigration, and they contribute in the same way to a family, firm, school, community or city.

More Young. Unlike New York, Tokyo is still a growing city, and the first thing a visiting New Yorker notices is that the pace is swifter than at home. Crowds are bigger and street traffic moves faster. Subway trains are packed and commuters burst from them as if shot from a cannon. Everyone is on time or compulsively apologetic about five minutes delay. "Run, don't walk" seems to be the rule for service people in stores and restaurants. People smile more, and they seem to be having more fun. The pleasure quarters sparkle. New York seems slow, gray, and sad by comparison. How come?

Then it dawns on you. Everyone on the street is young. During rush hours, commuter trains are full of young males. Both of these world's biggest cities, New York and Tokyo, have a higher proportion of single people than their nations as a whole, but Tokyo has more people under 30, and more of them are men. Superficially, at least, the city problems of crowding and pollution are statistically worse in Tokyo. They are simply endured more cheerfully by a population that is young and bettering itself.

A higher proportion of young men means more of what young men do. One of these things is to look for a first job. Better educated, and choosier than their Depression-bred fathers, the young men who had been born in the post World War II baby boom confronted an economy that had mechanized most of the beginning jobs. Unemployment rates rose for the younger ages. Colleges filled up with unemployed and underemployed young men who were quick to see that the curriculum was irrelevant to the jobs for which employers were demanding "more education." No wonder they were more rebellious than the small "silent generation" of Depression-born babies who came of age in the prosperous 1950s, when new hands were not only few, but badly needed!

Another thing young men do is to commit crimes. In spite of the reluctance to charge youngsters, almost half of all the people arrested for serious crime in 1969 were under 18 years of age. It is true that young people were more apt to commit crimes, or at least be caught for it, than formerly. But it is also true that there were more of them. If the proportion of young people ages 13 to 20 had remained the same in 1967 as in 1958, for instance, the annual rate of increase in crime would have been 7.5 percent rather than the 8.7 percent reported by the FBI Uniform Crime Statistics.

More Newcomers. A growing community has more young, and more newcomers. Both are geographically more mobile than the old and the settled. Young adults move away to new jobs and new marriages. California is growing so fast that it is full of people who have learned how to move and are willing to move again for reasons which seem trivial to those who have never pulled up stakes.

Migrating runs in families. It can also become a habit. There is some evidence that people who move to another community are more apt to move again than those who stay put. Communities with a lot of newcomers also have a lot of people moving out. This is particularly dramatic in suburban communities, some of which have streets on which the oldest resident on the block has lived there only two or three years.

60

Habitual movers give California its restless, experimental quality. Those who find it easy to move learn the tricks of making and breaking friendships fast. They are not necessarily dropouts, or flower people. On the contrary, they are apt to be opportunists, pulled by news of better opportunities or the offer of a slightly better job in another community, or moved by their employers to new and presumably better jobs.

Expanding firms suffer in the same way as expanding cities, or more recently, suburbs inundated by newcomers from the central city. The newcomers are eager, young, ambitious, and they impress the people on the ground as ill-mannered, brash, untrustworthy, and likely to ruin the reputation of the community or the firm.

When colleges were expanding in the late 1960s, younger faculty members learned to shop around for better pay and promotion from one institution to another. Tenured professors complained, with some justice, that the young instructors were "commercial" and "opportunistic." They were also distressed by the need to make rules about practices which could be left to the discretion of individuals in smaller and more stable faculty groups.

Resentment of the newcomers is sometimes unwittingly encouraged by managers when they bring in "new blood" to make changes they cannot get the incumbent employees to make. The "systems specialist" is often hired to do the dirty work of restructuring obsolete work practices under the guise of computerizing them, and he is hated accordingly by those accustomed to the old ways.

There is a pattern to the complaints against the newcomers, whether to a college, a company, the city, or more recently, the suburbs, and it is remarkably similar to the objections raised against the immigrants from Europe a century ago. The newcomers are seen as "dirty" in their personal habits, likely to "run down" the neighborhood, property values, the quality of the product a firm manufactures, or the reputation of the college. They are personally uncouth and not "friendly." No one gets to "know them" anyway because they "don't care" about their present neighbors and associates, but only about making money and advancing themselves. The loyalties of the newcomers are with those they left behind.

What is disrupting is not the eventual size of a city, town, or country, but the process of getting there; the difficulty is caused by growing. Growing pains, however, are by definition, less serious than problems of size, because in the nature of things, they cure themselves. They may seem unbearable, but like labor pains, they don't last forever, even if you do nothing about them. Statisticians as well as biologists are familiar with the natural law which provides, in the words of the old German proverb, that the trees do not grow into the sky.

• *Size and Density Are Different*

Size means the total number of people, while density refers to the number within a certain area.

The population of a submarine is small, but dense even for a ship. The population of the United States is large, but its square-mile density is no more than that of the world as a whole. As nations go, Japan's population is also big, but denser than that of the United States. Japan's population is big and dense, but Holland's is small and dense, and Australia's is small and sparse.

There's also a difference between density and growing density. Growing density alarms because it violates, in a very personal way, the expectations of personal space in which individuals have been reared. Few Japanese boys have a bedroom of their own, so they don't mind living in company barracks, but middle-class Americans brought up in suburban privacy are uncomfortable when they are drafted into the armed forces, where they have to adjust to less physical and psychic elbowroom than they have had at home. What we call "crowding" is not necessarily dependent on numbers, but so much is blamed on it that it deserves to be considered by itself.

Chapter IV

Too Crowded

There is nothing abstract about doom by "population bomb." The prospect which generates popular support for population control and moves scientists to fantasize cannibalism is all too concrete. There are faces, faces everywhere and none you care to meet.

Everyone can imagine the horror. *Life* magazine pictured it by printing a photograph of bassinets rowed up in a big maternity ward next to a photograph of thickly set tombstones in one of the Long Island cemeteries that limousines pass on their way to New York airports. The implication was no room at birth, no room at death, and no room in between.

A small inconvenience, the very thought of which tenses the shoulder muscles, is the calculation that shoppers will have to wait four or five times as long for a department store elevator in the year 2000—three and half to four minutes instead of the average of 45 seconds clocked by traffic engineers in stores of the 1960s. And there will be no escape, say those who anticipate a packed planet. After a morning of shopping, lunch will be at a counter with two or three hungry people watching for your seat over your shoulder. Traffic in restrooms will be so heavy that they will have to take the doors off toilet stalls or line toilets up against the wall. If you want a moment to yourself you will have to rent a special room for a half hour of solitude. The price will be high, but those who can afford it will find it worthwhile; during the impacted sixties seasoned air travelers on expense accounts learned to rent motel rooms to wait out daytime weather delays away from the bustling anonymity of even the most spanking-new airport buildings.

The search for solitude suggests that it's not the mere jamming together of people that causes problems, but the relationships that this density sets up—the encounters between people. Crowding is the discomfort that develops when people must endure more encounters with each other than they are accustomed to.

"People pollution" is the phrase Dr. Milton Greenblatt, Mental Health Commissioner for Massachusetts uses. "There is a toxic reaction caused in an individual when over-crowded by others," he told the 1970 meeting of the American Medical Association.

What he has in mind is the situation facing people who live in the densely populated inner city.

• *Urban Blight*

Central cities seem to have more of everything bad; more schizophrenia, alcoholism, crime, delinquency, suicide, family desertion, infant mortality, and rejection for service in the armed forces. These pathologies are often ascribed to "crowding" itself, rather than to the poverty and under-privilege which forces ghetto dwellers to accept inadequate

65

housing. When he was asked to explain an increase in the cases of children battered and abused by their parents, Dr. William Barton of Children's Hospital, Washington, blamed ghetto crowding. He said that the poor live in cramped quarters and can't get away from their children when they are angry with them.

Many behavioral scientists, among them Ashley Montagu, the anthropologist, said that riots and demonstrations were not expressions of man's innate aggressiveness, but were learned and exacerbated by the "cramped conditions" of modern cities.

To middle-class social workers, the crowding of slum life seems sufficient cause for the breakup of families. Little children are cooped up inside, kept from sleep, and atrophied by long hours of watching television. Older children and fathers escape as often and as long as they can, if only to avoid family fights that are intolerable in close quarters.

In the United States, we have always looked upon cities as a source of evil. We shudder at the plight of generation after generation of country boys and girls who migrate to urban areas where they have to adapt to the "bad" ways of city life.

Louis Wirth, the great Chicago sociologist, labeled this process "urbanization," and his description of 1938 is still the most articulate statement of our traditional distrust of expanding cities:

> The recency and rapidity of urbanization in the United States accounts for the acuteness of our urban problems. . . . Large numbers account for individual variability, the relative absence of intimate personal acquaintanceship, the segmentalization of human relations which are largely anonymous, superficial, and transitory. . . . Density involves diversification and specialization, the coincidence of close

physical contact and distant social relations, glaring contrasts, a complex pattern of segregation, the predominance of formal social control, and accentuated friction. . . . Heterogeneity tends to break down social structures and to produce increased mobility, instability, and insecurity, and the affiliation of the individuals with a variety of intersecting and tangential social groups with a high rate of membership turnover. The pecuniary nexus tends to displace personal relations, and institutions tend to cater to mass rather than to individual requirements.

Wirth saw danger in the "relative absence of intimate personal acquaintanceship, the segmentalization of human relations which are largely anonymous, superficial, and transitory."

• *Back to the Country*

If crowding in the cities creates so many problems, the obvious solution seems to be to encourage people to move back to the small towns and the country where the desirable virtues of community spirit, neighborliness, "friendliness," and personal loyalty seem to flourish.

The United States has been moving people into the backwoods since land was offered to Revolutionary War veterans. We have been so successful that our distribution policies may well go down in history as the reason why we became the richest country in the world.

During the nineteenth century, the Federal Government used its public lands to subsidize settlers, railroads, and the land-grant colleges which have been the spearhead of our agricultural revolution. The New Deal revived the dying Tennessee Valley by providing it with cheap electric power. During World War II, Federally financed war plants and Army camps were built in the boondocks, where they rescued many a declining community. Mortgage loans insured by the FHA and the Veterans Administration made it possible for people to move out of the cities after the war.

The most dramatic people-relocation policy of the 1960s has been in education. Eastern states have followed the example of California in developing their state universities into a network of branches. Although the original idea was to put colleges where the students lived, many of the branches were located instead in dying small towns, such as Oneonta and New Paltz in New York, and the students have been coming to them. In the 1970s, nearly half the students at the State University of New York at New Paltz were from New York City, and the State University of Tennessee, at Martin, a stagnant little farming town in the Bible Belt, drew a substantial portion of its students from Memphis.

Population relocation is more attractive than population control because it is, in the officialese of President Nixon's former counsellor, Daniel P. Moynihan, more "policy-responsive,"—easier for the government to influence.

In 1967 Secretary of the Interior Stewart Udall under President Johnson suggested that the United States would be better off if half the population could somehow or other be eliminated. His successor, Walter B. Hickel, was less Draconian. "We don't have too many people," he announced. "The trouble is that they are concentrated in the wrong places."

In his 1970 State of the Union message President Nixon called for a "new rural environment which will not only stem the migration to urban centers, but reverse it." Rural areas and small towns have, of course, been traditionally Republican and they are losing population.

Nixon's "rural alternative" to crowded cities stimulated a new set of back-to-the-country policies. Specialists in the Department of Agriculture identified 300 small towns and cities with growth potential and tried to get business to move to them. Some economists talked of revitalizing the rural areas with little canneries that would make food specialities, or leather goods operations that would make economic use of semi-skilled labor supplied by people who did not want to work hard or full time in the city. William H. Crook, Ambassador to Australia, suggested a "New Homestead Act" to develop the 400 million acres of remaining public land, most of it non-arable, for manufacturing, towns, colleges, or whatever land-use research could suggest. If the Israelis can make the desert bloom, why can't we?

The friends of the country have argued that depressed farm and mining towns ought by rights to be getting the money the Federal Government was spending on job training, housing, and welfare in the ghetto. Specialists in the Department of Agriculture proposed programs that would keep farmers on the land. Business could be lured to small towns with investment tax credits, liberalized depreciation allowances, and highways built with Federal money.

Those who advocate these "back to the country" policies are as distressed about the decline of the farms and small towns, which epitomize the old-fashioned virtues, as they are about the evils of concentrating people in the cities.

Although most Americans now live in metropolitan areas, policy-makers in business and government still tend to come from farms or small towns. Down to 1972, Kennedy has been our only really urban president. Johnson thinks of himself as a rancher and Nixon grew up in a small town. Both inherit the agrarian tradition which moved Thomas Jefferson to fear that "men and women would one day live together in such numbers that they would become indifferent to one another's needs or cares." According to this tradition, the city is not merely the place where problems erupt, but the basic problem itself.

The reasoning is straightforward: people are crowded in cities, and "crowding" is a self-evident source of trouble. Both propositions are questionable.

• *Cities Are Thinning Out*

If spreading people out geographically would really make things better, we should never have had the breakdowns of the 1960s. Most people who experienced a change in the population density in which they lived during the decade of the 1960s moved from high density to low density, rather than from low density to high density, as the "crowding alarmists" assumed.

According to the Census of 1970, three-quarters of the population growth between 1960 and 1970 was in the metropolitan areas, but virtually all of that growth was in the suburbs, where population density wasn't high by any standards. The central cities where population density is a problem grew only one percent!

Where did the new people in the suburbs come from? A great many of them were babies who had been born there. If they moved from somewhere else, they were much more likely to have come from the more densely populated central city than from the less densely populated country. The people moving into the suburbs were spreading out from high-density to low-density living.

The spreadout was nothing new. Cities always grow faster around the edges, where the density is lowest. American cities have been overflowing their boundaries and annexing the overflow for years. When you try to find out how much a city has grown between two census years, you're likely to discover that the population figures can't be compared because the city limits have been extended. To make comparisons possible, the Census reports compare population on the basis of Standard Metropolitan Statistical

Areas, (SMSAs), which stay put geographically. The average density of SMSAs was highest in 1930, and has been declining since. Much of the spreadout, of course, has been inside the areas, as people move from the more densely settled neighborhoods downtown to less densely settled neighborhoods a little farther out. Between 1950 and 1960, for instance, the number of people living in "urbanized areas" of more than 1000 to a square mile increased by 30 percent, but they had spread out so that they were occupying 80 percent more acreage. This meant that the most densely packed urbanized areas were thinning out.

Americans have been spreading out now for several generations. Manhattan, our densest county, now has about 70,000 people per square mile. In 1910 people were packed into the lower East Side 320,000 per square mile. According to one source, the density of cities and towns in New York, New Jersey, and Connecticut has been declining since 1860. Urbanized places were fewer then, and they didn't cover as much ground, but they were jampacked with people inside the city boundaries.

The "ant hill" society which "piles humanity on itself" is disappearing, yet city authorities continue to blame urban unrest on new arrivals "crowding in" to their slums. Politicians in Los Angeles and Cleveland were so sure of it that in 1965 these cities undertook a special census to measure the tide of newcomers. To their embarrassment, they found that the black areas of Watts and Hough, which had been torn by riots in the early 1960s, had actually suffered a net loss of population.

If getting people out of densely populated cities is the way to improve the quality of life, the Census of 1970 provided grounds for hope. More than half of the nation's 25 biggest cities lost population. St. Louis lost a fifth of its population. Other big cities which lost were Pittsburgh, down 15 percent; Detroit, down 11 percent; Boston, down 10 percent. Smaller losses were registered for New Orleans, Chicago, Seattle, San Francisco, Baltimore, Milwaukee, and Philadelphia.

The worst cities lost considerably. Few had more troubles than East St. Louis, Illinois. In 1969, 21 percent of the labor force was unemployed, a quarter of the population was on public assistance, and half the families were living on less than $3,000. None of this could be blamed on newly crowded conditions. Its residents had been moving out faster than any Federal program of population redistribution could have sent them. Between 1960 and 1970, East St. Louis had lost 17 percent of its miserable population.

The same thing happened in Newark, whose awful condition is beyond question. Its unemployment rate and nonwhite infant mortality rate, a sensitive indicator of ghetto wretchedness, were among the highest recorded in the 1960s. But the Census of 1970 reported that Newark had actually lost 7 percent of its people during the decade.

The loss has done little to improve the quality of Newark life. It hasn't even relieved the housing shortage: the black community still feels so squeezed for space that it bitterly opposed a plan to tear down part of the ghetto and build a college on the site.

Harlem, the black capital of the United States, also seems to be thinning out. Blacks are getting out of the dilapidated buildings and moving to the suburbs, or to other parts of the city where it is now possible for them to find places to live. The thinning out of Harlem is hard to establish however, because unlike Newark, Harlem is a neighborhood lost in the dense and various populations of Manhattan, and its black population has been grossly underestimated in the past because single black males are notoriously hard for the census takers to find.

In 1970 there were 17,000 fewer blacks in Manhattan than there were in 1960, but whether the loss meant an improvement in housing is a controversial issue. Buildings are being abandoned throughout New York, and a large proportion of them seem to be in Harlem, where boarded-up houses are very visible. The blacks who still live there could be more crowded in the remaining units than before. The issue will be settled when the block-by-block data from the Census of 1970 is finally published sometime in 1972, but, on balance, many students of population movement believe that Harlem, like other ghettoes, is less crowded than it used to be.

• *Thinning Out Hasn't Helped*

Cities losing population do not feel that they are better off for the uncrowding. Their mayors are not happy about the declines. To them, thinning out is not a remedy, but a symptom of trouble, the same trouble that causes some of the breakdowns. One cause is physical deterioration. The old plants in the central cities become costly to run, so employers move out of them, taking jobs out of the neighborhood. When middle-class residents move out of the old housing nearby, poor people crowd in to get cheap rent by sharing the vacated old quarters, but since the jobs have gone, they are unemployed.

In Watts, the black suburb of Los Angeles, unemployment was at a 20 percent rate all through the 1960s, and there was no industrial construction in the area for thirty years, until the Department of Commerce underwrote the development of an industrial park in 1969.

But plants and residences are not all that wear out in the central city. Schools, firehouses, police stations, hospitals, power plants, and other public facilities of the central city get old and costly to operate, too, but unlike the industrial plants, they cannot be abandoned. On the contrary, they get harder usage. As the neighborhood runs down, there are more fires, more crimes, more emergency hospital admissions, more demand for special school services. Those who remain in the rundown neighborhood are a dead loss to the city treasury. They use more public services, especially welfare services, but they cannot afford to pay taxes.

If low-density living were a magic solution, those who had "escaped" to the suburbs should be better off, but it has not worked out that way. Companies who move their offices out of town often discover that they have merely taken the problems of the city with them. After the initial local labor supply has been tapped, skilled help is hard to find, and frequently has to be bused, sometimes from long distances, and fed subsidized lunches. Local facilities for traffic, phone service, electric power, and other essentials of corporate life quickly reach saturation.

Families moving to the suburbs for space are soon surrounded by apartment houses, gas stations, rising taxes, and old residents willing to protect, by zoning laws or even by force, the former character of the neighborhood. In the late 1960s, welfare expenditures were rising faster in many suburbs of New York than they were rising inside the city itself. Westchester, once the home of the rich, is coping with pockets of poverty, race problems, pollution, and crime. Shopping centers are targets for teen-age vandals, and middle-class parents are horrified to discover that drug addiction is no longer confined to black teen-agers in the big city ghetto, but has spread to their well-brought-up children as well.

The space between suburban houses which had looked so attractive has turned out to be awkward and expensive for many purposes. In some suburbs, kindergarten children spend as much time on the school bus as they do in school. Suburban sprawl is not only costly to service, but as destructive of community feeling as the "piling of people on people" in the heart of the city.

Too Crowded

In the 1970s, crime, family breakup, pollution, welfare costs, and race conflict are following people to the low-density suburbs, where "crowding" can no longer be the culprit. Critics of the suburbs have a new word which sounds like the slippery evils it symbolizes: the slurbs.

The troubles of the suburbs make it easier to see the hitherto disregarded advantages of the high-density life.

• *Cities Create Wealth*

The friends of the city challenge the traditional agrarian view that cities are parasites on the countryside. A strong case can be made for the city as the original and true creator of progress and prosperity.

"Concentration is the genius of the city, its reason for being," says William H. Whyte, conservationist and author of *The Last Landscape*. "What it needs is not less people, but more." He thinks that density actually creates wealth because it forces people to use scarce land more efficiently. Jane Jacobs takes much the same view in her books, *The Death and Life of Great American Cities* and *The Economy of Cities*. She says that cities have problems because they have stopped growing, and are not applying new technology to traffic jams and pollution. Thinning the city out is "subtracting the problem," not solving it.

When people "rub elbows" with each other, the theory goes, the enterprising among them see new work to be done, new ways to do the old work better. They are near enough to capital, suppliers, and customers to try the new ideas. Jane Jacobs describes how the brassiere industry was founded by a dressmaker, who used the resources she found in New York City to mass produce a garment most women need.

Cities do seem to grow big by taking in their own washing, so to speak, and by making possible more encounters between people. The bigger the city, the more of its workers are selling to or serving each other or the industries regarded as "basic" because they bring money into the city. Big cities can support diamond cutters, umbrella repair shops, advertising agencies, and many specialties which are not economic in small cities. In *Urban Structure: The Social and Spatial Character of Cities*, Ralph Thomlinson quotes a study made some time ago of the proportion of basic to nonbasic workers in various cities. For every 10 "basic" workers, little Oshkosh, a manufacturing city in Wisconsin, had six nonbasic workers, but New York City had 21.

It's easy to see how nonbasic work multiplies. In a small business, the owner doesn't need a secretary. He can carry the paperwork around in his hat, leaving both hands free to pitch in and help where he's needed. He can write the few letters required in odd moments and greet all visitors personally. But as his business grows, he delegates some of this work to a secretary. When other businessmen prosper and hire secretaries, it becomes profitable for someone to specialize in the training of secretaries.

At first the secretarial school may serve the whole community as a placement service, but when the number of graduates and jobs grow too big, it is worth someone's while to specialize in placing secretaries, and it becomes worth the time of employers and job applicants to pay for this placement service.

The business community grows, presumably in part at least, because of the time that the secretaries are saving their bosses, and eventually the secretaries form an association to promote the interests of their occupation and possibly to seek better pay and working conditions. At first the work of the association is unpaid; members pitch in and help. But eventually the association becomes so big that contributions from members are enough to support a paid secretary for the Secretaries Association.

Too Crowded

Paid help enables the Secretaries Association to gather information and perform new services on behalf of all secretaries. At first, these activities are reported informally to the membership. But the report grows, and soon it has become a periodic newsletter, and then a regular magazine. Manufacturers of typewriters and other products that secretaries have a voice in buying, are willing to buy advertising space to reach secretaries, so the Association magazine eventually becomes a separate commercial enterprise. The specialization and the spinoffs continue as the number of secretarial jobs, and the encounters between secretaries, increase.

Manhattan is an interesting case to study. It is the perfect example of the upward spiral produced by more and more encounters between people until the encounter specialists themselves take over. Because it has the densest concentration of highly salaried workers, it also has the highest rents of any central business district in the country. Even though new skyscrapers continue to be built, the high rates force out workers of lesser productivity.

You can see what has happened on almost every street. Secondhand bookstores, small manufacturing that used to be carried on in loft buildings, handicraft shops and other establishments have had to go. Routine clerical work, such as insurance records, magazine subscriptions, and mail order, have been mechanized to use smaller space, or moved to places where rent and wages are lower.

Who is left? Those whose work is worth the high rent can be described as *encounter specialists*, people who must be close to the greatest possible concentration of other people. They are increasingly people who make a living by knowing the "right man to see." They are, primarily, men who sell ideas: advertising men, promoters, brokers, publishers, radio and television people, and program packagers, in addition, of course, to the people who frankly admit they are salesmen, and want to be close to a large number of customers. People who mediate between enterprises, such as lawyers, who must be close enough to each other to pass papers back and forth and talk face-to-face. Bankers who are essentially brokers of money, and must be in constant touch with people who have money to invest and people who can make good use of borrowed capital. Agents of every kind—travel, employment, executive recruiting, talent, literary, sales, publicity. Consultants of specialized services who must be near their clients; lawyers, accountants, management specialists, public relations advisors. Specialized services which cater to all of those we have mentioned, such as typesetting enterprises and office machine repair services.

Although some big companies have moved their headquarters out of New York, the city is still the "headquarters town" for many leading American corporations. More presidents of large corporations can be assembled by phone for lunch in New York than in any other city of the world, which is one of the reasons why they are there. Even companies that have moved most of the head office to the suburbs find that they have to maintain some facilities in the city for the advertising, marketing, financial, and legal heads.

New York City is the biggest auction market not only for stocks and bonds and sugar and coffee and silver, but for Maine potatoes, frozen concentrated orange juice, rare metals such as platinum and palladium, and ship charters. It is the place where small groups of brokers, well known to each other, make markets for products so esoteric that those who need them would not know where to look for them. When flood threatens a populated riverbank, dealers in burlap bags can phone each other up and locate the nearest source of sandbags in a nonbureaucratic hurry. Encounters have to be cheap and easy to make these transactions possible.

The contact industry has to be in one place—and it is so productive that it has driven just about every other kind of work out of New York. Professor Benjamin Chinitz, an economist at the University of Pittsburgh, has estimated that 40 percent of all U.S. jobs in national-market whole-saling, more than a third of the jobs in finance, and almost a quarter of the business and professional service jobs are located in the New York metropolitan area. Half of these jobs are within five miles of Times Square.

• *Metropolis, U.S.A.*

The opportunities provided by the encounters of high-density living are still more attractive to most people than the drawbacks. Though the inner city cores may be thinning out, the metropolitan areas continue to increase their popu-lations at the expense of the rural sections of the United States. In 1970, there were more people living in metropoli-tan New York than on all the farms in the country put together.

We are becoming—indeed, we already are—a metro-politan nation. If the shift continues, more than half the population of the year 2000 will live in "Bos-Wash," the cor-ridor from Boston to Washington; "Chi-Pitts" the area be-tween Chicago and Pittsburgh; or "San-San," the region from San Francisco to San Diego. A fourth rapidly growing region is "Ja-Mi" the belt of people from Jacksonville to Miami.

Outside of the expending metropolitan areas, all is de-cay and decline. Over half the counties in the United States had fewer people in 1970 than in 1960, and so many young people had moved out of some of them that they had more deaths than births. One of these was Loving County, Texas. A local newspaper headline writer could not resist the pun: NO LOVING IN LOVING COUNTY.

The Crowding Syndrome

Fly from New York to Los Angeles on a clear day and you realize that most of the country is as empty as the interior of an atom. Drive out of the city into any of the midcontinent communities fondly known as the "heartlands," and you see deserted villages, rotting farmhouses, and scrawny, second-growth trees where once was crop or pasture.

Only two percent of the United States is "urbanized" to a density of 1000 inhabitants per square mile, but more than three-quarters of the population lives in this two percent of land.

The overloads of the city are the underloads of the country. In the cities, congestion raises the cost of essential services, but Victor Fuchs, a specialist on the cost of services at the National Bureau of Economic Research, points out these costs also rise in places so sparsely populated that there are not enough people to support them. Costs rise astronomically when children have to be bused long distances to school, or patients flown to hospitals, as is the practice in Alaska.

West Virginia, North Dakota, South Dakota, and Wyoming lost population in the Census of 1970, and Mississippi was the same. People were leaving these states because they wanted schooling, medical care, entertainment, and other services of a caliber that was generally not available in these places at any price. "Most states in this country suffer from having too small a population," Fuchs asserts flatly. "The case for attempting to influence the geographic distribution of population in the United States is stronger than for trying to control the total size." Fuchs is supporting the Government's relocation policies, but he's also saying that some things that people want are only available in metropolitan areas.

Chapter V

Not Enough
Elbowroom

So far, we've been talking about "crowding" in terms of number of people per square mile, or density. There's another aspect to it however. "Crowding" can also refer to a lack of significant personal space, or "elbowroom," which can be measured in square or cubic feet per person.

The two concepts frequently go together, but they are not the same. Manhattan has more inhabitants per square mile than any other area in the United States, but some of its most heavily populated blocks are occupied by people in high-rise luxury apartments who enjoy personal space befitting the prince who built the Taj Mahal. They are not "crowded" in the same way as are the ten or fifteen families who live together in an East Harlem tenement apartment designed for one family.

The general indictment of "crowding" implies an intolerable restriction of personal space. It is based on the notion that every human being needs a certain amount of "breath-

81

ing room" in order to be human, and that without it, social order breaks down.

The proposition sounds plausible until you try to find out the square or cubic footage human beings need to be human, and what happens when this is restricted. As you hunt for this evidence, it dawns on you that the discomfort described as "crowdedness" is social, not spatial, and that in the past ten years complaints of crowding have become a polite way for the rich, the cultivated, and the white-skinned to express their fear of physical contact with the poor, the uneducated, and above all, the black.

Listen carefully to complaints of "crowding" and you detect a snobbish overtone that the complainers don't want to admit even to themselves. Middle-class families move away to the suburbs not so much to get away from "too many people," but to get away from the need to "rub elbows" with the "wrong kind of people." In their new homes they frequently seek out opportunities to meet the "right sort." The blacks made a rule out of it long ago: "In the South they don't care how close you get, just so as you don't get too high; in the North they don't care how high you get, just so as you don't get too close." White intellectuals don't dare admit their uneasiness at the extent to which blacks are getting both close and high, but they complain instead about the inhumanity that seems to result when people are forced into close contact with each other.

Language discloses how strongly people feel about personal space. A "close" friend is one who can come close, but others who try "breathe down your neck," "get in your hair" or "under your skin," and if they become too "pushy" we may treat them in an "aloof" manner designed to warn them to "keep their distance," which turns out to be "at arm's length," or the range within which we could hit them.

Violations of personal space arouse acute discomfort.

Not Enough Elbowroom

We sympathize with the member of the Women's Army Corps who spent her first 24-hour leave up in a hotel room with the "Do Not Disturb" sign on the door. We pity royalty because they cannot always retire from public view when they please, and we wonder how submariners and Arctic explorers stand being cooped up with each other.

People have very definite feelings about the personal space they need, feelings that reveal themselves in explicit action. You "move over" to give a stranger room without being conscious of what you are doing, and the "room" you make for him can be measured precisely. People in queues space themselves as neatly and as unconsciously as sparrows on a telephone wire.

Dr. Milton Greenblatt of the Massachusetts Mental Health Commission, tells us that the response to the approach of another person is physiological: "The galvanic skin resistance decreases, the skeletal muscles tense, the heart accelerates, the skin vessels contract, the blood pressure rises."

• The Right Distance

Since the days when galleys were rowed by banks of slaves, human affairs have been arranged on the assumption that human beings "have" to have a certain amount or kind of space. Building codes require that buildings be set back from the street and that ceilings be of a certain height so that individuals will have "enough room." There are safety rules limiting the number of persons to a restaurant, a theatre, an elevator, even a subway car, and whatever the reasons for the limit, the number must be less than the physical capacity of the space or it would not be necessary to have a rule.

The space a person needs seems so self-evident that it

comes as something of a shock to discover that behavioral scientists can't really give architects and institutional managers a universal square or cubic-foot per-person figure as a guideline. We can be explicit about how much we need in one particular situation, but the amount varies as soon as the circumstances change.

Edward T. Hall, Professor of Anthropology at Northwestern University in Evanston, Illinois, measured the space people unconsciously adopt between each other in different cultures and situations. He discovered very distinct zones, based on their relationships with one another.

The *intimate* zone is within arm's reach, and it's for lovemaking, comforting, and protecting. The *personal* zone is the distance for conversation, about four feet. The *social* zone is for most work and play involving a group. The *public* zone is the distance of public lectures. It can sometimes be determined by the distance beyond which a casual greeting is regarded as necessary.

You don't realize how rigid and how arbitrary the "right distance" is until you go to another country where the "right distance" is different. A South American will push a North American across a room trying to maintain the close distance that is normal in South America between acquaintances, while the North American backs away to attain the somewhat bigger distance comfortable in his country. The maneuver is visible only to a bystander: the men themselves are unaware of it. It's hard to express the "right distance" with a tape measure, because it depends on who's talking. "Far" means out of reach, "near" means close enough to touch, and the actual feet and inches involved depend not only on the length of the observer's arm, but on his feelings about the person or thing to be touched.

"Crowding," then, is not a simple or universally measurable evil. Before blaming it, you have to know who's crowded, and under what conditions. Early social workers who were sure that slum crowding was the cause of slum behavior, were never able to prove it. William C. Loring, Jr., a sociologist, tried to find out what characterized families who were brought to the attention of the authorities in Boston during the 1940s by comparing them with untroubled families similar in size, composition, income, occupation, length of residence, and housing. He found that the troubled families averaged a little less total space, number of rooms, and heated space, but not enough to make much difference.

More recent investigators have had no better luck in finding a straightforward connection between houseroom and well-being when income and occupation are held constant. The French investigator Paul Henry Chombart de Lauwes found that Parisian workers averaging 86 to 108 square feet of houseroom had twice as many measurable social and psychological troubles as those averaging 108 to 150 square feet per person, but it is obvious that big families with the same income and occupational status as small families have not only less houseroom per family member, but less of everything else that money can buy as well. Halliman H. Winsborough of Duke University found that population density didn't make a signficant difference in the infant mortality, welfare dependency, and tuberculosis rates of neighborhoods in Chicago. There are worse things about being poor than the crowded housing that usually goes with it.

Families who are moved from crowded slum dwellings to new housing projects should enjoy improved family life at the very least, but attempts to prove the worth of housing projects by before-and-after studies have also been inconclusive. Some relocated slumdwellers miss the old neighborhood so much that they feel they are actually worse off in their spacious new quarters, and a few social workers, obviously piqued, have suggested that the reason might be that the poor are more territorial, in the animal behavior sense, than middle-class families who range farther from home "territory" in their daily lives.

Still another attempt to prove a connection between crowding and behavior failed when defense planners set out to determine just how little space it was safe to provide Americans in air raid shelters. Experiments in which people volunteered to coop themselves up in prototypes of air raid shelters for weeks on end invariably proved only that people who volunteer for experiments are on their best behavior, and in any case, are not subjected to the strains of the real thing.

Since experiments can't duplicate the conditions of demoralization likely to occur in a real air raid or crowding disaster, the Bureau of Social Science Research, Inc., in Washington, D.C., undertook to find out what happened when people were crowded in concentration camps, prisons, the coolie trade, slums, immigrant ships, mental hospitals, natural disasters, shipwrecks, sieges, troop transports, and the Middle Passage of the African slave trade. The conclusion to the massive compilation *Historical Incidents of Extreme Overcrowding* is anticlimactic: "Physical density, per se, is not a fruitful unitary concept for use in scientific study. For all but those extreme values approaching the physical displacement of the human body, density of occupancy has significance only in interdependent relationship with many other variables of the situation: environment, structural, temporal, psychological and social."

What happens when you crowd beyond endurance? Designers of space vehicles, air raid shelters, undersea chambers, and even schools and hospitals want to know. During the late 1950s and 1960s various defense agencies made an

Not Enough Elbowroom

effort to find out. The answers were disappointing. The consensus seemed to be "less space is needed than we thought," followed by "it all depends on the circumstances." Early air raid shelter designs recommended by the Office of Civil and Defense Mobilization allocated 12 square feet of space per person—little more than grave space, but volunteers who tested group shelters with only eight feet per person came through in good health and good cheer. They seem to be buoyed up by the challenge they have undertaken, and they quickly develop what J. W. Altman, one of the analysts of shelter responses, calls a "new morality." Men in prisons, in Antarctic stations, and in other confined places quickly learn to "cool it" when their emotions are aroused, and reports from prisoner-of-war camps indicate that people in general, including entire family groups, adapt to the pressure of enforced togetherness better than they would have thought possible before put to the test.

The worst overcrowding on record is 1.1 square feet per person—one-seventh of the space that air-raid shelter volunteers found acceptable—and it occurred on the African slave ships in which blacks were methodically stowed. They survived because they had given up hope and were content to lie "as if dead" in a state of trance which lowered their metabolic activity to a minimum. White immigrants in steerage accommodations had a little more space per person but they also were crowded by any reasonable standards. However, their morale was good and their adaptation high, like that of volunteers testing air-raid shelters, because they were buoyed up by hope of a better life in America. The highest death rates on record are in crowding disasters such as the Black Hole of Calcutta, in which all but 23 of 146 prisoners perished in 1756.

Panic is no respecter of nationality or degree. White Americans have not reacted as sensibly to involuntary confinement as the blacks who survived the Middle Passage. In his book, *Give Us This Day*, Sidney Stewart describes how a night of heat, suffocation, painful posture, extreme thirst, and physical pressure from the seething mass of bodies in the hold of a Japanese ship, drove American survivors of a Philippine prisoner-of-war camp to mad, mutual slaughter:

> The men began screaming and fighting. They tore at each other, they fought and pushed. Their screams of terror and laughter were terrible things. . . . I heard strange noises. . . . Men were choking each other. Then the awful truth dawned on me as I looked at a body lying beneath me on the floor. His throat had been cut and the blood was being drunk. . . . A few feet away I saw two men grappling. In the gloom I recognized who they were. They were father and son. I remember how they had protected and cared for each other in the years past. They were both West Point graduates. The son was killing his father.

The picture is a horrifying one, but reflects the lack of hope felt by these men as much as the discomfort of their quarters.

Neither the past nor the present, then, give us solid evidence about how much crowding human beings can stand, and still remain human.

It's even harder to prove that crowding causes the overloads and breakdowns that began to plague us in the 1960s. Actually, for most people, there is less crowding now than in the recent past. Everyone may feel crowded, but most people have more personal space than in earlier times that are recalled as more orderly.

• More Houseroom

Manhattan is a good example to take again. It's the most densely populated county in the United States, and has also become the most expensive in which to live and work. Yet the affluent individuals and enterprises who could afford the rent were generally using *more* space per person at the end of the decade than at its start.

Even though the final figures on Harlem are not yet in, in Manhattan as a whole, the Census of 1970 found that fewer people were occupying each home or apartment unit in the city than in 1960. It is the same story in Manhattan work places. New offices allot more space for each employee than the old offices.

There is, as a matter of fact, more room per person everywhere. The Department of Health, Education, and Welfare has documented the decline in the proportion of housing that fails to meet minimal standards of one person per room.

The rich are less crowded. Many have moved out of their big old houses, it is true, but they did so because they are maintaining establishments in several parts of the country or the world and frequently occupying hotel space much of the year in addition.

Middle-income families are less crowded, too. Development houses built during the 1960s averaged two baths and three times the space of the boxlike one-bathroom development houses thrown up to accommodate returning soldiers after World War II.

There is more room at work. Factories now spread out horizontally in one-story plants with generous parking lots. Inside, the machinery that replaces workers leaves more elbowroom for the men who remain. In the New York metropolitan area, plants built since World War II frequently have used an acre of land for every ten workers.

Retailers use more space also. Supermarkets have grown big enough to provide food shoppers with considerable exercise. Stock which was once piled compactly in the back room has to be spread out so that customers can get at it, and every year there are more products to stock. As stores grow bigger, they have to attract more customers to break even. More customers means bigger parking lots to accommodate peak loads. For the stores, it all adds up to more space per customer, however crowded the customers feel.

There is more room at school. Especially in the new suburbs, spread-out, one-story schools with many special purpose facilities replace the multi-storied, jail-like schools that were built a generation ago in the central cities to prepare children for factory work by containing them in a single room for the entire school day. New college dormitories provide a single room for each student. Older colleges convert their double rooms into single rooms when they can, and an increasing number of college students move out of college housing to apartments which offer even more space and privacy.

Europeans are also using more space per person. According to a study prepared in 1970 for a European Conservation Conference for which Prince Philip of England was one of the sponsors, each European now uses five to ten times as much space for housing, employment and recreation as in 1900. Nineteenth-century Europeans lived in less than six square meters per person. In the 1960s they felt crowded because they were living at this same density when, in the words of a World Health Organization report, "Europe's need is for 14 to 16 square meters a person."

There is more space everywhere, according to the measuring rods, but people honestly don't feel as if they have more room. There seems to be a Parkinson's Law that says that not only do people spread out to fill the space available, but that the more space they have, the more space they need.

• *Role Density*

Why do we feel so crowded when we are really spreading out to more spacious quarters? Why do we "need" more space all the time? William C. Loring, the sociologist who failed to show that crowding broke down family life in Boston has a clue. The amount of space a family needs, Loring suggests, is determined by what they do at home, or the number of "social or cultural roles simultaneously acting in a given physical space." Anyone who has tried to conduct an adult conversation while teen-agers are playing records, knows what "role density" can do to a small apartment.

Role density increases with the diversity of the family. Girls need more space than boys, because they typically spend more time inside at home and do more things there than boys. The rich and the well educated need more room because they have more interests (records, books, hobbies, entertaining, collecting) and market surveys have shown that people who have one hobby are more apt to have several others than those who report none at all. Finally, the rich and well educated need more houseroom because they expect individual family members to "do their own things" on their own schedules. As any housewife knows, it takes a bigger refrigerator and a bigger kitchen to feed a family on short orders than it does when they all come to meals at the same time. And as many American families have discovered, a bigger house and another TV set is the only permanent solution to chronic differences of taste.

Television makes the poor feel crowded because it keeps them apprised of the activities they do not have room for as well as those they cannot afford. Reducing exercises don't cost money, but very few apartment bedrooms are big enough to accommodate big swings without disaster, to say nothing of the inhibition provided by a family audience even if it happens to be sympathetic. Many boys who live in apartments would have bicycles if their mothers could think where to keep them. And as one ghetto wife told a social worker: "One of the things I hate about this place is, a man comes home from work and takes off his pants and there is no place to hang them. No closets, no place even to throw them down. All you can do, you must eat and go to bed, and maybe look at television."

Loring points out that people get along with less space in army barracks or a submarine because "each person has but one or at most a few specific roles or functions and those mostly integrated into a common interest of the group." A mission helps morale. The five women Aquanauts who spent 20 days in the Navy's underwater Sealab reported that they were "too busy" to feel the confinement. There wasn't much space in the Sealab, but its "role density" was down to one role of high status: scientific investigator.

• *Why We Feel Crowded*

Although architects and designers have not been able to find a magic number of square feet per person, there are a number of subjective principles that affect how people feel about their spacing.

Experts at planning meetings know something about these principles. They can make a small group seem larger by booking it in a small room, or a large group smaller by booking it in a big room.

Any space seems more crowded if it is being used *for more than one purpose.* A bedroom-study is more crowded than a bedroom or a study seems to be. A multi-purpose gym, auditorium, dining hall, and play yard seems "too small" for the school because the mind's eye recalls all these activities at once even though they occur one at a time. Several things going on at the same time in the same space during the affluent 1960s is the main reason Americans were feeling crowded although they had more space at home.

Any space seems more crowded if it is being used *in a way for which it was not designed.* Space capsules and sealed "environments" accommodate astronauts and aquanauts comfortably because their design has anticipated their every activity. At the opposite end of the spectrum are slum residences, most of which have been designed for far fewer people living in an entirely different manner than their present occupants. Old mansions have space, but it is broken up in a way that makes unnecessary traffic when it is adapted for occupancy by many families. When public housing replaces slums of this type, the new apartments sometimes have no more square feet of space than the old substandard units. They seem more spacious because they are better arranged.

Any given space seems more crowded if it is confining because *you can't get very far out of it.* Prison cells seem smaller than any other rooms their size. Ghetto flats—and the cramped quarters in European cities—are bearable because their residents live more of their lives on the street than Americans in middle-class neighborhoods. According to Edward T. Hall, the anthropologist who studied how people space themselves, New York is less oppressive than smaller cities which do not have similar networks of escape routes. Samoan children don't feel crowded because they can slip out under the wall mats of the huts and escape from surveillance.

A room with a view seems bigger than a room without a view, as anyone can attest who has "borrowed space" from the outside by installing a picture window. Office space affording a view is highly prized, and nicely evaluated in the assignment of desks by employment status. What you see out of the window makes a difference, too. According to Hall, Washington seems less crowded than other cities its size because it has trees on the streets to create an illusion of being in touch with nature.

The value of looking out has been a matter of controversy among those who design and build schools. The New York City Board of Education has been bitterly criticized for the design of I.S. 201 in Harlem, which has no windows. Windows are no longer necessary for light and ventilation, and they raise costs. Considering the drabness of the view, designers thought there might be an advantage in creating a self-contained, new environment for Harlem school children. Studies on a windowless school constructed entirely underground in the Southwest desert showed that the children were not adversely affected, and windowless schools have failed to produce any of the symptoms of claustrophobia feared for them. Interiors can be made interesting and changed so that they are more effective in stimulating the occupants than the static view of the street afforded by a conventional window, but the advocates of windows are not convinced. They continue to feel that a windowless building is a self-evident horror and that children in them are deprived of a deep-seated social or psychological need to "look out."

Any given space seems more crowded if you share it with people who are *strangers*. In the family dining room, you don't mind crowding at Thanksgiving, but such closeness at the table would be uncomfortable and dangerous as well as illegal in a restaurant serving all comers. Have you ever noticed how a restaurant table shrinks when you allow the hostess to seat a stranger at it during a rush period? A schoolroom seems most crowded the first day of school, when the children don't know each other.

Any space seems more crowded if the people in it are *uncertain of each other's status.* Parents and their teen-age children feel crowded in spacious suburban American homes not only because there is no street life in the suburbs into which children may escape, but because they don't know what to expect of each other. Submarines, barracks, and prisons accommodate high densities because discipline is strict and roles are not only few, but well defined.

Any space seems more crowded if the people in it are *unlike in age, and particularly social class.* Preteen girls seem able to "sleep" happily on slumber parties in space smaller than the law allows for passengers in an elevator. The telephone company has argued that it cannot have male and female operators working the same switchboard without allowing more than the 18-inch space for which the boards have been designed. Young people of the same sex don't mind sleeping together, but older people are often uncomfortable if they have to spend the night in a place where they don't have a bathroom to themselves.

Servants have become uncomfortable for middle-class Americans because the enforced intimacy of unlikes seems too undemocratic to be bearable.

"Crowding" it turns out, is a relative, not an absolute concept, and depends upon subjective, rather than objective factors which make it almost impossible to establish the personal space that any one individual must have.

Chapter VI

The Animal Analogy

During the 1960s, biological scientists took up the inquiry that sociologists had given up as hopeless. If you want to see what crowding really does to human beings, they reasoned, just look at what it does to animals!

If man is an animal, the argument runs, then he is subject to animal instincts, including the phenomena of animal territoriality and animal population control. The analogy is so appealing to intellectuals that it deserves a closer examination than it has usually received.

Ethology, or the sociology of animal life, attracted wide interest in the 1960s. Biological scientists wrote popular books: In 1965, there was *Man Adapting* by René Dubos, *Wild Heritage* by Sally Carrighar, and *On Aggression* by Konrad Lorenz; in 1967, *The Naked Ape*, by Desmond Morris. When John Leonard of the *New York Times* reviewed *The Human Animal* by Hans Hass, he speculated that "after a decade of assassinations, war, and civil strife" it was probably inevitable that "studies of animal behavior should excite the American intellectual appetite in the late 1960s, much as years ago we pounced so voraciously on the Freudian bone."

• *Self-Regulation in Animals*

Students of animal behavior have long known that starvation is rare in the wild. Animals seldom multiply to the point where they destroy their food supply, as human societies have frequently destroyed their pasture and farm lands. Tropical fish breed to the capacity of the tank and thereafter eat exactly as many of their young as is needed to keep the population steady. An increase in numbers will stimulate the adrenal glands of many animals to produce stress hormones, and these in turn trigger other hormones which interfere with the reproduction of sika deer, rabbits, mice, rats, voles, and other animals as well.

Animals regulate their numbers by instinctively apportioning their livable environment. Territorial animals limit breeding and feeding to individuals who have succeeded in establishing a territory. If the heather on which Scottish red grouse feed is thick, territories may shrink so that the moorland may support more grouse; if the heather is spare, territories will expand, dispossessing some grouse from breeding. Sea birds regulate breeding by competition for a fixed number of nesting places. Herd animals do it by a "peck order" which reserves food and mating for the dominant animals and extends these privileges down the line when the environment is favorable.

Male birds compete not for mates but for feeding and breeding territories. The song and plumage of birds warn rivals to keep off the incumbent's territory. The flocking of birds and the humming of insects are devices for communicating the size of the population to its members and triggering action to cut it if it is too high. Konrad Lorenz, the Austrian zoologist, says that the bright colors and grotesque shapes of tropical fish permit them to recognize and avoid their own species which compete for the available food in coral reefs that harbor many kinds of fish.

The general principle that animals regulate their own population was evolved by the British ecologist, Vero Copner Wynne-Edwards in the 1950s. "When I first saw the force of the deduction 10 years ago," he wrote in a *Science* article of 1965, "I felt that the scales had fallen from my eyes. . . . A whole series of unconnected natural phenomena seemed to click smoothly into place." Wynne-Edwards saw that the implications for mankind were as momentous as the principles of Darwin and Malthus which he was modifying. He redefined "society" as "an organization of individuals that is capable of providing conventional competition among its members." Under this definition, "status-seeking," "keeping up with the Joneses," social discrimination, and competition are no longer deprecated as wasteful and unworthy but become "an inseparable part of the substance of society" because they are methods humans use to restrict the numbers of those who prosper.

Aggressive impulses were similarly endowed with new prestige by the slightly different explanation for self regulation advanced by Konrad Lorenz. In his view, animal populations regulate themselves by "a mutual repulsion acting on the animal of the same species, effecting their regular spacing out, in much the same manner as electric charges are regularly distributed all over the surface of a spherical conductor." He studied the rituals by which tropical fish and birds establish territories and dominance orders to avoid fights to the finish and found in them the rudiments of human social systems. He concluded that aggression cannot safely be eliminated from human affairs but it can and must be redirected and sublimated. Animals have survived the negative consequences of their own instincts in the past by evolving new "inhibitory mechanisms" such as those which prevent most animal parents from attacking their young.

• *The Weak Must Die*

Robert Ardrey, an inspired playwright and screen writer, is the most popular of the animal analogists. His 1961 best-seller, *African Genesis*, reported archeological evidence of early man in Central Africa in such a way as to arouse new interest in the animal basis of human nature. This led him to speculate on the similarity between the territorial behavior of animals and the "home place" attachment of people long recognized in expressions such as the "turf" of a gang.

In *The Territorial Imperative* of 1966, Ardrey asserts that there is "no qualitative break between the moral nature of the animal and the moral nature of man."

The territorial imperative is, of course, the urge of males to compete for status, "place," and above all, real estate, and the urge of females to compete for the winning males. This simple, unifying concept makes many things plain to him: the population explosion arises because human females are permitted to copulate with males who have no property; the Jews marched to the gas chambers without fighting because they had no territory. His conclusion is somber: "Whether morality without territory is possible in man must remain as our final, unanswerable question."

In *The Social Contract* of 1970, Ardrey took the final step and predicted that the human population would "crash" as animal populations do, under the increasing stress of life in crowded communities protected from the self-regulating population controls of the territorial imperative.

For humanity, it's either compulsory contraception or control by the growing stress of city life, producing "more impotency due to acute alcoholism, more corpses, victims of crimes in the streets, and more couples living together in unreproductive sin." Ardrey's social contract protscts the advantages of the fittest in the interests of strengthening the race. The weak must be allowed to die, he says, in order to prevent overpopulation.

• *Why Lemmings Commit Suicide*

Ardrey bases his political philosophy on animal behavior. Scientists work the analogy the other way around. Even when they try, they can't help seeing animal behavior in human terms. And animal behavior, with its many similarities to human affairs, is subject to varying interpretations which shed as much light on the interpreters as on the animals. A cautionary example is provided by the history of the various and contradictory theories that have been proposed to explain the periodic population explosion and collapse of the lemmings.

Lemmings are arctic rodents, slightly larger, silkier, and more playful than house mice. Every four or five years they erupt from Scandinavian mountains, run down the valleys like a plague of locusts, and plunge to their death in the sea. This is the Rorschach picture. Now for the readings.

In Victorian England, naturalists proposed a political explanation. The lemmings were emigrating from Scandinavia in search of a lost home in the North Sea, or in the grip of a compulsion to move westward, toward America. But Swedish lemmings ran east, not west.

During the depressed 1930s, the dominant explanation was economic: the lemmings periodically outbred their predators, ate up their food supply, and ran frantically after more. The only trouble with this theory is that lemmings are not starving when they run and they ignore food in their path.

The stress theory emerged during World War II. According to Edward S. Deevey, a Navy biologist, scientists in the service saw similarities in several different war phenomenon. One was the symptoms of shell shock or battle fatigue which psychologists and physiologists were studying. Another was the behavior of laboratory rats under conditions simulating the confinement in close quarters on submarines. And still another was the observation that rats shipwrecked on Pacific islands sometimes dropped dead for no apparent reason.

After Hans Selye, Director of the Institute of Experimental Medicine and Surgery at the University of Montreal, published his general theory of stress, it was possible for biological scientists with experience in war service to see that overloaded rats and men broke down in the same way. Both experienced the sudden failure or shock which Selye describes as the final breakdown of the body's efforts to adapt. John Christian, a Navy researcher, verified that the adrenal glands of crowded mice were enlarged, showing that population density did act as a stressor.

Scientists now agree that whatever the cause of their population explosion, the lemmings die of shock induced by crowding. The explanation is good so far as it goes, but it may lead to scientific disregard of other data that now appear irrelevant, just as earlier naturalists had ignored the comment of observers that the lemmings seemed to be affected by the presence of each other. More than a century ago, the Norwegian naturalist, Robert Collett noted, but only of marginal interest, that "it is constantly stated by eyewitnesses, that they die from their great excitement."

• *Behavioral Sinks in the Lab*

While naturalists were seeing human behavior in animals, psychologists were using laboratory rats to prove something about people. They reported that ghetto conditions of crowding could make laboratory rats and mice behave remarkably like the residents of the human ghettos in our big cities. During the 1950s, John B. Calhoun, the psychologist, set out to study the social consequences of rapid population increases. He used rats because they resemble men, not only anatomically, but socially, too: for instance, they are one of the few animals that attack their own kind.

First, he created a quarter-acre rat heaven of conditions so ideal for wild Norway rats, that the only limitation on their numbers would be crowding itself. The stresses from too much sociability eventually stabilized this population by increasing the infant mortality rate: the rat mothers simply lost interest in their babies.

Next, Calhoun arranged for domesticated rats to breed to twice the normal density in inside pens, where they could be closely watched. What emerged was a microcosm of the social evils of big central cities. The death rate of babies rose dramatically. Mothers neglected and ate their young. They lost interest in their nests. "In the midst of transporting a bit of material they would drop it to engage in some other activity occasioned by contact and interaction with other individuals." Males fought, bit, and mounted each other. Some became frenetically overactive "probers" who neglected the conventions of rat courtship and followed females into their burrows to rape them. Others became "somnambulists" who simply gave up the struggle and withdrew.

"Behavioral sinks" developed when Calhoun encouraged rats to spend a lot of time close together at troughs where feeding took a long time. Eventually, they came to enjoy being together for its own sake and wouldn't eat alone. "Pathological togetherness," Calhoun called it. These crowds seduced females from the harems in which normal rat mothers bring up their babies under the watchful eye of a dominant male. All the pathologies were worse in these metropolitan "sinks." Practically all of the babies there died.

Calhoun's findings reminded zoologists that sika deer and other animals occasionally build up what look like behavioral sinks in the wild. Apes fight in zoos, but seldom in the wild. Rhesus monkeys protected in cities in India are more vicious, more responsive, shrewder, but no more intelligent than forest monkeys in solving problems set them by researchers with food as a payoff.

Calhoun is a psychologist, not a zoologist. His objective is to find out more about social behavior. His moral is clear: abundance attracts individuals into "behavioral sinks" in which females shun motherhood and males fight or withdraw. The population densities which make economic sense may induce physiological stress. Individuals may be attracted by the "easy living," and ultimately by the very crowd which degenerates its members.

Calhoun has become an outspoken advocate of population control. In 1970 he told a reporter that extreme overcrowding could bring doom. "People could be physically healthy but they'd still perish. They would begin by withdrawing from the mass, then lose all interest in life—and finally just sit aimlessly around waiting to die." His warning was based on the emergence of passive mice he called the "beautiful ones" when he put 2000 mice in a pen designed for 100. In 1971 the mice were dying, which is just what he thinks is going to happen to the human race if we keep on the way we are going.

The Crowding Syndrome

• *Man Is Not an Animal*

It is easy to make a modern Aesop's fable out of Calhoun's reports from the laboratory. His "somnambulists" and "beautiful ones" are hippies and dropouts. His "prober" rats are delinquents and criminals. His overstressed, homosexual rats are the casualties of big city competition. His distracted mothers, and especially the discontented harem females attracted to the excitement of the crowded pen are candidates for Women's Liberation. His dominant males holding down territories are the establishment, the powerful few. The feeding troughs which create behavioral sinks stand for the technology that makes ever denser population concentrations possible.

The animal analogy has had some useful scientific applications. During the 1960s, it encouraged sociologists to compare such diverse phenomena as the way teen-age gangs defend their territory against invasion, the conviction in sports that "the home team always wins," the hazing of newcomers and "black sheep" in schools, and the prejudging of outsiders of a different race or culture. It even stimulated psychiatrists to report cases in which neurotic behavior disappeared on the patient's "home ground" and to question committing mental patients to institutions.

Konrad Lorenz was quick to see the relationship between animal territoriality and the sentiments of nationalism and patriotism which had led to World War II, in the course of which he had been held a prisoner of war. He described in animal terms the physiological reactions of a man to a call to arms: "The tone of the entire striated musculature is raised, the carriage is stiffened, the arms are raised from the sides and slightly rotated inward so that the elbows point outward. The head is proudly raised, the chin stuck out, and the facial muscles mime the 'hero face' familiar from the films. On the back and along the outer surface of the arms the hair stands on end." No one recalling the biological picture of such an emotion could ever again think of it in the metaphysical terms which made patriotism unquestionably noble.

The animal analogy is useful, but it is safe only if it is recognized and understood. Man is, of course, an animal, subject to the same hormonal mechanisms, and carrying around in the lower brain a parcel of instincts left over from earlier evolutionary adaptations, among which may be an "instinctive" need for a certain amount of physical space. It is well to remember, however, that man has built an imposing cultural and symbolic edifice on this parcel of instincts and impulses.

A man may respond hormonally to a threat in the same way that the animal responds, but the man's hormones can be triggered by a flag, a word, a tune; the animal responds mainly to the threats for which the symbols stand. Animals can be social beings, dependent on their relations with other animals, but they do not have a learned culture, or at least not a very extensive one. Animals may have "sociology," but by definition they do not have an anthropology and even less a polity.

Ardrey and Calhoun seem to forget that human beings are not lions or tigers or rats or lemmings. Human beings can do something about their instincts and what they have done has been to create civilization. People can't go "back to nature" and become animals again even if Ardrey did succeed in convincing them that civilization has been a mistake.

Chapter VII

Too Rich

It is now fashionable to suggest that the breakdowns which began in the 1960s were caused not only by an overload of people, but also by an overload of things.

Prosperity made news during the long boom of the 1960s, but increasingly it became bad news. The media publicized frightening examples of the high price of providing affluence for all:

> On days when smog is thick, school children of Los Angeles have been excused from doing exercises that would require them to breathe deeply. Smog is the price Los Angeles pays for its rapid economic growth.

> Farm workers suffering from convulsions and tremors called the "walking death" are victims of pesticide poisoning. Public health sources estimate that pesticides kill several hundred human beings a year, many of them children vulnerable to poisoning adults can resist. These deaths are the price farmers pay for chemicals which greatly increase their income while keeping the price of food from rising as high as demand would otherwise push it.

Too Rich

Tourists report that plastic bags of garbage now decorate open fields in Italy. They are likely to remain there forever. Municipal incinerators don't like plastic because some kinds melt and foul their grates, while spewing hydrochloric acid into the air. The easiest thing to do with garbage tied up in a nice plastic bag is to leave it there, an eternal reminder of the price we pay for taking the smell out of handling garbage.

But for the most elegant example of the trouble affluence can cause it is necessary to go to Japan. Japan's spectacular economic growth did more than increase the amount of refuse that had to be handled. It actually created the problem of sewage disposal where none had existed before.

Before World War II, solid human waste was not a problem, but a valuable article of commerce collected from septic tanks by entrepreneurs who hauled it to the country and sold it to farmers. In the postwar years, Japan's farmers grew rich enough to turn up their noses at the collection of human manure, and when they had enough money to buy chemical fertilizers, sewage piled up ominously in Tokyo. To cope with the emergency, the Tokyo Metropolitan Government organized a "vacu truck" service which cleans out householders' cesspools twice a month and barges it out to sea, whence it sometimes washes back to pollute the seacoast. They've been laying sewage pipe as fast as they can, but a sewerage system for the world's biggest city is not built in a day. In 1968, sanitation was the biggest single expenditure per thousand inhabitants in the budget of Greater Tokyo, and the tinkle of the vacu truck was anxiously awaited by 70 percent of Tokyo's households.

Never has progress produced so much paradox. Oil tankers big enough to keep down the price of transporting oil foul miles of inhabited shorelines when they leak or break. The supersonic transport plane that was going to speed, and hopefully cut the cost of travel, produces sonic booms so destructive that it was abandoned after public and private agencies had put more than a billion dollars into its development.

Affluence rushes new technology to the market so fast that "bugs" are often worked out on the general public. By the time we discovered that detergents which wash clothes "whiter than white" also kill the waterways into which the wash water eventually drains, we had invested in textiles and washing machines that wouldn't work with old-fashioned soap.

Resistant strains of the germs causing diseases supposedly wiped out by broad-spectrum antibiotics brought back diseases such as meningitis and diphtheria. Hospitals were tight-lipped about the diseases they were bringing back, but the more responsible ones went back to tedious and expensive sterile procedures and old-fashioned scrubbing.

X-ray techniques that had enabled physicians to diagnose many disorders were found to cause cancer.

• *The Price of Affluence*

Affluence means a greater demand for utilities and services—and the supply isn't there.

The phone company, the stock exchange, the electric-power companies, and the airlines have blamed their breakdowns on a demand for their services they did not foresee. When called to account, leaders in these overloaded industries explain their shortfall with a single word: affluence.

There is a subtler horror that sounds merely funny to men but is grim to women. All those wonderful things that money can buy turn out to be a burden once you get them home. They break down. They take more time than they are worth. And most houses haven't been designed to store them.

Living the good life turns out to be a lot of work. That backyard pool—no one tells you that you will spend more time cleaning it than swimming in it. And even if you are rich enough or lucky enough to find someone to clean it for you, it takes you the proverbial "minute" to see that he does it. A "minute" here to make out the warranty of a new appliance. A "minute" there to remember to clean out the trap in the washing machine. The pampered woman at home can easily spend a whole day of her life on these "minutes" and have nothing to show for it that commands the prestige of a paid job. A woman who does work for pay often looks to the hours spent in a well-organized friendly, and appreciative office for relief from the unstructured demands of the personal work which eats up that part of her time which is supposed to be "free."

Abundance for almost everybody means that services cost so much that most people have to wait on themselves. In many communities you now have to be your own grocery clerk and delivery boy in order to get a time-saving TV dinner into your kitchen. More things come knocked down for supposedly easy assembly at home. Postal patrons help sort the mail by looking up zip codes, bank depositors make out deposit slips, mothers fill out the medical history forms pediatricians have to certify for school records, and during the Christmas season shoppers in some of the proudest old New York stores have to make out sales slips for clerks unable or unwilling to write.

The final blow has been inflation. Affluence for all turns out to cost too much.

Prices have been rising along with wages, so that the extra money in paychecks doesn't buy as much more as expected, and the disappointment is keen because of the false hope that rising incomes inspire. In spite of rising incomes, luxuries have a tantalizing way of pricing themselves just out of reach. The reason is that many things formerly enjoyed by only the rich are subject to steeply rising costs when there is a moderate increase in demand— an increase in the number of people with money to buy them.

The costs which soar the fastest are the status items to which families with rising incomes are aspiring. During the last few years of the 1960s, the larger house, the better college remained as far out of reach after a couple of raises as before.

The overload of affluence is easiest to see in medicine, where the first serious steps towards financing high quality medical care under the present system for all spiraled hospital costs up and beyond the capabilities of Blue Cross, Blue Shield, and the Government funding plans.

President Nixon summed it up in his State of the Union address of 1970: "Never has a Nation seemed to have had more and enjoyed it less." He spoke for an increasing number of Americans who were blaming a wide variety of troubles on prosperity.

The attack on affluence is something new for a country that has always worshipped the almighty dollar. J. Kenneth Galbraith was all alone when he attacked the basic American dream of abundance for everyone through economic growth in his 1958 book, *The Affluent Society*. Most people thought that good times were just beginning.

"The next ten years will see more material progress than the last fifty years," General David Sarnoff, then chairman of the board of Radio Corporation of America declared on June 4, 1961. "Global television in full color, thermo-electric home heating and cooling systems with no moving parts, electronic tools for medicine, and computers 1000 times faster than present models will be part of the world a decade hence," he predicted.

Forecasts breathed unconditional faith in the magic of technology. "The no-hands phone, so sensitive it can pick up your voice across a room, is already on the market, and will be widespread by 1970," Norman Ginsberg, President of the National Design Center told reporters on January 21, 1961.

"We will cross the continent or the Atlantic in one hour and 15 minutes beginning in about 1970," Victor Cohn, a science reporter, wrote in 1961. "In the various vehicles of 1970, we will fly at three times the speed of sound. We will fly straight up. We will ride on a cushion of air just off the ground. We may own compact cars with a new kind of battery, the fuel cell, driving a tiny electric motor at each wheel."

Economic growth was a complete defense in the minds of most people for such inconveniences as the exaggerations of advertising and wasteful defense spending. Like traffic congestion, a bit of public untidiness could be excused as the inevitable price of progress and full employment. Smoke meant jobs, not pollution.

But not for long. As the price of affluence became increasingly high, the mood changed, and the young people have led the way.

Since 1968, they have become increasingly bored by economic theory. They confound their elders by asking "What's so good about affluence?" It seems as if the broken phonograph records, obsolete toys, unstrung tennis rackets, dirty clothes, and private bedlam of their childhood rooms have finally turned their own stomachs. Rather than pick the stuff up, they decide to throw it all out—or at least kick it out of their way.

Students rally for population control, Women's Liberation, consumer revolts, and also demonstrate against thruways and housing projects. Attacks on the "military-industrial complex" supposedly responsible for the Vietnam War swept the college campuses in 1968. In one way or another, all these movements challenge the mystique of abundance for all through economic growth. And while the young have been attracting national attention, the challenge has been taken up by older specialists in the social and biological sciences who have long harbored doubts about the viability of the American dream. The goal of abundance for all has come under full-scale attack.

- ## Affluence and Vietnam

"If the U.S. were to double its Gross National Product, I would think it would be a much less livable society than it is today," Richard A. Falk, Milbank Professor of International Law at Princeton, told the Reuss Committee in October 1969. The attackers blame the mystique of economic growth for three of our most pervasive problems: the Vietnam war; declining quality of goods and services; and the degradation of the environment.

The unpopularity of the war in Vietnam took a new twist with the charge that it was artificially stimulating the economy. The war's staunchest supporters were accused of profiting from it.

"War is good business, invest your son" the young draft protesters chant. Their indictment of the military-industrial complex is supported by maverick economists. Galbraith has pointed out that the military budget is an ideal Keynesian tool for maintaining prosperity. It is secret, sacred, nonproductive, under total government control, and above all, big enough to make a difference to the rest of the economy.

The attacks on the war itself have expanded to include

attacks on local enterprises that profit from it. Communities which had formerly welcomed military installations because of the business that came from them, now protest the construction of missile sites in their midst. College students who would actually benefit from military support of research in their institutions demand that their schools refuse this source of funds. Housewives boycott Dow Chemical Company's consumer products to protest its former production of napalm fire bombs. The protests have not been wholly ineffective. They speeded cutbacks in defense contracts and closing of military installations which idled thousands and whittled down the substantial sector of Gross National Product contributed by the Department of Defense.

* **Consumer Revolt**

"We don't need more things, we need better things," said Esther Peterson, Assistant Secretary of Labor under President Johnson and the first consumer advisor to the President. Everything that money buys seems to wear out faster, break down sooner, and do more harm than good.

Disaffected consumers now talk back to the deaf seducers who bombard them on television. Virginia Knauer, President Nixon's Advisor on Consumer Affairs reported that she was getting 3000 complaints a month as of February, 1972. Bess Myerson, her opposite number for New York City, received 90,000 complaints in 1970 and 120,000 in 1971. Commuters organize to protest the train service, in some cases by getting on trains and refusing, en masse, to pay their fares. Tenants organize rent strikes.

Regulatory agencies have begun to respond. DDT was banned. The Food and Drug Administration stopped ignoring the suspicions of doctors and women, and publicly investigated the side effects of the pill. Doubts about the safety of artificial sweeteners and the claims of breakfast foods were publicized. Despite its advertising clout, the tobacco industry was unable to prevent edicts requiring health warnings on cigarette packages. Publications have begun to refuse the lucrative cigarette advertising which has been a major support of the American press, and cigarette commercials were banned from television beginning with 1971.

• *Pollution*

The most telling indictment against economic growth is its degradation of the environment. "Population growth may be half the cause," Dr. Roger Revelle, Director of the Center for Population Studies at Harvard, testified at the Reuss Committee hearings. "Increased affluence and filthy habits are the other half of the cause." Biologist Wayne H. Davis has calculated that because of American affluence, an American baby creates 25 times the impact on the environment of an Indian baby.

There was a time when men talked with pride about mastering nature. But mastery has turned into potential destruction, and there has been a widespread call to eliminate the polluting by-products of affluence.

The earth, say the environmentalists, is a spaceship. It is our home and we have to keep it tidy or perish. Thousands of local and scores of national groups have been organized to pick up roadside litter, use returnable bottles instead of non-degradable plastic containers, clean up lakes and rivers, fight smog, reduce noise, conserve depleted natural resources, outlaw unsightly billboards, regulate junkyards, preserve wild rivers and natural spots such as the Grand Canyon, Storm King Mountain on the Hudson, the Everglades of Florida, and the redwoods of California.

114

Too Rich

Led by biologists, zoologists, social scientists, lawyers, and leaders in academic and political life, the environmental movement staged a nationwide "environmental teach-in" or E (for "Earth") Day in 1970 to acquaint local communities with their own ecological conditions and mobilize support for a mammoth national cleanup. *The Environmental Handbook*, a paperback anthology of warnings prepared for the event, sold thousands of copies a week during the spring of 1970.

Politicians have responded to the concern. President Nixon urged "a quest not for a greater quantity of what we have but for a new quality of life in America." At a meeting in February, 1970, of the Joint Economic Committee, Congressman Henry S. Reuss suggested modifying the goal of "maximum production for the economy" with which the Council of Economic Advisers is charged by the Employment Act of 1946, because it "can mean that as our GNP grows, national pollution also grows every year." Elsewhere he suggested setting up a "Council of Environmental Advisers" charged with seeing that the "Council of Economic Advisers" doesn't let sheer growth ruin the country.

The intense concern of Earth Day, 1970 has ebbed, but the consciousness of ecology it stimulated cannot be erased. Communities of young people pledge themselves to ride bicycles instead of cars, save water by putting bricks in toilet tanks, save paper by carrying groceries home in reusable net bags instead of paper sacks, and wear tattle-tale gray shirts rather than use detergents that pollute waterways. Colleges organize seminars, courses, and whole schools or centers devoted to the study of the environment.

Europe is also awakening to its environmental problems. Rising incomes have polluted the Rhine River, and the Baltic, a sluggish shallow inland sea, is dying as fast as Lake Erie. Industrial interests shook the foundations of beautiful Venice, Italy, by dredging a canal there big enough to carry oil tankers.

Pollution follows wherever people take the industries that produce wealth. An aluminum plant brought both prosperity and pollution to Sunndal, a city located at one end of a remote fjord on the north coast of Norway. Discovery of oil on the north shore of Alaska aroused conservationists who warned that almost any human intervention could upset the fragile and rare wildlife of the Arctic. A pipeline across the frozen northern tundra could melt the frozen earth, making it unstable, interfere with the migration of caribou, and flood thousands of acres with polluting oil if it should break.

• *The Industrial Villains*

Three American industries have borne the brunt of the new concern: the automobile industry, the national symbol of rising living standards; the paper industry, the economy's most sensitive indicator of prosperity and chief source of trash; and the electrical-power industry, the basic supplier of energy for all other enterprise.

America has fallen out of love with the automobile. Its many new enemies hold it responsible for more deaths a year than the Vietnam war at its height. It causes air pollution, junk pollution, view pollution, urban sprawl, and traffic congestion that make America ugly. In California, the state most dependent on the automobile, the Senate voted 10 to 1 to outlaw internal combustion engines by 1975. Cars not only pollute when they run, but also when they are no longer usable. It used to be worthwhile to disassemble them for scrap. But now, complex mixtures of materials, plus steel-making methods that cut the demand for scrap, make it cheaper for owners to abandon old cars where they die.

More than any other industry, the automobile industry lives in an ivory tower of its own fantasies. It continued to make big cars because they yielded higher profit per unit long after the success of the little Volkswagen had shown that a substantial number of Americans wanted a small, cheap, economical car without the frills of annual model changes. Before the campaigns of Ralph Nader, the young consumer advocate, car makers did not even bother to recall models known to have dangerous mechanical defects. In 1970, Nader succeeded in getting General Motors to let its stockholders vote on adding members representing environmental and consumer interests to the board and establishing a Shareholders' Committee on Corporate Responsibility.

The motions were defeated, but Nader and his young associates had introduced a daring new theory of shareholder responsibility. They contended that all but a handful of big stockholders of General Motors were more affected by what General Motors did to them as drivers and citizens than as dividend receivers. They urged stockholders to demand that General Motors support mass transportation at the expense of the bigger profit it makes on private cars and to spend more money than the law required eliminating air and water pollution. The attacks came at a time when car sales were slipping and the competition of smaller, cheaper, less polluting foreign imports had finally forced Detroit to change its cars and reconsider corporate strategies.

It is an economic fact of life that the amount of paper consumed sensitively distinguishes rich from poor nations, and good times from bad. In the United States, consumption moves with the business cycle at a remarkably constant rate per $1,000 of real GNP, and the industry sees steady expansion ahead. Edwin A. Locke, Jr., president of the American Paper Institute, expects paper consumption per capita to grow more than two percent a year indefinitely—enough to cover the finite landscape with a visible paperfall by the magic year 2000.

Manufacturers of packaging are accused of contributing to the rising per capita tonnage of garbage overloading municipal dumps. Many students of solid waste disposal advise a tax on disposable containers that will encourage a return to the more economic deposit bottle, or less elaborate packing. René Dubos, the French biologist, is shocked at the waste of wrapping each after-dinner mint in its own transparent paper envelope. He grew up in a country whose housewives carry bread home with both ends of the loaf protruding from the wrapper.

Environmentalists charge American packaging with adding to costs, litter, and the chore of hauling in the groceries.

The electric power industry is charged with even more damage. Demand for electric power doubled during the 1960s and there is no letup in sight for the 1970s. According to Donald C. Cook, president of American Electric Power Company, Inc., serving the Midwest and near South, the country will need 400 or 500 new power plants by the year 2000. The big blackout of 1965 was just the beginning. Power reductions, local blackouts, and stoppages continue to grow in spite of a ban imposed by some public service commissions on the promotion of new uses for electric power.

Power companies are damned for polluting if they build capacity to meet the market, and damned for falling short of power if they don't. "We're not constructing a single plant that someone is not objecting to," Con Edison's board chairman, Charles F. Luce told reporters. Oil-fired plants are charged with polluting the air and the view, and nuclear plants with emitting radioactive wastes and heating up rivers to the peril of fish. Tapping clean hydroelectric power in faraway Canada would require overhead high-tension wires that would raise objections in hundreds of communities along the way.

In 1970, Con Ed stopped promoting the wider usage of electricity. It spent advertising money on a campaign to "Save a Watt." It urged its consumers to turn off lights and appliances.

• *The Cure-All Is Cut Back*

Con Edison has found itself in the unthinkable position of asking people to use less of its product. The giant utility is not alone. "Cut" has now become the official, overall national economic policy.

It began in 1969 when the Federal Reserve used its control of the nation's monetary supply to cool the speculative boom on Wall Street, which reminded old hands of the frenetic weeks before the crash of 1929. When tight money failed to slow the inflation, the administration cut back on government spending for health, education, and welfare as well as the war in Vietnam.

Nothing much happened. The "game plan" for slowing inflation either was not working or what amounts to the same thing, was taking too long. Nixon reluctantly declared an economic emergency in the fall of 1971 and froze wages and prices for 90 days.

Big companies accepted the freeze, even though it meant a curb on sales and even profits. General Motors may not have had prior knowledge of the freeze, as Ralph Nader alleged, but it certainly had more to gain by preserving the status quo than risking continued growth which might force it to change. Better to sell a few less cars than shoulder some of the costs of fume pollution now borne by others, for instance.

119

Economic times have changed. Farmers who might profit from inflationary growth no longer have the political base that they had when they opposed President McKinley's sound money policy before the turn of the century. Today, only Wright Patman of Texas, the last of the populists, attacks Nixon for raising interest rates in language reminiscent of William Jennings Bryan who charged McKinley with "crucifying" the American farmer on "a cross of gold."

Farmers are now down to less than 5 percent of the labor force, and wage workers who are represented by unions capable of demanding pay to keep pace with prices, are a declining minority of workers. The biggest part of the labor force is salaried, and except for the handful caught in cutbacks, the salaried are sympathetic with the Nixon plan for slowing economic growth.

• *Making the Rich More Comfortable*

Economists now say we have to choose between inflation and unemployment. Inflation hurts the rich because it makes their money worth less. Unemployment hurts the poor, particularly the non-union poor at the bottom of the barrel. Whenever confronted with the choice, the Nixon administration has chosen unemployment as the lesser of the two evils.

The Nixon recession of 1970 and 1971 has had the intended effect. It has made life more comfortable for the rich. For those who have the price, it is nice to be able to get a taxi, an airplane seat, a hospital bed, or admission to college without unseemly jostling. Cooling the economy has slowed the increase in the proportion of affluent families. When too many people "have money," the things that money can buy become scarcer. During the 1960s, for instance, the rich complained that you could not walk into a popular Broadway show on the spur of the moment any more. You could not get a taxi or a seat in a little French restaurant. Those whose dollar incomes were newly high enough to afford these amenities felt cheated. More unsettling even than the personal disappointment was the dawning realization that no redistribution of wealth could ever make it physically possible for everyone to ride around Manhattan in taxis, dine in intimate French restaurants, or enjoy unobstructed views.

It has become apparent that everybody can't be rich, at least in the way the rich have traditionally lived. Money will never buy enough kidney transplants to go around, for example. The most elusive luxury of all is access to places that the masses cannot get to. Wilderness is intrinsically limited to a few, and everywhere it is being threatened by the increase in the small numbers of wilderness enthusiasts with funds to get into it. There are now so many visitors to Yellowstone Park that the officials have to shoot the more ornery grizzlies to make the place safe for humans, and it is only a matter of time until the authorities will have to choose between bears and people. An even more dramatic case is the plight of the famous Lascaux caves in France. The French Government has had to bar tourists from visiting them in groups because the hot breath of several people at a time causes a biological growth to form on the Stone Age paintings on its walls. To observe some things is to destroy them.

Preserving the environment sounds so right-minded that it is hard to see the elitism it conceals. One of the first to spy it was Senator Edmund S. Muskie of Maine, who began working on water pollution long before it became cocktail conversation, and has sponsored virtually every major piece of Federal legislation on the environment since he started the Senate Public Works Subcommittee on Air

121

and Water Pollution in 1963. In 1970 he warned that the issue of environmental protection might become a smoke-screen for the unmet challenge of equal opportunity. He urged changing national priorities to "give up the luxury of absolute and unlimited freedom of choice" and produce more of the kinds of things that are desperately needed, such as housing and public works.

• *Poverty Is Not the Answer*

Would the environment improve if Americans went back to the simple life practised by the East Indians who are so poor that they are supposed to cause only one-twenty-fifth the damage to the environment of an American baby? Poverty may be good for the soul, but it offers no sure-fire salvation for the environment. If anything, the poor pollute, ravage, and waste more than the rich.

The most wasteful ravage of timber may be the cut-and-burn agriculture of primitive African and Amazon tribes who simply move on when they've ruined the place, as the nomads did in the Biblical lands.

The privies of the poor, though few and modest, pollute mountain streams faster than the plumbing of modern houses equipped with septic tanks or a whole housing project for which proper sewerage and sewage disposal have been provided. Pollution in Catskill mountain streams could be cleaned up by imposing sanitary regulations on all houses in the region. However, rather than vote this expense for householders, the local taxpayers are trying to keep city people from coming up and building summer houses that "ruin the place."

We cannot go back to the questionable ecological virtues of soft coal instead of oil, privies instead of plumbing, and horses manuring the streets instead of cars fouling the air. We cannot go back to the simpler economy in which air, water, and space were "free" and the time of the poor was cheap enough to support personal services on a custom basis. Cut won't work because growth is a physical law, not a moral imperative. Living systems, whether small boys or social systems, do not grow backward. They decay if they do not grow, or at least maintain themselves.

When the strapped Los Angeles school system proposed to cut out school busing in 1968, older people reminded each other that it would do the spoiled kids good to walk. But engineers figured that the city would have to add police both to take care of the children who would be in considerable danger in areas where sidewalks had not been installed, and to regulate the jam of private cars delivering children to school one or two at a time. Busing was basically cheaper and safer than any attempt to "go back" to the "good old" alternatives, and it was retained.

The trouble is not prosperity itself, but an economic system whose faults become unbearable in affluence. The American economy is concerned primarily with products. It considers people in the role of producer and consumer. It ignores what happens to the innocent bystanders of production and consumption, and it ignores the poor, who cannot produce or consume.

The gains come more slowly as the system grows bigger. We will have to work harder in the future to maintain the standard of living to which we have become accustomed. One reason is that it's going to take an increasing amount of time and money to clean up after ourselves. Another reason is that just about everything we want more of is subject to *diseconomy of scale*, which means that it costs more per person to supply larger numbers of people with everything they want. We'll look at these problems one at a time.

• *Cleaning Up*

The cost that has most dramatically punctured the American dream of abundance for all is what Henry H. Villard, the economist at the City College of New York, calls the "social cost of clearing up the debris of production." Villard has pointed out that the economic textbook most widely used in American colleges ignores as irrelevant the cost of the damage private enterprise inflicts on the nation's air, water, resources, and scenic beauty. Business firms regard these costs as *"external"*: a factory includes fuel in its production costs, but not the damage caused by the fuel when it burns. The laundry, repainting, time lost through disease, and shrubbery replacement due to smoke that comes out of the chimney are not charged against production. If they were, manufacturers would find it cheaper to avoid pollution.

The British economist Edward J. Mishan, who calls external costs "spillovers" suggests that quiet around airports and silence overhead could be obtained by requiring airline passengers to pay for disturbing the peace of householders over whose property they fly. The British are sometimes more alert to political issues than Americans. Mishan's paper, "The Spillover Enemy" is subtitled "The Coming Struggle for Amenity Rights."

Government is as much to blame as private enterprise. In order to avoid the cost of trucking snow away from streets, the City of New York simply piles it in the center, so that passing traffic will slice it up for easy hosing into sewers. According to Daniel Bell, the sociologist who uses this illustration, passers-by spend more on cleaning bills than the city saves on trucking.

Some consumer advocates maintain that cleaning up the pollution or preventing it before it occurs would be cheaper than paying for the damage. Even so, it is going to take huge sums of capital simply to make the change. New factories and new equipment will be needed. And some companies may have to be indemnified for the losses incurred in the changeover, or permitted to go out of business. All this means higher prices and higher taxes. And as both business and Government policy-makers have pointed out to the ecologists, it would be hard to raise the capital at a time that we were trying to slow economic growth to prevent new pollution.

• *Diseconomy of Scale*

The most important reason that more wealth, rather than less, will be needed in the future is that it costs more per person to supply larger numbers of people with everything they want. This diseconomy of scale is a novel concept to Americans. It is the opposite of mass production. Instead of units getting cheaper as volume rises, each additional unit costs more than the one before. Americans have been reared on the economics of scale. Cars are cheaper by the million, and Lillian Gilbreth, the pioneer management consultant asserted that even children were cheaper by the dozen. The fact is, however, that economy of scale is a special case that applies only to manufactured goods, and not even to all of them.

Diseconomy of scale is the general rule for services— health, education, insurance, banking, communications, transportation, hotels and restaurants, retailing, repairs, personal service, and the manifold services performed by Federal, state, and local authorities. Haircuts, for instance, are not cheaper when more people need or want them. Haircuts tend to go up in price as wages rise. More people can afford them which increases the demand, but at the same time higher paying jobs lure barbers away from barbering.

Services which, like barbering, cannot easily increase

their productivity, loom larger in family budgets all the time. Hospitals, schooling, government, welfare cost more as more people are served, and it is hard to find an acceptable way to make them cheaper.

Diseconomy of scale is the iron fact of life for all *network services*. Anything supplied through a system of wires, pipes, tracks, patrols, or routes grows more costly per customer added, not less. Some networks can offer added value for the added unit: each new telephone added to a system means someone else you can call; each new stop added to the busline is an additional place you can get off. But the added cost of facilities is much greater than the value of the increased service. For most networks, particularly those that service cities, there is only grief in numbers.

One man can scoop a drink of water free from a mountain stream, but New York City has to build reservoirs and viaducts to get enough for millions. It costs more to get rid of the sewage and garbage in a big city than in a village, but it isn't worth any more to the individual householder, and the same unhappy economics apply to fire protection, police protection, and street maintenance. In 1968, the Mayor of Kansas City figured that if the population of the city doubled, it would cost $200 a head to provide the services that were costing $125.

Power companies, the post office, stockbrokers, and the phone company are all clamoring for rate rises in the face of declining service. It doesn't seem fair, but customers are going to have to pay more simply because there are so many of them. Utilities are going to have to find more capital to build more line and more equipment per customer. Donald C. Cook, President of American Electric Power Company estimates that the electric power industry will need a *trillion* dollars for new plants before the end of the century. Demand for capital will keep interest rates high. Meanwhile, for consumers, the outlook is gloomy. Service is bound to go down while the bills go up, not only for power, but for all the other network services as well.

The arithmetic is inexorable. Beyond a low break-even point, each additional car on the road requires not only more roadway, but more traffic rules, more safety devices, and more policing per car than before. Garaging and parking costs more per car.

The high cost of numbers has been creeping up on big cities for a long time. In 1910, for instance, "transportation" was not a big item in a city worker's budget. If you couldn't walk to work or school, you could go by inexpensive, surface trolley car. By 1966, however, "transportation" was an essential to every family and took nine percent of the budgets of city families, more than medical care, and almost as much as clothing. And to the direct costs of daily travel has to be added the paid time lost in traffic tie-ups. A truck with more than 100 horses under its hood now takes nearly twice as long to make a delivery in Manhattan as a vehicle drawn by a single horse in 1910. It costs more and does a poorer job.

In the 1960s, traffic engineers figured that the city of Washington, D.C. had to spend $23,000 in capital investment to accommodate each additional commuter car coming into the city each working day. The incremental cost of traffic works vertically, too. Elevator shafts, steel, and construction costs rise with each added floor in a skyscraper raising the rent for everyone in the building.

It all means that a continued increase in the standard of living will have to cost more per person in the future than it has in the past. The question that inevitably arises then, is what are the advantages of being rich?

• *The Real Consequences of Wealth*

In the United States we are not as rich as we sometimes imagine, but we are clearly richer than we have ever been before. What difference does affluence really make? A quick way to a more realistic appreciation is to list some of the obvious differences between countries with high per capita consumption, as measured by Gross National Product, and those with low per capita consumption. The GNP may not be a perfect yardstick, but it is the best one we now have.

Many of the differences turn out, after a moment's thought, to distinguish rich from poor individuals and cities, as well as effective from ineffective human enterprises, whether the stated measures of effectiveness are profit, productivity, health, or subjective states as vague as "happiness" or "wellbeing."

In 1968, the latest year for which international statistics were available, the United States had the highest per capita GNP in the world, about a third higher than Sweden, the second richest. Closely following in order were Canada, Switzerland, Denmark, France, Norway, Australia, Belgium, the Netherlands, United Kingdom, Finland, New Zealand, Israel, Austria, and Japan. Generally speaking, the rich countries were increasing per capita consumption fastest, too, with Japan ahead of the United States in growth rate.

We can make some very simple statements that distinguish these countries from the rest of the world and the richer of them from the poorer:

Spending. Rich countries and individuals spend more of their money on intangible services—retail trade, transportation, utilities, communications, health, education, brokerage insurance, banking, government, entertainment, and all personal services from barbering to labor saving devices including those programmed into products, such as precooked, frozen meals. They spend less of their money on products.

Rich countries (people, cities, companies) exchange for money many of the services which the poor provide for themselves or each other outside the money system. The poor mind each other's babies, teach each other to drive, do their own laundry, counsel, comfort, and entertain each other for free. The commercial services in rich countries are usually better in quality, create new avenues of employment, and extend the human contacts of individuals.

Rich countries (people, cities, companies) have more choice about what they spend. The income of the poor is predictable because it is committed to known necessities. (One of the aspects of affluence that proved very upsetting to marketers during the 1960s was the increase in discretionary spending after basic living expenses and taxes. Affluence makes thriving industries out of fashions or expenditures such as trips to Europe—but these industries are highly vulnerable to variations in the business cycle.) The rich make more choices.

Working. Rich countries, cities, companies, and people do more productive, more skilled, and less physical work than the poor. Their work requires longer and more formal training and education.

Rich countries have a more productive labor force, fewer unemployed and underemployed, and hence fewer domestic servants than poor countries.

The rich spend a higher proportion of their time on overhead, staff, coordination, liaison, and brokerage work required by a more complex organization and less on direct production tasks.

Rich individuals, and individuals in rich countries, cities, and companies work shorter hours and fewer years of their lives than the poor.

The rich have more capital and live less "hand to mouth" than the poor.

In poor countries, there is more of a gap between rich

and poor people—e.g., Spain and India, although some poor countries are, or appear to be, egalitarian, such as Communist China. Rich countries are relatively egalitarian, as for example, the United States, Sweden, Japan. The gap between rich and poor declined in the United States at the time of the Great Depression but has not declined since then as dramatically as in ethnically homogeneous countries such as Sweden, the Netherlands, Britain.

Life Styles. Rich countries and companies offer more opportunities for financial, occupational, and social advancement than poor countries.

Rich individuals and individuals in rich countries:

> have better health than the poor when health is measured by longevity, freedom from sickness, infant mortality and absenteeism due to illness.
>
> are better educated, but less religious than the poor.
>
> move more often and take more and longer trips away from home.
>
> know more people and interchange with a wider circle.

People who complain that we are "too rich" are either imprecise or hypocritical. Whatever "rich" means, and as we have seen, this is by no means clear, it has to be something you'd rather be than poor. Those who romanticize poverty as noble, usually haven't experienced it.

Poverty is not romantic and it is not a cure for what ails us.

Chapter VIII

Too Much Talk

A traffic violator recently got off in Chicago by contending that there were more lights, signs, and signals at the intersection where he went wrong than the human brain could handle. There were, he testified, twenty-four in all.

"Twenty-four?" queried the judge, aghast. "Case dismissed."

Times have changed since Charley Chaplin struggled to keep up with the automobile assembly line in his 1936 movie, *Modern Times*. Union demands and industrial engineering have adapted machines to human physical capacity. Today, the speed-up is in the mind.

There seems to be too much talk, too much data, too much noise, and too many decisions to make. Floor traders on the stock exchange, air-traffic controllers, and the directors who decide which of the television cameras recording an event shall be cued in during a live news broadcast have to react as fast as is humanly possible. All the rest of us are being forced to think faster and faster, too.

Information systems overload us at home as well as at work. Computerized mailing lists bombard consumers with more circulars than they can read. Computerized inventory systems put more brands on the grocery shelves than Madison Avenue artists can get us to tell apart. At work, data-processing machinery makes room in the mind for more decisions, more input. The result is that more phone calls, letters, books, memos, and forms contest for the limited space inside the skull. Some days are just a blur.

It is becoming increasingly difficult to hear yourself think. Sound and message pursue you in cars, elevators, waiting rooms, hospital rooms, outdoors. A sober-sided experiment at the University of Nebraska proved that notices posted on the inside of toilet doors were better read than on bulletin boards, and the investigators commended this new location to educators.

Somebody wants to fill up every moment of silence or place of blankness. Billboards, television commercials, telephone salesmen, sound trucks, Muzak, intercom systems, view-shattering buildings, sonic booms, and the rising decibels of machinery of every kind make it harder and harder for individuals to control and make sense of the sights and sounds claiming their attention.

Computers are the arch villains. They do all the easy work and leave the hard work of deciding to mere humans who increasingly feel they are forced to think faster than humanly possible. At the computer millennium, the prophets warn, duller-than-average wits will find it hard to get around the new mechanized world safely, even as many are already finding it hard to get across the street. Eventually, the brightest will have to support a huge, useless majority of ordinary mortals. The intellectual elite will do all the work and wield all of the power, but at the imminent risk of blowing their minds.

Too Much Talk

The ultimate horror, death by overthink, has been vividly imagined by the astronomer, Fred Hoyle. In his science fiction novel, *The Black Cloud*, a superior intelligence from outer space undertakes to communicate the real principles of the universe to two earthling scientists, but succeeds only in burning out their brains so that one after another of the candidates for wisdom dies in fevered agony.

Like more population, more information and communications have always seemed like a good thing. Now, in the 1970s, we aren't so sure.

• *Loquacious Americans*

As a people, Americans have, in the past, been notoriously unwilling to leave each others' minds alone. We invented the quiz show. We revere education. We are "friendly" to the point of foolishness, suspicious of loners, and convinced that there are few personal or social ills that cannot be cured by increasing the flow of information to the afflicted.

We prescribe stimulation for most of the difficulties of everyday life. Take a walk or trip, make new friends to shake a bad mood, a neurosis, a bereavement. Talk to your child to raise his I.Q. Visit the shut-ins. Get involved, it's good for you. Learn more and you'll earn more. Fight gossip with disclosures. Talk away your fears, talk out your differences. Check for a "breakdown in communications" if there is trouble with a spouse, your child, your employees, the public, foreign countries. Improve communications to wipe out prejudice, neurosis, nationalism, and war.

During the 1950s, the magic remedy was "participate." During the 1960s, some of the most active participators were having second thoughts.

"There may also be a danger in sensory overload," Hall

T. Sprague, a behavioral scientist, wrote in a circular letter to his friends. "I find myself—and I think I see others—asking for it—by simultaneously reading, listening to hi-fi, thinking of work tomorrow, glancing at the kids' choice of TV programs, and monitoring my daughter's phone conversation. Or I make an explicit overload choice—like going to a gripping, militant cocktail party with participators—when a more appropriate move would be to unload with a sauna, massage, and aimless day dreaming."

Alvin Toffler coined the term "future shock" for the overstimulation to which modern Americans were subjecting themselves, and he presented convincing evidence that it was making individuals as well as societies literally ill. The concept rang so true to overloaded intellectuals that his book *Future Shock* stayed on the best seller list for months after its publication in 1970.

Like other intellectuals, Toffler advises slowing down and cutting out the threatening overloads. He suggests that we "cope with tomorrow" by "destimulating tactics" such as storming into your teen-ager's room and turning off the stereo, reducing psychological stress by making deliberate attempts to forget trivia, establishing "personal stability zones" such as the well-worn old jacket or the habit of napping after lunch, and "taming technology" by assessing the impact of an innovation and giving it up if it looks as if it is likely to overload the power of human beings to adjust.

• *The Search for Privacy*

The problem that affects most active people in their everyday lives is not to cut down on the quantity of information, but to keep *unwanted information out*. Many active participators solve it by maintaining two residences—one in the thick of metropolitan action, another in a hideaway in the country for solitary work or unwinding.

"Don't answer fan mail," Marya Mannes, a successful writer advised beginners. "Don't get on committees. Don't make speeches." An investigator discovered that Nobel prizewinners are less productive after winning the prize than before, even when they have many productive years ahead of them and thought it was because of heavy demands on their time for nonscientific public service.

"Never look at incoming mail until you have time to read it at leisure," C. Northcote Parkinson said in his 1968 book, *Mrs. Parkinson's Law.* "Never answer the telephone if you are in the middle of something more important."

Telephone solicitation has in fact, become such a nuisance that the New York Telephone Company ran a commercial showing a young mother trying to get rid of a salesman on the phone so that she could take care of her baby. It advised subscribers to hang up on persistent uninvited callers. Obscene and threatening phone calls from strangers have become so big a problem in metropolitan areas that the company developed a special detective service to track these unwanted callers down and prosecute them. Unlisted telephones increase every year in spite of the effort of the phone company to discourage them because they are hard to service. Telephone answering services report a rise in the number of customers who use them to screen calls rather than merely to catch calls they might otherwise miss.

One of the attractions of travel by car seems to be that it is the last refuge of privacy. Many overstimulated professionals cheerfully drive to meetings they could reach faster by air because the trip gives them uninterrupted time to think and plan. A surprising number of corporation presidents do all their reading, and dispatch correspondence by dictaphone while being driven to work or to and from airports. Many pick up associates for confidential talks in the car. Like the restaurant table protected by the white noise of nearby unintelligible chatter, the automobile is a private conference room that needs no secretarial guard.

During the 1960s, architects and product designers discovered the privacy market. Doors, dining rooms, and partitions which architects had banished during the postwar age of togetherness have returned by popular demand, and radio and television manufacturers put out "personal" sets with earphones for use in places where noise would disturb others. A memorable Sony advertisement shows a couple back to back in bed with their "His and Hers" TV sets for the times you want to be "alone with the one you love,"— without having to listen to the beloved's program. And airlines provide special seats for transcontinental passengers who want nothing at all piped into their ears or flickering before their faces.

• *"Quiet, Please!"*

Noise has always been especially distracting to intellectuals because, as Norman Cousins, the former editor of *The Saturday Review* points out, it "interrupts the train of thought." During the 1960s professionals fought back. Dr. Joseph Buckley, Professor of Pharmacology at the University of Pittsburgh, induced ulcers, high blood pressure, irritability, and increased output of stress hormones in rats by putting them in a pen which simulated city stresses with flashing lights, loud bursts of sound, and periodic oscillation similar to a commuter ride. A psychiatrist suggested that noise could cause psychosis by interfering with dreams essential to mental health. A doctor charged that the sudden ring of a doorbell could bring on epileptic seizure. A study of several hundred sixth graders near Washington, D.C. disclosed that what these kids most wanted was "quiet."

Overloaded intellectuals fight "data pollution" as emotionally as they fight noise. One medical researcher was so enraged at the pollution of his mailbox by "preprints" of scientific journals mailed by drug houses that he had a rubber stamp made up and threw them back into the mail marked "Return to Sender." Infuriated by the unstoppable avalanche of unwanted advertising, an English teacher at Eastern Michigan University invoked a postal regulation that leaves the definition of obscenity to the addressee, and forced the Post Office to make Sears Roebuck and J.C. Penney take their catalogues back.

But the charge against "too much talk" is more serious than its intrusion on personal privacy. Too much talk inevitably gives currency to information whose impact is unpredictable because it has never been widely disseminated before. In 1972, the indictment against "too much talk" takes the form of a running feud against the media, in which intellectuals privately concede that Vice-President Spiro Agnew "has something" in blaming the press for riots and unrest as well as hamstringing the government in negotiations with foreign nations. In the 1970s, there is sincere doubt that a free press and universal education will improve the kind of understanding that smooths relationships. More information seems to lead to more complaints. It is blamed for the rise in crime, riots, race problems, teen-age rebellion, political protests, and a visible decline in public morality.

The indictment is broad, and there is some truth to it. A lot of talk creates discomforts of many different kinds. It speeds change. It makes noise both literal and figurative. It creates crime and stirs up dissent. And it raises the aspirations of people who were formerly content with their lot.

• *Faster Change*

The more information passed around, the faster word of new things spreads and the faster innovations are adopted. The more information, the less attention is paid to each individual item. People tend to make room for a faster flow of messages by attending a shorter time to each one and forgetting the stray ones faster. Children brought up in information-rich homes where books, magazines, records, phone calls, and competing conversations, personal radios, and television sets blare at all times, don't stick with tasks as patiently as children brought up in old-fashioned homes where television is rationed and turned off when the phone rings.

Declining attention spans could account for the shorter life of fashions, personalities, slang words, and not only pop music hits, but whole styles of popular music as well. No contemporary singers are as popular for as long a time as Rudy Vallee was a generation ago. No television personalities are popular as long as movie stars like Joan Crawford. Public personalities have a progressively shorter life all the time.

Breakfast food manufacturers capitalize on the new tempo of change by bringing out the same old grains in a succession of new shapes, textures, tastes, and boxes. In economic terms, they have moved out of the low-profit food industry, and into the lusher communications industry.

Shorter attention spans, faster forgetting, means that the young embrace and abandon causes, problems, and particularly tactics of protest with a speed that upsets people accustomed to a world of lower information flow. Veteran politicians did not foresee that voters would so quickly forget Nelson Rockefeller's 1962 divorce, or the tantrums Richard Nixon threw in his 1964 press conference.

Too Much Talk

The sheer volume of news flowing through the media makes it hard to find out what is "real" and what is press-generated. Is there, for instance, a "real" rise in crime, or is crime merely better reported? Are parents really battering their children more frequently than formerly in response to demoralizing urban conditions, as some social critics maintain, or is this crime merely becoming better known?

• More Noise

More information means more "noise"—the word communications engineers use to describe signals that get in the way of the message being sent over a wire. Many of the meaningless sounds are mistakes in transmission. A lot of talk means a lot of error, as in the children's game in which a message is whispered around a circle of people and usually comes out garbled at the end.

When a television message goes wrong, it can result in accident, controversy, violence, and crime. Programmers really cannot predict who will receive the message, or what the message will suggest. Television is charged with teaching teen-agers to smoke pot, wear their hair long, defy school authorities, and otherwise behave as teen-agers. The critics say that news reports have presented irresistible models of abnormal behaviour to young people.

Increasingly, authorities complain that television not only magnifies crime, so that New York is seen as less safe than it is, but spreads it as well. For instance, New York Transit authorities find that news reports of vandalism on a particular subway line inevitably attract new, similar acts of vandalism on that very line. Museums hesitate to report thefts of paintings because the reports so often stimulate new thefts.

Airplane hijackings spawned each other all through the

1960s. The kidnapping of hostages, an extremist political tactic originating in South America, was closely followed by the spectacular capture and destruction of several neutral airliners by Palestinian guerrillas. Weeks after the maneuver succeeded, French separatists in Canada kidnapped two cabinet ministers and killed one when the political demands of the separatists were not honored.

• *More Dissent*

No longer does anyone really believe the optimistic doctrine of the 1950s that disagreements are due to "misunderstandings" that can be cleared up by "education." We now know that it's the other way around: the more information, the more protests. Television exposure made it harder for Presidents Johnson and Nixon to muster the consensuses enjoyed by all previous presidents, and the new freedom to quote the President directly without permission simply made the exposure more difficult for them.

The new communications channels bring together people who had been too scattered or too ignorant of each other to make common cause. Many political pressure groups have literally been created by the news media. News correspondents noticed that Arab nationalism became a force only after the importation of cheap transistor radios from Japan enabled leaders to reach nomad shepherds isolated in the desert. The political emergence of French separatists in Canada, homosexuals, welfare mothers, retired people, and American Indians has come about in the same way. Until everyone had television, the blacks, the poor, and the young weren't able to get together. They are now aware not only of each other, but of what they have been missing that is enjoyed by more privileged groups.

The complaints of the protest movements are not new

or even more grievous than formerly (although the protesters undoubtedly think so). In addition, the complaints often seem abstract, as if the placard carriers were not personally involved. Increasingly, minorities are protesting in purely ideological terms. They respond to symbols, or to news events that have been made symbolic in their minds. Racial disorders are a good example because they have been studied, sometimes while in progress, by many different teams of behavioral scientists, but the principles also apply to campus disorders, crime, and consumer campaigns against business.

• **Rising Expectations**

First, of course, comes the obvious fact that however blacks feel about it, their actual situation has been improving, though some of the gains did not last. In a scholarly study for President Johnson's Task Force on Historical and Comparative Perspectives, James C. Davies concluded that Negroes made rapid progress toward economic equality with whites between 1940 and the early 1950s, but lost nearly half of their gains by the early 1960s.

According to Davies, an increase in violent repression of blacks—the celebrated "white backlash"—triggered the black revolts which culminated in full-fledged riots in Watts, Newark, and Detroit in the mid-1960s. Like other rebels, the blacks had reached the breaking point after "a rather long period of rising expectations followed by a relatively brief period of frustration that struck deep into the psyches of black people." Davies documented a similar gap between rising expectations and reality just before the French Revolution, the American Civil War, the Nazi revolution in Germany, and the civil rights movement in the United States. It was the same with the college protesters. The best

141

students, those who wanted the most out of college, were the ones who mounted the most militant protests. Their targets were not the worst schools, but the best schools.

The theory of the revolution of rising expectations is convincing because studies have failed to show any connection between living conditions, unemployment, low income, or unresponsive government of cities on the one hand, and their incidence of racial disorders on the other hand. As we have seen, several studies of racial disorders have suggested that the critical element may be the number of blacks in a city. If there are a lot of blacks, then disorders are likely, and according to University of Wisconsin sociologist Seymour Spilerman, who studied 341 racial disturbances between 1961 and 1968, they are frequently triggered by telecasts. "The sight of Negroes being beaten up in Selma, Alabama, is as visible and galling to Negroes in Newark and Madison as in Selma itself," he says. "Likewise, TV highlights from Congressional debates on whether to fund a rat control program must provoke similar frustrations in every ghetto." It's not my rat problem that spurs me to protest, but the *idea* of rat infestation of black housing. Revolutions are made with ideas.

• The "Power Structure"

The new popularity of the term "power structure" amuses people old enough to remember when most people weren't well-enough informed to realize that there *was* a power structure controlling their lives. Now everyone sees the powerful on television, and everyone understands that the power structure is actually a communications network. The old revolutionaries seized the telegraph stations. In the 1970s, they seize the infinitely faster and more powerful tube. Never before have so few been able to grab the attention of so many.

Veteran reporters say there is a reversal of influence. Instead of ideas and causes trickling down from the intellectuals or the authorities, the "power structure," they seem to well up from nowhere. A protest or an idea will start somewhere locally, as Women's Liberation started when a few unaffiliated New York women protested the Miss America contest of 1968, and in a few weeks it will be all over the country. Sometimes there will be a big national blowoff, as there was on Earth Day 1970, which seemed to exhaust everybody's concern for the subject.

One of the unforeseen hazards of total, instant information is that serious public issues suffer from the same kind of overexposure that tarnishes the glamour of politicians who appear too often on television. People hear so much about national problems that they get tired of them long before any steps are taken toward solving them. Many intellectuals discharge their guilt over discrimination against blacks, or the war in Vietnam, by talking these problems to death.

Universal literacy and the availability of more information create discontent by informing the disadvantaged of their disadvantages, but they also strike at the power structure much more directly. They deprive the elite of their "mysteries" by making knowledge available to everyone, or at least reducing its price. Intellectuals who have controlled the dissemination of knowledge have the most to lose, and they have been among the most vociferous in attacking technological advances that reduce their knowledge monopoly.

The "humanists" deplore computerization of libraries and information. Educators claim that Evelyn Wood's rapid reading method is a fraud, and the very communications

143

specialists who practice rapid reading without calling it
that, say aloud that it would be better if people read less and
thought more. Information is no help, they say, unless you
know "what to do with it."

If knowledge is power, as the intellectuals themselves
are fond of boasting, than the power structure is by definition a communications network, and politics is the art of
getting control of the network. The more people who have
access to the network, the more people who can grab a
minute on the television screen, the greater the threat to
those now in control.

Power depends on keeping some things secret, and you
can't keep much of anything secret when there's a lot of talk
going around. Attempts at censorship break down under the
sheer volume of information flying around.

● *The New Censorship*

Quiet! sounds heavenly to the haves, but the program
is a form of complaint, not a remedy. American intellectuals
have never been adept in the art of keeping information
"confidential," or limited to safe hands, but even the experts
at censorship can't do it anymore. The Russians tried, for a
time, to jam Radio Free Europe, but for several years now
governments have just given up the attempt. Like it or not,
diplomats and businessmen and even intellectuals have to
think in public. The newly sworn-in President of the United
States had no jump on millions of televiewers who saw the
murder of the assassin whose murder had elevated him to
that office.

When the Government attempted to enjoin *The New
York Times* from publishing Pentagon papers obtained
through undisclosed channels, the first reaction of most educated Americans was that the issue itself was an anachro-

nism. Hadn't we solved all that back in the seventeenth century in England? Did we really have to go over all that ground about the freedom of the press again?

It seems that we did. The dispute over the Pentagon papers neatly divided those who wanted to change the system from those who had stakes in preserving it, and it was no accident that the issue which polarized the division of interest was the issue of access to information.

The issue had been brewing for years. The blacks, the young, the poor, consumers, doves—any group with complaints against the establishment devote their energy to catching the television camera crews. Public discussion of the merits of their causes increasingly centers on their ability to "get control of the tube."

No one fully appreciates how much difference television makes. In New York City, for instance, even reformers have concluded that the city is basically "ungovernable." It is not the problems of the city that are new, but the informed voices of the deprived who had been ignorant and silent before national saturation of the television market in the 1950s.

The issue of access to public information has nothing to do with the political party in power. President Johnson, an avowed reformer in domestic affairs, inherited an unpopular foreign policy that had been developed back in the days when negotiations between governments were made in private by so-called "gentlemen," and nobody really cared enough about these state secrets to object. When past wars had been unpopular—and all but World Wars I and II were just as unpopular as the war in Vietnam—Presidents had been able to marshal support from Congress and the people by appeals to patriotism. President Johnson couldn't do it in part, at least, because his efforts to silence dissident Government officials in the interest of national consensus on foreign affairs became the substantive issue itself. Hostility from the press and harrassment from doves, largely young people successful in getting attention, convinced President Johnson that he could not unite the country through a second term.

The lesson was not lost on President Nixon. In line with a proclaimed policy of national quiet, Presidential Counsellor Daniel P. Moynihan advised treating the blacks to a season of "benign neglect." The new President announced early in his term that he would make no startling reforms. He delayed making any public pronouncements for months after his election. He limited news conferences. Newsmen fumed against the "public relations" types President Nixon employed to buffer him from their questions, and his choice of televised settings in which he himself could control the scene.

Nixon correctly sensed the national mood. The new high levels of information flow, the intensifying "rat race," had the newly affluent searching for relief from stimulation in everyday life as well as in public affairs. During the 1960s something new was added to the American dream: the search for peace and quiet.

• *Quiet Is Not the Answer*

Talk may create trouble both private and public, but shutting up is as fruitless a remedy as "don't worry." For one thing, we know too much already to go back to consensus. We can never go back to the innocence of pre-television America. Once you know something, you can't unknow it.

Cutting down won't help for a more important reason. It is not the sheer quantity of information alone that causes trouble, but its meaning. When people say they need privacy to get away from too much stimulation, what they really mean is that they want to get away from messages they don't

146

want to hear. It's not only the interruption of the phone call, but who and what is on the other end of the line. When executives say they are overworked, it's not only the stacks of computer printouts that they mean, but trying to decide what to do about the data in them. When those in power— and that includes the intellectuals—complain about too much television, they are really concerned about what the programs are saying.

"Quiet please!" Who asks for it? The rich, the entrenched, the people who like things the way they are or were and don't want to be "bothered." To these privileged people, too much talk is as threatening as too many people. The same conservatives who want to slow population growth, and the concentration of people in metropolitan areas, and even economic growth itself, in order to maintain an agrarian-type economy, also want to cut the avalanche of words which disrupt the prevailing methods of control, words that seem to disrupt "law and order." Daniel P. Moynihan, a Democrat who served a Republican President, sincerely fears that too much talk will dissolve civilization.

Rap enough, the critics warn, and things will surely come unstuck.

Chapter IX

The Arithmetic
of Growth

The maddening thing about the accelerating break-downs is that every simple explanation evaporates when you really look at it. So far, it's been easier to say what did *not* cause the breakdowns than what did cause them. Yet there are a few things that we do know.

First, the timing. The breakdowns began to snowball in 1965. The year of the big Northeastern power blackout was also the year of the Vietnam build-up, when inflation began to gallop ahead of productivity. The problems of the cities reached the boiling point in the next few years. Dollars kept increasing, whether of sales or income. The GNP kept going up and so did the stockmarket, but most people could see that it wasn't doing anybody much good.

Second, the sense of overload. The problem seemed to come from increasing numbers, from more people, things, and talk than we knew what to do with. And of course, it was true. While no specific overload was the sole cause, each contributed something to the snowballing problems.

Take the rise in crime. Crime rises with population

because population growth increases the proportion of young males who commit most of the crime; with affluence, because more money means more and higher-priced personal property exposed to theft; with expanding communications, which suggests crimes and make them easier to commit.

The most disturbing thing about a world of large numbers is that it blows up problems that don't exist or can be ignored when the numbers are smaller. Mistakes hurt more people. Accidents are not only more damaging, but more apt to happen. Expectations of improvement in the standard of life rise faster, but so many are involved that they are harder to satisfy. A high volume of talk undermines authority and promotes demands for equality of status at the same time that organizations get bigger and require more rules and more differentiation of people's roles.

As long as numbers, things, money, and talk go up together, a high volume of one implies a high volume of the others, and these volumes set up contradictions. A lot of people generate a lot of talk and heat up demand for change while at the same time making it harder to get agreement on any course of action. This is what has been happening in many communities where minorities are beginning to make their voices heard. Much of this is the role that sheer numbers play.

Where did all the unanticipated people, things, and ideas come from? Why have they piled up so inexorably? And why in the middle 1960s? The answer lies in their relationship to each other, and in some laws of mathematics.

• *The J-Curve of Growth*

What started the snowball rolling? The domestic population explosion that overloaded schools in the 1960s, may have started when Federally insured mortgage money made houseroom in the suburbs broadly accessible after World War II. The information explosion, the most powerful multiplier of all, was touched off by modest sums for scientific research and education voted by Congress after the Russians put up Sputnik in 1957, and the incredibly speedy saturation of the American market for television sets.

It's very tempting to plot this growth on a graph—and try and see where it's going.

Population alarmists point out that the growth of human numbers describes a curve that looks like the letter "J." Their charts show the long, slow rise of the population of the planet up to a few hundred years ago, when it started gathering speed. It is our fate to live in the crook of the J-curve, where it seems to point straight up, and out of sight to standing room only. This comes about because human beings increase by compound interest.

Talk may multiply even faster. Information increases the range of choices. According to one management consultant, the number of decisions an administrator has to make increases not by the square of the options facing him, but by the square of the square. Administrators will readily agree that the increase in data showered on their desks is the root cause of the syndrome of discomforts called the "rat race."

Not only do people, things, and talk grow by compound interest, but they also stimulate each other's growth. Rising wealth—"means of subsistence" Malthus called it—increases the population, whether in the new lands of colonial America, the postwar United States, or even, as we have seen, in India, where recent population rises have followed closely on increases in per capita wealth.

Increase real per capita wealth by any means (such as an invention) that increases productivity, and the birth rate rises.

There is a lot of popular misconception about population and poverty. "Overpopulation" simply doesn't happen in countries where conditions are getting worse. It doesn't make rich people poor. It simply multiplies the number of people living in unacceptable poverty, and makes it harder for them to get rich as fast as the Japanese and Swedes have been doing in this century. For what it's worth, Gross National Product per capita has been rising slowly in "overpopulated" countries.

Talk and wealth stimulate each other as well. Start with anything that makes talk cheaper (such as a computer or television) and you encourage more efficient speculation as well as increase the ambition and productivity of more people so that real per capita GNP increases. (Under the umbrella "education" this increase in information flow is the general prescription of the experts for the underdeveloped nations. If we are right, this "education" will help them not so much by lowering their birth rate, but by increasing their wealth.)

• The Peanut Principle

There's another reason why people, and especially things and talk mushroom so ominously. The desire and the need for things and talk—perhaps even the desire and need for babies—increases with their availability. The appetite for money and information grows on the peanut principle— the more you have, the more you want and need.

Psychologists sometimes refer to this principle as "the more, the more." The more money you have, the more you want and the easier it is to make it. The wider the road, the more traffic it attracts and the wider it has to be. The bigger and faster the planes, the more trips, and the more trips, the more big and fast planes. Crowds in big cities attract people by their very size. The leading brand attracts customers by its very popularity.

Every child knows about peanuts. Eat one, and you want another. Eat another, and it whets your appetite for a third. The more you eat, the more you want. Left alone, an innocent child will go on eating peanuts until every last one is gone, or his stomach literally ejects them.

Psychologists can't explain the appetite that whets itself. It doesn't make any kind of physiological sense. Thirst is more rational. The first glass of water slakes your need for the second and the third is dispensable. In economic terms, supply "satisfies" and so reduces demand. But not peanuts. With peanuts, supply *creates* its own demand.

Mysterious as it is, the peanut principle governs the most characteristically human appetites. The more you know, the more you want to know. Travel increases curiosity about distant scenes. The more golf you play, the more ardently you desire to play more. The more clothes you have, the more you want. Move once, and you're more apt to move again. Those who enjoy wealth, power, prestige, insight, affection, and a wide circle of friends are more willing than the rest of us to put themselves out to get still more—even though the additional unit cannot add significantly to their existing store.

Human sexuality is a revealing example. Orgasm reduces desire in the human male, but increases it in the human female. Male orgasm is essential to reproduction. Human males share it with animal males. Female orgasm, on the other hand, appears to be a human embellishment on the reproductive machinery. It works on the peanut principle.

When asked how he managed to meet all the demands on his time, the president of a big insurance company replied that he had found he could regulate the number of people in the organization who wanted to see him by the amount of attention he was willing to give them. He had, of course, restated an application of the Peanut Principle: the more receptive, the more callers; the more you listen, the longer people talk.

• Encounters

The common feature of people, things, and talk through which they spark each other's growth is the encounter. The more people, the more encounters, especially if the people are crowded spatially. The more encounters, the more economic transactions, as every merchant who sets out to catch impulse sales well knows. The more dollars or wealth, or things, the more encounters, because they all represent a particular kind of encounter, the exchange of goods or services. The more talk, the more encounters, for talk is another kind of meeting between speaker and listener or writer and reader. And as we saw in analyzing crowding, it is the encounters between people, not their spatial propinquity, that causes all the good and evil ascribed to population density. Encounters are the common denominator.

Encounters grow much faster than the number of people, dollars, or messages that produce them. The rate of encounters that can be anticipated for molecules, cars, skaters, people in a city, or any other collection of interacting things rises as the square of the number of these things. That's why traffic jumps up so fast in response to even a modest increase in the number of cars. That's why the problems of the city grow so much faster than the city itself.

The arithmetic of encounters is important because encounters themselves are the source of wealth.

• Encounters Make Wealth

It is the encounters, not the crowding of people together that encourages the division of labor which is generally credited for the wealth of cities. Back in 1893, Emile Durkheim, the French sociologist, suggested that people in densely populated societies become specialists in order to avoid head-on competition with each other. "The division of labor varies in direct ratio with the volume and density of societies," he wrote in his classic work *The Division of Labor*, "and if it progresses in a continuous manner in the course of social development, it is because societies become regularly denser and more voluminous." Durkheim made clear that he meant social, not physical density. He pointed out, for instance, that the poor people in densely settled parts of China and the oriental Russia of his day were not really exceptions to the rule because they had very little contact with each other. The same is true, of course, of present day India which is poor primarily because its people are more isolated from each other than Americans can easily imagine.

The Indians are poor, not because they are too many, but because they don't talk to each other. Some students of that unhappy country say that it has enough resources to feed all of its people. It is poor primarily because of the caste system that cuts the population up into little pockets of people, so that resources cannot be mobilized or organized. Hong Kong is more densely populated than New York, but not as rich because its people do not have as many relationships with each other as New Yorkers can maintain through cars and phones.

Famine, the ultimate in poverty, is almost always caused by inadequate transmission of information and lack of transportation. Communication of knowledge is the quickest way to increase the food supply, and as we have seen, increased food supply means more people. Word of the plow and the innovations following it, right down to the "Green Revolution" of increasing agricultural yields, are real reason why world population has steadily risen.

The Arithmetic of Growth

Encounters make wealth, and information flow is, of course, the quickest way to increase the number of encounters and the biggest encounter bargain. Intuitively we all realize that information has a dollar value. Rich countries and cities and people have more information flowing through them than poor ones. Vocabulary correlates with income. The more relevant information a businessman has, the more profitable his decisions. That's why it pays insurance companies and banks to specialize in certain kinds of risks. Computer-based credit-card systems increase sales by making it safe for a merchant to extend credit to customers he does not know.

For merchants looking for business (and young people looking for mates) the arithmetic of urban encounter is stimulating. Stanley Milgram, a mathematically inclined Professor of Psychology at the City University of New York has calculated that a resident of Nassau County, a suburb of New York, can reach 11,111 other people in a ten-minute walk or drive, but he can reach 220,000 in the same time if he moves to the densely populated center of Manhattan. Milgram also reports that people in big cities move faster than people in small cities, and so increase their potential for meeting others.

When Richard L. Meier was studying the application of information theory at the University of Michigan, he became convinced that the increased information flow in cities is the cause, rather than the effect of their growth and wealth. He states the relationship rigorously, as a general law: "A sector of society that grows in influence, wealth or power, measured in absolute terms, must experience a growth in information flow that occurred prior to or simultaneously with the recorded growth."

The theory checks out with the recent spurt of growth in the American economy. Between 1950 and 1955, when television sets per capita quadrupled and air travel doubled, our Gross National Product per capita rose 28 percent. Between 1960 and 1965, the boom period for books, scientific research, and computers, GNP per capita went up 26 percent and the total of profits earned by all U.S. business enterprises nearly doubled.

Nothing that has ever happened in human history so far has stimulated the encounters that produce wealth as much as the communication explosion that gathered steam in the 1950s. Since talk is the fastest multiplier of the growth of everything else, the overloads may well have begun in a drastic change in the way information is passed around.

• *Information Explosion*

At the turn of the century, when my father entered the University of Wisconsin, the most distinguished citizen of Madison, Wisconsin was Senator William F. Vilas. He was, of course, rich. But he was rich with style. His simple brick mansion on Lake Mendota shamed its pretentious neighbors. His children went East to school. But the thing that most impressed my father at the time was that Senator Vilas had a standing order with the local bookstore to send up one copy of "everything new."

It was an extravagant but not impossible policy. By getting hold of every new book published in the United States at that time, his eager bookseller could have scraped together a manageable number of items a day.

In 1970 no bookseller could fill the order and no customer would have wanted it. By then, the daily tide had risen to more than 70 volumes a day—far more than the speediest demonstrators of rapid reading methods could skim. No library today has the space, manpower, or resources to take in everything.

The Arithmetic of Growth

A list of the innovations that changed everyday life is always an interesting project, sure to suggest many explanations of puzzling phenomena. If the innovations made between 1920 and 1940 are compared with those made between 1950 and 1970, it is striking how many of the recent ones have been systems for greatly increasing the transmission of information or facilitating social transactions.

Everyone's lists will differ a little, but mine looks like this:

1920–1940	1950–1970
Mechanization of agriculture	Frozen foods
Refrigeration	Air conditioning
Electrification of homes	Plastics and light metals
Synthetic textiles	Antibiotics and "wonder" drugs
Hospitalization of childbirth	Contraceptive pill
°Radio	°Transistors (solid-state circuits)
Mass-production techniques	°Television
°National advertising	°Computerized data processing
°Automobile	°Jet air travel
Comprehensive public welfare	°Large-scale consumer credit
°Free, public-supported high schooling	°Free, public-supported college systems
	Mortgages paid like rent
	Widespread health insurance
	°Massive investment on research and development

° communications-oriented advances

Of the most recent list, antibiotics and the pill have not as yet substantially affected the age or size of the population, while the principal impact of air conditioning and frozen foods has been to reduce dependence on the seasons and redistribute people to big buildings in central cities, and hinterlands worth cultivating. None of the non-communications-oriented advances of 1950–1970 changed everyday life as radically as the electrification of homes or even refrigeration.

157

High school education, the radio, and the automobile transformed everyday life in the period between the two world wars, but they did not increase the information as much as college education, television, jet air travel, and the computer. And just as it took a little while for high schooling, radio, and cars to change everyday life, so it is taking a few years (though fewer all the time) for the more recent innovations to make themselves felt. The recent innovations have come in two waves: first an increase in the transmission of information that hit the masses, and more recently an explosion of information-dense media that hit the specialists.

In the first wave, a series of technological advances between 1950 and 1955 made information-rich activities a much bigger bargain for the average American than alternative ways of spending money. During this five year period, long-distance phone rates fell, jet service cut air fares, and a series of technically minor improvements in the reproduction of printed material, such as offset printing, cut the relative cost of mass mailings. The result was that the average American made 23 percent more phone calls, received a third more pieces of third-class mail (printed matter, advertising circulars, etc.), and flew twice as many air miles in 1955 than in 1950.

The increase made a big difference in the national economy. According to one measurement, the calculations of Fritz Machlup, an internationally known economist at Princeton University, "knowledge producing industries" accounted for 29 percent of the economy of 1958 and had grown twice as fast as the rest of the economy between 1954 and 1958. He counted as "knowledge producing" all educational activities wherever found: the communication media, information machines (typewriters, cameras), information services (stockbrokers, insurance, wholesaling, and professions). But in 1958 the big multipliers of knowledge were yet to come.

• Books and More Books

The book explosion and the computer didn't blossom until the 1960s, and although spending on research and development and college attendance began rising in the 1950s, the new knowledge and the new college graduates didn't hit the world at large until the 1960s either. The new communication channels, physical and human, were much richer in information than the phone calls, television shows, and advertising circulars that had first inundated the average American in the late 1950s. Books and computerized data reach far fewer people, but the few who receive them are strategically located to make things happen, and it all happened very fast.

Like the J-curve of population rise, the increase in the number of book titles has been remarkably recent. As late as 1957, American publishers actually issued fewer new titles than in 1910. But that year the Russians put up Sputnik and jolted Congress into appropriating Federal money for research, education, and libraries to help the United States catch up. New book titles nearly doubled between 1960 and 1965, and by 1967 Americans were spending twice as much money on books as in 1957.

Publishers, printers, and reviewers were overwhelmed. A book that wasn't ready on time lost its place in line at the printers and might have to wait six months. There weren't enough bookbinders to go around, and inexperienced copy processors left a trail of typographical errors behind them. *Publishers' Weekly*, the trade magazine of the book business, thickened to handle the new titles and finally increased its page size. Reviewers serving readers lacked time and space to report even "good books," and *The New York Times* had to ration advertising space among publishing houses. Prosperity was hard on the ego of authors.

Public libraries couldn't begin to keep up with the titles. In 1966, the proud New York Public Library sold $1.2 million of its endowment capital to buy new books, but it couldn't find the help or space to catalogue and shelve 70,000 of the new arrivals or even to move into larger quarters where they could be accommodated. In Detroit, the Public Library extended its stacks and put its messenger boys on roller skates.

College libraries were worse off because they had more money. Although modest by comparison with the billions of dollars newly appropriated for research, development and education in the name of national defense, the millions included for the libraries gave most college librarians more book-buying money than they had ever dreamed of spending.

Word of the windfall traveled fast. Every professor had a little list of books he expected to see on the shelves by return mail. Administrators eyed the millions available for library construction and expected instant libraries equipped to serve the graduate students attracted by Federal grants. Most of the books a graduate student needs are out of print, and college libraries had to compete on the secondhand market for them with new public libraries funded under the Library Services and Construction Act of 1964. Some of the 3000 new libraries founded between 1966 and 1968 were in such a hurry that they bought out whole bookstores without stopping to inventory the books they were getting or considering what they would do with them. Reproduction services boomed.

The Arithmetic of Growth

- *Computers*

Computers didn't get going on everyday life until the 1960s, but they eventually affected more institutions. In 1955, computers were largely confined to the Census, the Pentagon, the Social Security Administration, and research institutions. By 1960, they had taken over billing, order processing, insurance records, check clearing, magazine subscriptions, and inventory control in companies with massive numbers of employees, suppliers, customers, or products. Between 1960 and 1965, they took over airline and hotel reservations, motor vehicle license renewals, and routing of telephone calls, freight and plane flights; calculation of the GNP; the listing of telephone subscribers, freight rates, and mail order inventories. A strike of computers today would ground all planes, knock out electric power and phone service, and create a painful shortage of cash.

Everyday life now depends on a score of new institutions that were impractical before paperwork could be mechanized, among them credit cards, revolving charge accounts, and rented cars that can be dropped off in the city of destination. More than 70,000 computers are at work.

Few activities have been left untouched. An alphabet of what computers do today would include, among many others, baseball batting averages, credit ratings, crime reports, dating, dog registrations, examination scoring, handwriting analyses, hospital bed schedules, income tax auditing, insurance planning, job matching, list making, menu planning, quotations of stock prices, royalty statements, security analyses, type-setting, and weather forecasting. Computer specialists are not impressed. They say computers haven't begun to show what they can do.

The books, the mailings, and particularly the computers eat up paper and multiply the paperwork of business

161

and Government "red tape" even more. Between 1960 and 1965 consumption of "printing paper" that goes into books rose 19 percent per capita, but the "fine papers" that go into stationery, ledgers, mimeograph machines, computers, photocopies, office forms and other documents generated by business and Government went up 28 percent per capita. In 1958, for instance, the Federal income tax return of The Monsanto Company was a compact 66 pages; its 1967 return took 1067.

The paperwork proliferates even when ruthless measures are taken to cut it. In 1964 the Federal government was spending $6 to $7 billion on paperwork, up from $4 billion in 1955. In order to hold the rise in this level, the Government had simplified and standardized the two *billion* forms it had people filling out, and was holding the Federal record to four million filing cases by destroying old records at a cost of $30 million a year. But it is like bailing out the sea.

The new information machines are in themselves powerful multipliers of the demand for information. Computers and other automatic data processors demand more information than was necessary when clerks did their work, because the machines are incapable of the minor judgments which clerks can make when information they are processing is incomplete. And just as washing machines make more washing, highways attract more traffic, and labor-saving devices make it possible to do more work, so the snowstorm of data issuing from computers, closed-circuit television, audio-visual material on tape, dataphone, and conference telephone setups raise more questions than they solve, questions which decision makers, already overwhelmed, tend to buck along to others in their organizations who either set the machines to turning out new facts, or feel obligated to retaliate with new words and opinions of their own. As an increasing proportion of the work done in offices consists in moving information around inside it, especially when the information required to make decisions expands to the point where it has to be assembled from many different sources, it is not a Parkinson-Law type joke to point out that the more people employed, the more work they create for each other.

Anyone who worked at a profession through the 1950s and 1960s felt the speed-up. There were more eyeball-to-eyeball encounters: more trips, meetings, interviews, seminars, conferences, conventions, panels, buzz sessions, guided tours, community projects, and visits to stores, doctors, beauty parlors, psychiatrists, gyms, courts, welfare offices, and income tax adjusters.

• *News Makes News*

Communications media also underestimate the extent to which they create business for each other. News creates news. The more you know, the more you want to know. On July 20, 1969, the streets of New York City were deserted as more than a million New Yorkers watched literally every step the Apollo 11 Astronauts took on the moon, with their own eyes and ears as it was actually happening. They got reports on the heart rates of the Astronauts, which was more than the men themselves knew. There seemed little for newspapers to add, yet the next morning, every newspaper in New York was sold out by ten o'clock.

What happened on Moon Day was that information supplied by one channel created a demand for information on the same topic supplied by all other channels. And typically the media did not realize it. Newspapers did not increase their print runs.

The Crowding Syndrome

The history of media demonstrates that new media give the old ones a new lease on life more frequently than they supplant them. The tractor did replace the horse, but radio did not replace newspapers. "Extras" were just about the only casualty. Instead of replacing phonograph records, the radio music built a whole new record industry and introduced millions of people to classical music. Magazine circulation has continued to grow in spite of the competition of television. And first-class mail has continued to grow in spite of the spectacular increase in per capita phone calling.

Television turned out to be less of a threat to other media than the prophets of doom expected. It seemed to stimulate rather than supplant radio: the number of AM radio stations increased fastest during the fastest growth of television stations between 1950 and 1955. It hasn't killed the lecture business, but has created a new interest in personal appearances by television personalities. Television took a lot of advertising dollars that would otherwise have gone to national magazines, but magazines attract more advertising dollars every year just the same. And while television keeps the passive mass audience glued to the tube Saturday nights, it seems to propel a growing active young audience to patronize the new art films.

The radio-television audience buys the newspapers for the program listings, day in and day out. During the 1950s, airline executives liked to boast that they were competing with A.T. & T. more than with each other. They hoped to steal from the phones the affluent businessmen they imagined that A.T. & T. had induced to phone instead of write. But phone calls and plane trips rose together. A businessman is more apt to hop on a plane as a result of a phone call than in place of it, just as phone calls generate confirming letters and letters lead to phone calls.

The Arithmetic of Growth

• Speed-up on Wall Street

The most dramatic and most instructive example of the multiplier effect of information and the interaction between information and wealth, is what happened to the stockmarket. During the 1960s, the high-speed ticker and other information machines boomed volume to the verge of back-office breakdown. The break resulted from information that fed the boom.

The stockmarket is essentially an information-processing institution. It automatically and instantaneously weighs a broad diversity of opinions and registers a consensus. Over the years the stockmarket has been a fairly good barometer of what is going to happen if only because the influence of investors with poor judgment is automatically eliminated: they lose their money or get out. Since "the market lives on news," as they say in Wall Street, it has been remarkably sensitive, over its long history, to improvements in communication technology.

Traditionally, stock prices moved as fast and as far as human brains could deal with numbers transmitted by wire. During the affluent 1950s, the volume on the New York Stock Exchange inched up about five percent a year. News of fabulous developments in electronics contributed to that growth, but however clearly stockbrokers saw the value of electronic data processing to industry in general, they were slow to automate the complicated information processing of the brokerage business itself. Tickers were improved and "wires" increased to speed orders from distant cities, but it was not until 1960 that the exchanges themselves invested in expensive new hardware. Then, the numbers that men had to handle multiplied beyond anyone's expectations.

In 1960, the American Stock Exchange speeded the

165

ticker to 500 characters a minute. In 1962, it installed the Teleregister—a device to print out current stock price information—in the board rooms of major firms and in 1964 AMEX inaugurated Telequote III which permitted a broker to dial on a computer the symbol of the stock that interests him and get its up-to-the-minute bid, asking, opening price, price of last sale, its high-low, volume up-to-the-minute, all relayed via a talking computer.

Meanwhile, the securities markets broadened and quickened. Turnover—the number of times a year a stock certificate changes hands—had been declining for a half century, but in the early 1960s it began to pick up: in 1964 the Big Board sold twice as many shares as in 1960. Old hands who remembered 1929 warned against "churning" portfolios just to earn commissions, and the Street was cautious about investing in facilities for the new high volumes. In 1965 the New York Stock Exchange estimated that it would take ten years for volume to double. But the doubling came only three years later, in 1968.

"What we missed was the impact of technological information change," explained the economist who made the projection, Leon T. Kendall. It was a new kind of market. "There were no high peaks or deep valleys in trading," *Fortune* marveled in May 1968, "just heavy, sustained volume, day after day." One reason was that the number of stockholders had doubled in less than a decade.

Wall Street had wooed them. Security analysts skilled in applying sophisticated new mathematical techniques to the rising tide of business data used them to "educate" prospective investors. Computers capable of printing out whole tables of figures on command replaced the rows of comptometer clerks formerly engaged in producing the simpler indices, and made it easy to invent new measures. "The Dow," a statistical average of stock prices, flashed along the ticker and blinked on the windows of brokers all over the country as the computers compiled it minute to minute from the ticker. Investors could respond faster to smaller fluctuations than formerly.

Financial information became a growth industry. Murray Bloom, the author of a book on Wall Street called *Rogues to Riches*, estimates that the new shareholders attracted to the market during the 1960s generated a geometric increase in the flow of financial information. He found twice as many stockmarket letters in the 1960s as in the 1950s. Syndicated columnists began talking about specific stocks rather than in generalities. Books on investing appeared on best-seller lists.

The larger brokers and information services used the machines of the same electronic companies whose stocks were contributing to the market rise, and new services were advertised, analysis of portfolios "by computer." Big brokers also installed order-handling machines which increased the volume of trades a floor broker could make, thus stepping up his efficiency.

Money poured into the market. Mutual funds competed with each other for stocks to buy, and in spite of a record number of new issues (advertising agencies and even stockbrokers now raise capital by incorporating and issuing stock), there simply weren't enough stocks to supply the new investors. In 1966, daily volume of The New York Stock Exchange averaged 7.5 million shares; in 1967, 10.1 million; on April 1, 1968, The New York Stock Exchange exceeded the 1929 Crash Day record by exchanging 17.7 million shares, and the backlog of undelivered securities Wall Streeters had treated as a private problem became a public concern.

As we have seen, the backrooms of brokerage houses breathed easier after May 26, 1970, when the Dow-Jones stock price index broke sharply, ushering in the doldrums that distracted Wall Street from its housekeeping problems. But though not the major worry of the investment community, the backroom problem did not go away. Although investors stayed away in droves, the millions who had been newly "educated" to the virtues of stock ownership and the delights of trading could not help responding to the faintest breath of hope for a revival of the bull markets of the early 1960s. Between April 1, 1968, and November 9, 1970, a period during which brokerage houses merged, closed offices, and dismissed employees for lack of business, the 1929 Crash Day record of 16.4 million shares traded was exceeded 44 times.

Volume did not bring prosperity back to Wall Street. In the 1970s it is obvious that the old private-club system of voice trading among gentlemen can no longer handle the sheer volume of securities transactions required by the economy, even when that economy is depressed. Brokerage firms are permitted and even encouraged to incoporate. Negotiable commissions have replaced the fixed commission system which penalized big institutions and subsidized the small investor, whose business cost more in paperwork than it paid. And brokers who have resisted such obvious reforms as a standard machinable stock certificate agree in private that floor trading can not last forever. Sooner or later, securities will be exchanged through a single giant computer which will automatically and instantaneously match any number of bids and askeds. In the stockmarket, as well as in less dramatic institutions, the information explosion fed on itself to the point of breakdown. Information and wealth had set up a beneficent spiral. The information machines increased stockmarket transactions and created the dollars to pay for more machines to speed transactions even further until human beings couldn't keep up with themselves.

Luckily, the recession that slowed stockmarket volume has provided a short reprieve from collapse during which it is possible to think about the many new systems required not only on Wall Street, but everywhere.

Chapter **X**

The Slowdown

The population alarmists have been telling us only part of the story with the J-curve, the first half of it. During that phase, growth feeds on itself; the bigger anything gets, the faster it grows. Fruit flies in a test-tube, the population of India, a plant, a child, the sales of a new product, the Gross National Product of an industralizing nation, all grow slowly at first, then by compound interest faster and faster. At the crook of the J-curve it is easy to look straight up, up and off the graph to an infinity of human beings. But we should remember that there comes a time when there's a slowdown in all growth, a willow tree, the sales of a new product, or the economy of nations. That straight upward line of the J-curve eventually slopes off into an S-curve.

A half century ago, the great statistician, Raymond Pearl, documented that there comes a time in all living systems when growth rounds off to a steady plateau of relative equilibrium.

The evidence seems to indicate that we are already in this S-curve phase of growth in the United States.

Additional people, things, dollars, or knowledge come more slowly, and cost more after a certain point. This is true even in the mass production of automobiles. All four American automobile manufacturers are making so many cars already that increasing production can't make them any cheaper. On the contrary, making more cars subjects them to rising overhead, and particularly to rising sales costs. Cars sell themselves to people who can afford and need them, but it costs increasingly more to sell additional cars to people who need other things more urgently.

Rising "costs"—many of them measurable in money—are already slowing the growth of our population, wealth, and information flow.

● *Fewer Babies*

The year 1957 was the high watermark of our postwar childbearing spree. The general fertility rate of women of childbearing age has been declining ever since, and in 1971 it was getting down close to the all-time lows of the Great Depression of the 1930s, when for brief periods at least, we did not, as a nation, have enough babies to reproduce ourselves.

Now, the baby-boom girls have come of childbearing age, and while there are a lot of them, they have been having fewer babies apiece.

Births might drop even further. The clue is the number of babies born to women who are 20 to 24 years of age, the years when most women have the most first babies. Between 1965 and 1969, the birth rate of this group dropped 15 percent, and the decline has continued. Women seemed to be marrying later and waiting longer to have their children. Professor Donald J. Bogue, a sociologist at the University of Chicago, calls it a "fertility recession" and he ascribes it to changing values and life styles.

Most young wives now expect to have two children or fewer. The change has been recent and sudden. Between 1967 and 1971, the percentage of women 18 to 24 who expected two children or fewer rose from 44 percent to 64 percent. Family size expectation dropped from 3.1 to 2.8 children, but the drop was sharper for the young wives.

American women are putting on the population brakes, but we don't know how far they are going to go. Judith Blake Davis, Chairman of the Department of Demography at the University of California, Berkeley, maintains that all of the poor people won't use the birth control the Federal Government plans to give them because some of them really want big families. Some of them, of course, really do. But the fact is that the most dramatic reductions in births have been among the blacks and poor who are just now bettering themselves and learning how to avoid unwanted babies. Contraception isn't perfect yet, in spite of the pill, and unwanted or at least unplanned babies are still born to the well off and the well informed as well as to the poor and ignorant. Wider knowledge of birth control, better methods, and easy abortion will all help slow growth even further.

It has become clear that there simply are not going to be 300 million Americans by the Year 2000. In August, 1970, the Census Bureau dropped its highest projection and announced that there would be only 281 million in 2000 at the current birth rate, and only 266 million if births fell to the replacement rate.

Why the decline? The population movement can't claim credit, because the movement didn't become popular until ten years or more after the decline started. If anything, the relationship was the other way around: Zero Population Growth and abortion reform have spread like wildfire because they provide a rationale for the growing preference for small families. And while the pill is a more efficient and acceptable contraceptive than those previously used, and has cut down on the number of accidental pregnancies, it has not really helped those women who don't really want to have children, but feel compelled to rear families because of social pressures. The all-time low fertility rate was in 1933, and it was attained by condoms, diaphragms, abstinence, coitus interruptus, and a loss of spontaneity.

• *Have One, Adopt One*

I ran into "Have One, Adopt One" in the spring of 1970. A student bride from Syracuse explained that she and her husband wanted to see what a child of theirs would look like, but they thought they should add only one to the over-burdened earth. Rather than rear an only child, they had decided to adopt a second. The adopted child would probably be black, not because they were out to prove anything about race relations, but because there were more black children available for adoption. The scheme was logical, but so bizarre that I wrote it off to one woman's hyperactive conscience. Then I got the same story from a Boston bride.

I was reporting trends for a magazine, and two cases, I told myself, were a coincidence and not a trend. But when a third turned up in Gainesville, Florida, I asked a college textbook salesman reading the *Environmental Handbook* beside me on a plane whether he had encountered the idea on any of the college campuses he had visited.

"No," he said slowly, "but it's funny. My wife and I are ready for a second baby, and we've been thinking of adopting it—because of the environment, you know." Back home in Poughkeepsie, I asked a high-school girl acquaintance how many children she wanted to have and discovered that she, too, had decided that the only way to cut down the population of the earth without foregoing children was to have one child and adopt a companion for it.

Did they mean it? A majority of adoption agencies queried by postcard across the country said yes, there had been a perceptible increase in requests for adoptive children from young couples who were able to have children of their own. For a small but well-distributed minority of young couples, adoption has become a logical form of parentage in an overpopulated world. So far as I have been able to find out, no one is "behind" this movement. "Have One, Adopt One" has just emerged everywhere at once, seemingly out of its own logic and a general change in attitude.

Other young couples, less idealistic, are planning no more than two children. Their reasons are usually economic: they can't afford more. They are no worse off than the young couples of the 1950s who wanted, and actually had three or four. If anything, the young families of the 1970s are better equipped to be parents because they have more knowledge and more money. They are postponing babies because there are other things that they want more urgently, frequently more education or more freedom for themselves.

Another way to say this, in economic terms, is that if you consider a baby as an expenditure, alternative expenditures are getting relatively cheaper, and are more attractive "buys" than children. In 1971, the Commission on Population Growth and the American Future figured that it costs $80,000 to bring up two children and send them through college, and the tab rises to $150,000 if you count the money the mother could have earned if she had worked at a job instead of staying home to rear them. Young couples don't need the details to realize that babies are an expensive luxury—more expensive than boats, electrical appliances, travel, a vacation home, and many other manufactured products that have become easier to acquire than they were in the 1950s.

The costs that are "pricing babies out of the market" are precisely those which cost more per capita as the population rises. Schooling, water, sewerage, local government, and other services take a sizable portion of the budgets of growing families. Medical care and college costs have risen even faster.

Babies "cost" more but they are also "worth" less, to their parents, and as we have seen, to our economic system. The new technology demands fewer workers, but those few must be well educated, highly trained workers. Some portion of the costs of supplying these highly trained workers devolves on their parents, and the extra expenses are deterrents to the production of people. Extra hands have long since ceased to be an economic asset to families, but in the 1970s, they cost much more than in the recent past.

For things as well as people, overhead rises with numbers.

• *Not So Rich So Fast*

During the 1960s, it certainly looked as if we were getting rich—even "too rich"—but closer examination raises questions as to how *really* rich we were getting. It looked good on the books, all right. Between 1960 and 1970, spending by families and individuals rose 50 percent, and little more than a third of the extra money was due to the increase in the number of consumers. According to Herman P. Miller, Chief of the Population Division of Bureau of the Census and author of *Rich Man, Poor Man*, nearly two thirds of the increase was due to the fact that each family was spending about 30 percent more money after allowing for higher prices.

It was a creditable performance. Cars on the road, personal consumption, and Gross National Product in constant dollars were not wide of the forecasts. Housing starts were the exception; they were just about the same in 1970 as in 1960. But beginning in 1965, the year of the Big Blackout which inaugurated our time of troubles, the growth of productivity began to lag sharply and corporate profits began to decline. At the same time, prices rose about twice as fast as the forecasters had predicted, knocking out the dollar estimates of 1970 business.

During the last half of the 1960s, most people ascribed the rising prices to the Vietnam War, which was being waged without the price controls of World War II, but some economists pointed to the disappointing productivity records as evidence that peace would not automatically bring back the effervescent economic growth of the 1950s. We were indeed entering the S-curve phase of declining economic growth, and by the end of the decade, economic philosophers, like Leonard Silk of The Brookings Institution and *Fortune* writers, were wondering out loud whether the fast growth rate of the 1950s could be maintained.

There are two aspects to the slowdown. One is inflation —the riches we have aren't worth as much. The other is recession, a slowdown in sales and employment. Both are beginning to afflict England, Germany, and Japan. The upsetting thing about this inflation-recession pattern is that it has begun to look like a permanent, worldwide condition.

Under these circumstances, it is hard to argue, as the environmentalists sometimes do, that we are "too rich." On the contrary. The trouble is that we aren't really rich enough to take care of the additional costs of raising the standard of living of a large number of people.

Malthus was right in saying that the population depended on the availability of the means of subsistence. As we have seen, even in India which is a poor country, population has risen only after an increase in *per capita* GNP sufficient to bear the costs of supporting larger numbers. One of the additional costs has been the cost of new agricultural methods that have made it possible to bring less productive land under cultivation.

As the poor grow richer, their needs change. Much of the persistent inflation which has troubled our economy in its affluence merely reflects the rising cost per unit of goods and services once available only to a few. "Cooling the economy" by raising interest rates deflated the stockmarket in 1969, but it did not improve phone service, make trains run, or slow the rise in consumer prices, and the wage-price freeze President Nixon ordered in the fall of 1971 succeeded no better.

• *How Rich Can We Get?*

Theoretically, of course, economic growth can't go on forever. The trouble is, we don't know how far it can go and when it will stop. The theoretical limit on wealth is worth considering because, as we have seen, it controls the size as well as the welfare of the population.

There are two kinds of liimitations. "Human wants may be insatiable, but the wherewithal to satisfy them is finite," points out Leonard Silk, author of a leading text on economic history. "The limit on goods is ultimately the amount of energy we can produce. The limit on services is human time."

It's not the time of the doctors, teachers, barbers, and other renderers of services, but the time of those who use them—the consumer.

The prospect of cheap atomic power means that we won't have to worry about the matter-energy base for quite a while. This means that the limit on how rich we can get is not going to be capacity to produce, but capacity to consume. Machines can offer wider and wider choice of consumption, and choice itself is an economic good. But in the end, a machine cannot consume. Only a human being can consume, and while you can (and more people do) consume dinner simultaneously with a symphony, there is a finite limit to the amount any one person can consume. A machine might teach you a foreign language, and save the time of the teacher, but it will still take you time to learn.

Another way to say this is that one of the limitations on wealth is time, because it takes time to spend money, and we are bumping up against the time limitation before energy will limit us. The ceiling on how rich you can get is the 24 hours a day you have in which to consume. Machines can work for you, but they cannot enjoy for you.

In the 1960s, economists were taking a new interest in the value consumers put on their "free" time. Gary S. Becker, an economist with the National Bureau of Economic Research, distinguished between "time intensive" expenditures, which take a lot of time per dollar, such as reading a book, and "earnings-intensive" commodities, which take a lot of dollars (presumably earned) per hour, such as night-clubbing. The concept of "foregone earnings" was being used by designers of public works. In deciding whether it is worth while to shorten the trip between two points, highway engineers figure the travel time of the person who will use it over its lifetime and attach a flat dollar value to each man hour saved. One rule put it at $2.82 an hour.

The richer you are, the more your time is worth to you. Swedish economist Staffan B. Linder points out that the rich have less leisure than the poor because they spend more of their income on services which take up their time. Americans are simply thrifty, not sloppy, when they throw away socks instead of spending the time to darn them, refuse to hunt for lost golf balls, or return deposit bottles, and risk buying shoddy goods over the phone rather than making a trip to the store. Rich consumers can afford poorer buying decisions than poor consumers, and they have so many more decisions to make that it doesn't really "pay" to shop around.

The rising value of consumption time is the real reason why the super-rich are giving up personal servants. They can afford to pay the cook $10,000 a year, but that rate of pay makes *her* time so valuable to *her* that she isn't willing to work the long irregular hours that make a resident cook worth maintaining. The potential employers may find it easier to eat out—or even cook simple meals themselves—than to schedule and supervise live-in service on a shift basis.

One way to increase consumption in the 24 hours a day available to each person, is to make better use of space. Like matter and energy, time and space are interchangeable. Families trade commuting time for housing space. Moviegoers trade time waiting in line for the scarce time-space of a seat at a premiere. The space-time of the restaurant table you occupy is narrowly calculated by restauranteurs. The bigger the table and the more leisurely the service, the more you pay for the meal. You pay a premium to be served in time to get to the theater, and enjoy a cut-rate supper special at midnight, when the crowd has thinned out.

You "save" time by moving activities into less crowded time-space. Executives read while being driven to work, and men who use electric shavers find that they can shave themselves in the morning while stalled in traffic. You can save time at airports by taking a suitcase that fits in the space under your seat, and you can "make" space in files by cleaning them out so that papers occupy their time-space for a shorter time. Even the grave is not always forever. In some Latin countries, the dead are evicted if no one pays their cemetery fees.

We are learning about space-time because it is getting scarcer. Of all the people who have ever walked the space of the United States since time began, almost half are walking around in it today. The trouble is that all of them want to be in the same place at the same time. We are used to shortages of matter-energy, but the limit on human time is not creating shortages. It is creating bottlenecks. More people, living more abundantly, have overloaded facilities designed for fewer people, living frugally.

The new pinch is translated into money. Things which use up resources of matter-energy—manufactured products —are generally cheaper than services which must be squeezed into a time-space bottleneck. It is that bottleneck which makes inflation a persistent economic problem in a time of affluence.

• *The Deceptive GNP*

One of the reasons it took so long to recognize the extent of the economic slowdown was because we have been measuring wealth almost entirely by the size of the Gross National Product.

This method of counting any country's national income was invented by Dr. Simon Kuznets in the 1930s. He received the Nobel Prize in Economics in 1971, just as other economists were beginning to question the value of his yardstick.

Gross National Product measures the dollar value of a nation's output. It is the sum total of all the money paid for all the goods and services that change hands in the country during the course of a year. Its value as a measure is based on the assumption that the more dollars being passed around, the better. This is not necessarily so. Neighbors who take in each other's washing, and pay each other for it, add to the GNP without creating any real new wealth. And it is obvious that the difference in the GNPs of the United States and India is much greater than the difference in wealth because Americans buy for money many services that Indian families perform without pay for themselves or each other. By the same token, the difference in dollars spent on education between the United States and the Netherlands is inflated because the Dutch don't feed and transport school children at public expense.

The GNP is an unsatisfactory yardstick because it leaves out three important classes of wealth:

1. GNP does not measure the quality of goods and services, merely what you paid for them. Like a cost-plus contract, it actually fattens on inefficiency. Delays, wastes, unnecessary repairs, redundant or short-lived products increase, or perhaps we should say, inflate the Gross National Product.

Professor A. J. Jaffe, manpower and population specialist at Columbia's Bureau of Applied Social Research uses traffic congestion to illustrate this point. "You sit in a taxi trying to get to Kennedy Airport, and the GNP goes up every time you can't move." A shuttle train that got there faster and cheaper would cut the GNP. Some economists point out that if we counted the laundry bill caused by factory and power plant smoke in the cost of production, we might find it cheaper to catch the dirt in the stack than wash it out of and off everything on which it settles. We'd all be better off, even if we had to pay extra taxes or utility bills to pay for the new stack equipment, but the GNP would be lower.

2. GNP leaves out all the good things that money cannot buy. It does not register the value of a beautiful view,

the sweetness of the air, access to fishing or boating on clean water, freedom from lung cancer caused by smog, peace of mind, privacy, quiet, and a lot of other "qualities of life" for which more and more Americans seem willing to give up dollar income.

3. GNP is amoral. A war increases defense spending and, with it, the GNP, but it would be hard to find anyone in this country who seriously believes we are better off for it.

Thus, economists readily acknowledge that the GNP isn't telling us all we should know. It is a measure of our gross production of goods and services, but makes no provision for the wearing out or obsolescence of the nation's economic capital—such as its buildings, machinery and natural resources.

Gross National Product is a relatively new concept. It became a tool of national economic policy during World War II, when 30 to 40 percent of the GNP went for defense, and the key problem was sheer output. In 1971, only 7 percent went for defense.

Changes in the economy since World War II have badly distorted how well the GNP reflects economic performance. A bigger piece of the national pie is now spent on services—wholesale and retail trade, finance, insurance, real estate, government and military, as well as professional and personal services—and these are so inefficient that we've had to spend extra money on them. At the same time, we've saved money on food production and manufacturing, which take a smaller bite out of the GNP because they have dramatically improved their productivity. There's no way of adding up how much smaller the GNP would be if services were efficient.

Dr. Arnold Sametz, Professor of Economics at New York University has undertaken to correct some of the failings of the GNP in order to find out how much better off we really are in the United States than we used to be. He tried to take into account changes in the quality and type of goods; leisure; the value of services, such as babysitting, which formerly were done for nothing and so did not get counted; the "ill fare" of congestion and pollution; the burden of traveling to and from work instead of walking to it, as was formerly the general practice; the rising cost of wars. He estimates that we are about twice as well off materially as our grandparents were in 1914, and *they* were about twice as well off as *their* grandparents in 1865. He thinks that real output per capita has risen about 50 percent since 1947, although its aggregate value is, of course, much bigger because we have so many more people.

All things considered, we're getting richer, all right, but not fast enough to support the full cost of production of the material things which are damaging the environment. In wealth, as in population, we seem to be at the stage where gains cost more and come slower.

• Not So Wise As We Sound

Information flow is subject to inflation, too. Although we have just absorbed important advances in communications, there is evidence that these new systems have their S-curve phase of diminishing gains, and that we may be getting to it soon.

Derek de Solla Price, the historian of science, has calculated that the cost of making a contribution to science increases with the number of scientists and their output. The reason is patent. In an Easter egg hunt, the first eggs are easier to find than the last.

This applies not only to the creation of new knowledge, but also to its storage and transmission. It's cheaper to file papers in a small filing system than in a big one with many breakdowns. Phone wires, mail services, the distribution of print, schools and other means of transmitting information are networks, subject to costs that rise with volume. New communication techniques, such as the automatic dial phone, are usually installed to accommodate larger volume, and even when operating costs are not higher, the initial investment required can be staggering.

The increasing cost per item of rising information is not confined to network systems such as the telephone. It turns up in printed matter like newspapers. Most people assume that producing more copies will reduce the cost per copy. But even for newspapers, there comes a time when an additional item of news is going to cost more to distribute.

Professor Reid A. Bryson of the University of Wisconsin figures that if newspaper readership doubles, advertisers will probably also double, so that newspapers will take up four times as much paper and require four times the waste-disposal effort of today. As the price of newspapers rise, the paper will be recycled, making possible even more newsprint. Eventually, of course, the transport of such huge quantities of paper will become too expensive, so news will be distributed electronically, under systems which will permit consumers to select what items they wish to keep in paper or physical form. Electronic distribution will make still greater arrays of news possible, at heavier investment. The new systems will "cost" consumers even more heavily in the energy required to choose among the many alternatives, so they will be sated, as with food, and find each additional piece of news less interesting than the one before. However efficient the transmission and display of news becomes, there is, after all, a limit to the news each person is willing to consume.

Even when the price of transmitting information drops,

the price of responding to it—or the value of not having to respond to it which we call privacy—increases.

Duplicate solicitations clog mailboxes. It may be cheaper to send both out than to edit the list, but the result may be that the recipient looks at neither of them. Just as a rising number of food products compete more fiercely for the limited space on grocery shelves and in human stomachs, so a rising number of advertising messages have to spend more to get a share of the limited broadcast time.

• *Saved by the Slowdown*

Slower growth of population, wealth, and information flow is giving us a breather. The worst crowding is over for primary schools. The overload of pupils who created a teacher shortage during the 1960s are now teachers themselves, and finding it hard to get jobs. The baby "boom" is over.

Nixon's economic game plan for fighting inflation has been giving us a taste of slower economic growth and some of it is welcome. No one has built a house in the orchard behind our house, so we have the view to ourselves. Neighbors stay put as big companies slow the feverish transfer of middle managers which goes with expansion. On my first trip in a 747 jet, a deadheading pilot and I had an entire section of the big plane to ourselves all the way from New York to Los Angeles. Colleges have empty places, and private schools can't afford to be as exclusive as formerly. And while traffic, phone, and electric service have not improved, slower growth has saved them from total breakdown.

Information systems have been saved by cuts in Federal spending on research and education. Libraries are restoring order, if not the full amenities of the pre-Sputnik days. An excess of Ph.Ds has slowed the hectic expansion of graduate schools and reduced the frantic production of scholarly papers below the insane level they would have attained under the forced draft of continued high research budgets. Meanwhile, on the popular front, advertising and promotion budgets have been trimmed, thinning publications that their money supports. The headlong rush to computerize paperwork systems has slowed, giving everyone a little more shakedown time.

Slower growth can relieve the tensions attributable to growth. It can ease the cost and disruption of a big crop of young, the turbulence of expanding sales and stockmarket speculation, the rising expectations generated by the swift expansion of television sets in the 1950s.

But slower growth can't bring back the past. Like it or not, we are going to have to live with more people, things, dollars, and words than our institutions are prepared to handle. Up till now, we have been doing it by a series of magnificent makeshifts.

Chapter XI

Makeshifts: Shrink, Share, Queue, Move . . . and Cut

Considering the overloads, there have been surprisingly few real breakdowns in the United States. People will do anything to shore up the familiar way of doing things. So when breakdowns threaten, people improvise solutions. Making shift is the uniquely human thing about human beings.

The breakdowns facing us now are of a new kind. They are caused not by scarcities of matter-energy, but by bottlenecks of space-time. The arts of thrift are known and prized, but they do not help us as much as they did during the Great Depression for instance. Thanks to our training in them, however, we're better at making a car with the least expenditure of materials and labor than we are at getting as many cars as possible over a bridge into Manhattan. Making a car requires the management of matter-energy. Getting cars over a bridge requires the management of space-time.

The striking common feature of all the breakdowns causing alarm is that they are caused by traffic overloading the physical capacity of wires, roads, pipes, or the human capacity of skilled people like doctors, teachers, policemen, and clerks to process large numbers of people, things, or data.

The problem is new, but we have developed magnificent makeshifts. There are not many different ways to get things through a bottleneck, and we exploit them for all they are worth.

You can *shrink* the thing or activity you want to get into the bottleneck. Put several of these units together so that they *share* the limited time-space. Line things up or *queue* them so that there's less waste of space or time. *Move* things out of the space or speed them through it to make room for more. Eventually you have to *cut* something out in order to make room for something more important.

Shrink, share, queue, move, or *cut* can get more of almost anything through almost any kind of bottleneck. Take a frivolous example. At least on weekends, a golf course is a space-time bottleneck. The problem: how to get more games of golf through it on Sunday. Consider the possibilities:

The games—the things to be put through—can be shortened. Traps can be eliminated. The hole can be doubled in size for easier putting. The course can even be shortened. That's *shrink.*

The course—that's the bottleneck—can be shared by more games at once by designing split tees and putting several holes on each fairway so that several foursomes can play the same set of holes at one time. That's *share.*

Foursomes can be lined up in order to save time, and fast players can be sorted out and allowed to start first. That's *queue.*

Players can be required to play faster. Slow players can be fined, penalized, or suspended. Some clubs insist that players cut down on practice swings, select clubs before a shared caddy walks to the other ball, leave the green before marking the scorecard, line up putts while others are putting. That's *move*.

Games played by children and beginners can be eliminated from the course or allowed to play only on slow days. That's *cut*.

Or take, for another example, the time-space bottleneck of public housing units. More tenants are accommodated by design that shrinks the size of the units, and by regulations that require units to be shared by families rather than single persons. Applicants are lined up in waiting lists to speed assignment of vacancies, tenants are moved out when their incomes rise, and people are cut out who fail to qualify in some way.

Parking is another bottleneck of space. It is critical because it limits the size of institutions and whole cities. We work hard to stretch parking. We consider *shrinking* the size of cars; *sharing* the space by many-storied buildings that stack parked cars above ground and below; *queuing* them in space by markers that line them up at the same angle, and in time by arrangements such as those churches sometimes make with supermarkets to use their parking lots on Sundays. Time limits which *move* parked cars to make way for others are enforced by penalties or fees. Many, of course, must be *cut out*. "No parking" is the most ubiquitous street sign in any city.

There are bottlenecks of the mind and there are bottlenecks of people-processing. Touring Europe is a people-processing operation. How can the given number of planes, hotels, guides, and sights be best deployed to accommodate more trips? You can shrink the trips by leaving out sights or making the total time shorter. Trips may be shared on group tours to load facilities more fully. Special rates and

189

other inducements can be arranged to queue trips more evenly through the year. Trips may be speeded up to cover the same schedule of sights faster. Tourists who are demanding or troublesome can be excluded and in any event, some must be cut out.

We are so good at breaking time-space bottlenecks that we are aware of them only when we fail. The record is impressive. Let's take a good look at each of the makeshifts, and then at some of the bottlenecks they have been busting.

• *Shrink*

Birth certificates, car registrations, credit cards, license plates, and even diplomas are shrinking in merciful recognition of the increasing number of such records people have to keep and carry around. Even garbage is being compacted and old autos crumpled to get more into dumps.

Not so many years ago, the demand was for big cars, big houses, big television screens, big parties, and big families. Now we are seeing how small we can make them.

Little, for-me-only-things appeal. They have been made possible by versatile transistors and spin-offs from research in space hardware. Radios, television sets, batteries, tape machines and even computers are made small enough to carry around or fit in places which couldn't accommodate the standard size. Space-thrifty housewives pass up the giant economy size for boxes of soap and cereal that fit on the shelf, the bulky cans of soup for the more storable dehydrated kind. We have compact models of pianos, typewriters, washing machines, dishwashers, and refrigerators. There is even a compact éclair for dieters.

Mothers are thankful for smaller toys. Toy trains now come in "N" for narrow gauge, with cabooses that could hide behind a postage stamp. Turkeys and watermelons have been miniaturized to fit into refrigerators; tomatoes, corn and cabbages to fit into suburban garden plots; parks to fit "vest pocket"-sized empty lots in cities. There are even "minipigs" (miniature swine) for laboratories without enough space for full-sized experimental animals.

Pets are getting smaller. Cats are gaining popularity on dogs because they take less houseroom, and the biologists have created jewel-sized, hibernating snails that can be sent as gifts through the mail. Miniature people could also have advantages. The Eskimos are reluctant to feed their children the nutritious diet advised by the Canadian government for fear they'll get too big and clumsy and need too much food in hard times.

Three out of every four Japanese corpses are cremated, and ultimately all the dead will have to be shrunk to keep the world from becoming a vast cemetery.

• *Share*

Cabs, beds, hotel rooms, college classes, jumbo jet planes, and even graves usually have room for more people than are in them. You can cook for two in the same pot you have to dirty cooking only for one. Two can often share the working time and office space of a single secretary.

Smart shoppers use their heads to save their heels and make lists, so that one trip shares many errands. Smart organizations make one record do two jobs. In 1969, the Army and the Air Force gave up serial numbers and began keeping all their records by Social Security number instead.

The things that go in the waste space around other things are surprisingly many. When you move you can put hangers in the wastebaskets and your socks in your shoes. Inner-city boys share the street with cars so expertly that they can play stickball without stopping traffic.

One of the design wonders of the world is the coexistence of recreational activities in New York City's Central Park. A little woods serves birdwatchers and treewatchers. Paths for walking, bicycling, and horseback riding wind over, under, and around each other. There's a lake for rowing, another for sailing toy boats, a pool for swimming, a rink for skating. You can grow a garden in Central Park, hear a concert, see a play, eat. You can play tennis, football, baseball, and other games. You can slide, swing, sit, climb, watch wild animals in the zoo or handle tame ones in the children's farm—all this and much, much more in a shared space less than two square miles in size.

The dead must share. In much of the world, they are buried in common graves, or several deep. The Japanese now stack the ashes of their ancestors in locker tombs in elevator-equipped buildings which can be visited for worship. In New York City, the cemetery of St. Mark's In The Bowery has been officially converted into a playground for neighborhood ghetto children.

• *Queue*

Queuing gets more things through a space-time bottleneck by lining them up in space or time. Schedules and appointment calendars line things and people up in time: queues, lists, or priority systems line them up in space. Like things can be lined up or queued to get more of them into a limited space. Canners do it when they line the anchovies up head by tail to get more into the can at a time (the anchovies *share* the time-space of the can when they are curled around something else, like a caper). You queue in space when you put all the tall books on one tall shelf so that you can get more shelves and hence more books on the wall at the same time.

Staggering is a form of queuing which lines things up in time to get them through a limited space. Billing is staggered through the month to get more bills through the time-space of the billing department. New York City welfare checks can no longer all be sent out on the same day. French resorts are overloaded and Parisian services understaffed because Frenchmen who get a vacation insist on taking the whole month of August off at once. Staggering will be eventually necessary to avert breakdown of the French economy.

People and things can be lined up by the speed at which they move so that fast movers are not slowed to the pace of slow movers ahead of them. High-speed lanes for cars, toll lines reserved for those with exact change, and express check-out counters in supermarkets line up or queue the fast movers.

People react strongly, and variously to being queued. Russians line themselves up without being told. Moscow theater audiences file out, last row first, like school children marching out of assemblies. In America, on the contrary, theatrical performances break up like the Arctic ice in springtime. Commuters and the constitutionally impatient gather themselves for a dash up the aisle, while the rest of the audience is still applauding. Fidgeters and people who can't bear having anyone ahead of them sidle across rows to emergency exits, while placid souls who seem to enjoy the presence of others drift happily up the aisle with the crowd. In Moscow, the theater is emptied faster. In New York, you can get out fast if you're willing to work at it.

Even on a first-come, first-served basis, Americans don't like queues. Rather than put some people in front of other people, we prefer to row them up horizontally on the starting line and let the best man win, the way they did when they shot off a gun to open the Oklahoma land rush. West Indians like queuing even less. There were so many bus-boarding accidents in Bridgetown that the British-bred Barbados Assembly passed a law requiring passengers to form a line of not more than two abreast whenever six or more persons were waiting for a bus.

Whether they like it or not, Americans are spending more time in queues. We now expect to queue for library books, cabs, movies, ski lifts, tees, subway tokens, and even campsites in the wilds of our national parks. Doctors, dentists, barbers, and employment interviewers line us up. So do headwaiters, sales clerks, cashiers, bank tellers, income tax adjusters, and the few remaining meat cutters. Lawn services line our lawns up for mowing. Plumbers line our emergencies up for fixing.

The queue is standing operating procedure for any transaction which may not be free at the time it is demanded. Freight cars queue for unloading, telephone calls for circuits, and stacked airplanes for permission to land. In order to get through a big organization, decisions may have to wait in one line after another, as they are bucked from desk to desk. Traffic control problems frequently involve similar queues of queues.

"Queuing theory" describes how queues grow and shrink. It has become a hot branch of mathematics practiced by operations researchers studying complicated traffic and transportation systems.

● *Move*

"Faster, faster!" gets more soldiers over the bridge and more people, things, or messages through any time-space bottleneck. Seconds saved per unit add up to big differences in the traffic that planes, phone wires, and computers can carry. At congested airports, airlines have a substantial stake in saving seconds on the time it takes to land a plane. Tele-type-like devices that move words faster are worth a big investment to news and business organizations.

Everyone knows how much it costs to stop moving. "Ground time" and "down time" severely limit the traffic a plane can carry or the units a factory can produce. Railings which wind a line of people back and forth actually save time as well as temper by keeping the stream moving at amusement parks, commuter train gates, and construction camps where workers are paid off in cash.

Planned obsolescence moves products and feeds on itself. The more new things you buy, the more new things you want. The more new popular tunes, the faster they are displaced. The more new clothes you buy, the sooner you throw them out. Women with limited closet space will move out an old pair of shoes to make room for a new one.

Services have to cut. Banks are too busy to give you your balance over the phone. Grocers can't bother to tell you whether the melons are ripe, and supermarkets don't have phones because their clerks are too busy to answer them. Phone some firms and you're told to write a letter, or they hang up, or the phone isn't answered at all. Motor Vehicle Bureaus urge the public to renew their licenses by mail rather than to come in person. Papers take less time-space than live bodies.

• Bottlenecks of Space

The nation's number one time-space bottleneck for traffic is midtown Manhattan in New York City, and all sorts of things are being tried to relieve it.

Commuters shrink the space they take by riding bicycles down Fifth Avenue instead of taking taxis, and light deliveries are made in minicars no bigger than glorified motorcycles. At rush hours, subways shrink people to the viable limit.

Commuters are queued for faster transit through bridges, tunnels, toll booths, and subway stations by barricades for motorists and pedestrians, and express highways, trains and buses queue the fast driver ahead of the slow.

Staggering working hours is frequently suggested to queue commuters in time. An "alternate people plan" would divide the population into "Monday-Wednesday-Friday" people who would stay home on alternate days to make room for the "Tuesday-Thursday-Saturday" people, with penalties for people who ventured out when it wasn't their day. On August 17, 1970, the Friends of Central Park sponsored a sightseeing tour of Manhattan which combined both shrink and stagger: 350 tourists on bicycles rode five miles down Fifth Avenue to the Battery at 2:30 A.M., when they had the heart of the city to themselves.

Ingenious devices "keep traffic moving." These include one-way streets, staggered stop lights, minimum speed limits, and limited access highways. In addition to rules against *parking* which protect the space available for cars to move, there are also rules against *stopping* to pick up pedestrians or drop off deliveries. Rules requiring exact change on buses were initiated to deter robberies, but they have had an added dividend. They keep buses moving by reducing loading time, as do buses designed with extra doors. One of the most persuasive arguments in favor of making mass transportation free is that it would do away with the delay at the fare box that slows traffic.

One "keep moving" rule forbids motorists on highways to get out of their cars. Service areas on many parkways around the city have signs at their access roads that warn "No charter buses 6 A.M. Saturday to midnight Sunday."

It's fast coming to cut. Trucks have long been banned from Fifth Avenue, and there are favorable reports on a trial ban of cars from Central Park over weekends and from Madison Avenue on Saturdays. Several narrow streets in the downtown financial district have been permanently reserved for pedestrians. And there's talk of eliminating private cars completely from the midtown section.

Another bottleneck is housing. We're getting more housing units on available land by shrinking their average size. A rising proportion of the new residential units built in the past few years have been trailers or high-rise apartments. Fewer have been single-family houses on their own lots.

Architects are finding new ways to make activities share the land. They are "making" more space by building up and down. Harvard's new library will be underneath the Harvard yard—all four stories of it. In New York, architects are using the air rights over highways and existing city property as sites for apartments and schools. Buildings straddle streets. New high-rise buildings combine office and apartments. Time, Inc.'s Chicago office has double-decker elevators so that people can get off on odd-numbered floors at the same time as people on even-numbered floors.

Housing units are bottlenecks for all the things and activities people want to put inside them. One way, of course, is to shrink the things, but the peanut principle of appetite prevents compact furniture and appliances from "making" as much space as advertised. What happens is that you buy more things and compound the closet clutter.

One answer is multiple-purpose furniture which shares the space it takes between two uses. Coffee tables that rise and unfurl for dining, and hassocks that hold records, have joined sofas that turn into beds and clothing chests that support lamps.

Things and activities are queued in space. They are designed so that you can move them out when you want the space for something else. Sleeping bags that fold up by day Japanese style, "stretch" space for guests; and they are popular with visiting (and sometimes resident) children. Avant-garde chairs and sofas inflate like balloons and pack away in drawers when they aren't needed. Chairs, tables, desks, toys and counters for work and play fold and stack themselves out of the way. Jogging machines are designed to slide under the bed to save embarrassing questions from visitors as well as space. Kitchen appliances that fold into walls or disappear into counter tops are offered at prices that reflect the high value cooks put on kitchen counter space.

Rental services queue the use of occasionally needed things in time. Householders let someone else store soup tureens, evening wraps, garden tractors, ladders, waxing machines, camping equipment, skis, garden furniture, and power tools, as well as the U-hauls to lug them around. But here, again, the solution compounds rather than solves the problem. Rentals make possible more of these bulky things than would exist if people had to maintain them between uses.

• *Bottlenecks of the Mind*

We mobilize all makeshifts to put more information through our time-space resources for handling it. Busy people get more into the day by shrinking the information in each letter, phone call, and meeting. They store and transmit as much information as possible in abstracts, digests, summaries, acronyms, abbreviations, and codes. Libraries shrink print with microfilm and microfiche, and more sophisticated miniaturization is in the offing, of which the ultimate is probably the Dove Data Device which puts 20,000 volumes on an 8 by 10 inch piece of nickel or aluminum foil. The Bell Laboratories have long been fascinated by the possibilities for condensation in the fact that you can understand words faster than you can speak them. Tapes that speed up speech sound funny, but they are intelligible and they conserve time, tape, and storage space.

Busy people divide their attention among several activities at the same time and that's not new. A young Dane who visited the seventeenth-century painter Peter Paul Rubens found him painting while dictating a letter and having Tacitus read aloud to him. His awed visitors reported that when they kept silent so as not to disturb him, "he himself began to talk to us while still continuing to work, to listen to the reading and to dictate his letter." Modern masters often share their attention among several visitors and receive at least two streams of information from split-screen movies and multi-media presentations that beam different messages to the eye than to the ear.

The young are developing superior powers for sharing their attention. Many youngsters watch one game on television while listening to another over the radio through transistor headphones. Brokers can watch the ticker while talking over the telephone, most adults can confer while eating lunch, and mothers learn to mend while keeping watch on a playground bully. Coaxial cables and microwave technology enables the telephone company to transmit scores of separate conversations over the same wire.

Queuing gets more activities and more information, as well as more soldiers through a bottleneck. Most people save time paying bills by letting them pile up in a queue and writing checks at one time. Libraries save access time by shelving together books on the same subject, or likely to appeal to the same kind of users, and by locating the most popular books nearest the door.

● *Cut*

As time goes on, bottlenecks will have to be busted by the simple process of cutting something out. The percentage of books unread, plays unseen, friends unvisited, letters unanswered, recipes untried, breakfast cereals unsampled, and ultimately babies unborn is bound to rise faster than the number of books, plays, friends, letters, recipes, breakfast foods, and nubile women respectively.

People are cutting out already. People who live in noise learn to screen it out. The Japanese are better at it than we are. They train themselves not to hear what's going on across their paper walls and are able to shut off intrusion seemingly at will. I once saw an entire Japanese family of four squatting in an intersection in the basement of the Daimaru department store in Tokyo, a scene more crowded than Macy's at Christmas. They were eating ice-cream cones, oblivious to the people literally stepping around them.

Paperwork is being cut. No one has room for archives any more. Offices send more and more of their records to the warehouse.

Red tape can be cut. Departments of the Federal Government have done it by the ruthless process of forbidding bureaucrats to buy new filing cases. Procedures can be cut. A few years ago Federated Purchaser, Inc., an electronics supplier in New Jersey, cut out most of its billing procedures. Customers simply sent signed blank checks with their order and the amounts were filled in when the order was delivered. The Metropolitan Opera requires blank signed checks from patrons who write in for tickets.

Telephone answering services line up incoming calls according to the number being called, so that they can be answered one after another. Heavily called parties, such as airlines and service organizations have installed devices that queue simultaneous calls automatically, informing the caller with a recording, "Your call has been placed in an automatic priority device and will be given to a salesman when one is available."

Busy people move faster. They shift gears from one activity to another faster. They shrink their letters by writing them shorter, but they also spend less time on each thought. If you don't believe it, consider the evidence that fast readers usually retain more than slow readers. Just before Earth Day, 1970, Stanford University environmentalist Paul Ehrlich was scheduling five-minute appointments. Libraries move books from one user to another faster by keeping them on reserve or letting them out for one week instead of two weeks at a time. The touch-tone system makes time for many more phone calls by connecting each call a few seconds faster than they can be connected by dialing.

Cutting out is the last resort. Efficient people are people who know which tasks to stint, which books to leave unread, which sleeping dogs to let lie. Bulging libraries make room for important new books by throwing out duplications, froth, and monographs on the mating habits of Antarctic penguins. They could, without loss, cut more. Too much chatter is frozen into print. Too little of the "literature" of scholarship is really worth keeping.

Presidents of major corporations bombarded with heavy mail use a lot of strategies to shrink it. They have it digested and abstracted for them; generally they combine reading mail with doing something else, such as traveling, waiting for visitors, phoning; their secretaries sort the mail into classes of like subjects, and line it up for easier physical handling. Most presidents learn to move the mail fast by absorbing the import of each letter at a glance and cutting the number to be answered by turning most of them over to somebody else for reply. Although methods and mail loads vary, few presidents actually cope with more than twelve pieces of mail in a working day.

People can make more different kinds of shifts than machines, but computers more than make up for what they cannot do. Computer memories *shrink* vast quantities of information. Tasks are *queued* to share computer time. Computers can *move* information with lightning speed, but they can't *share* two activities at the same time and above all they cannot *cut* anything presented to them cut.

• *People-Processing Bottlenecks*

The most uncomfortable time-space bottlenecks are those that limit things that have to be done to, for, or by people. The arithmetic of encounter says that the more people you know, the more people you meet; the more clients a lawyer or hairdresser already has, the more they will attract. The corollary says that the more clients the lawyer or hairdresser has to serve, the less time and attention they can devote to each. Big people-processors learn to treat their clients as non persons, or objects, and they move them along the way a practiced hostess moves her guests along a receiving line at an official occasion.

Health care is people-processing, and all the makeshifts are used to cram as many person-units of medical care into the available space-time of facilities for serving them. Hospitals do everything but shrink the size of their beds. In disasters, when patient load is high, emergency room service is limited to first aid. Almost all "private" hospital rooms now are shared. Patients are queued in time for visiting teams which wash, feed, treat, and medicate them as if they were chassis on an automobile assembly line. Hospitals get more patient-units into their facilities by moving patients out as fast as they can. New mothers go home three days after the baby is born instead of staying for a week. Inevitably, of course, it comes to cut. The chronically ill, those suffering from contagious diseases, and many other classes of sickness are arbitrarily excluded.

Education is a people-process that has had long experience in makeshifts. The law requires public schools to accept all children, whether facilities exist for them or not. When there's an overload, the course of instruction is quietly shrunk: English is taught, but pupils may not be required to write themes because there aren't enough teachers to correct them. Biology may be taught, but if there aren't enough microscopes to go around, laboratory work is abbreviated. Medical schools propose streamlining the curriculum to get more doctors faster.

More students mean bigger classes. More must share existing facilities. One teacher may have to watch two study halls.

More learning units can be queued through facilities by using teachers and classrooms night and day all year round. Some New York City schools have been so hard up for cafeteria facilities that they have had to start serving lunch at nine A.M. to get all the children fed before the end of the school day.

Learning units can be moved faster through existing instructional facilities. Courses can be speeded up so that students cover the same ground faster. Teachers may take on additional subjects, and so may space. The architect Jeh Johnson designed a multi-purpose room for the Poughkeepsie Day School his children attended. It stores dining tables, gym equipment, and theatrical props under the raised stage so that the room can serve as gym, dining room, assembly hall, and theater all in one day.

Budget-minded school boards "cut the frills." Even in public schools, supposedly open to all, qualifications for special courses such as vocational subjects may be quietly raised to cut some students out.

When large numbers of people have to be processed, the constraints of time-space have converted the pleasurable everyday activities of eating, dressing, talking, playing, and sleeping into engineering operations called feeding, clothing, seating, housing.

Consider the logistics of feeding. More people are fed per unit of feeding time-space by shrinking the menu. Most of the 10,000 restaurants in Tokyo offer little more than a single dish. Many American restaurants now serve only pancakes, sausages, hamburgers, or fried chicken, and airlines shrink the standard meal for the day to fit on a single, one-piece stackable unit.

Large numbers of people can be fed by requiring them to share eating space with each other at counters or cafeteria tables, or with other uses. Eating spills over to desks, cars, airline seats, living rooms, and beds. Cafeterias and buffet tables queue diners, and institutions stagger them by feeding in shifts. Restaurants speed service and hurry diners to move more through their time-space. Unfortunately for the national girth, most people manage to eat somewhere or somehow. Those cut out of one facility squeeze into another.

These are some of the ways we are making shift to cope with the time-space bottlenecks of affluence and numbers. We do a good job of it.

We shrink, share, queue, move, and cut to accommodate more passengers, lawsuits, diners, golfers, corpses, prisoners, furniture, residents, mail pieces, patients, messages, decisions, phone calls, records, students, sales, and commuters through existing facilities.

• *"Cut" Discriminates*

Eventually, of course, the improvisations fail. More and more frequently it comes to cut.

Cutting out is always discriminatory.

When a restaurant is crowded, the hat-check girl won't take the coats of women—a discrimination that should be getting attention now that women are speaking up for equal treatment. The academic establishment has long protected its privileges by adjusting the admission of students to the capacity of the institutions and the volume of scholarly publications to the capacity of the journals that the academic establishment manages. They have done it so automatically that they have not themselves been aware of the distinctions they have made until they have been protested.

The police do it, too. When the jails are full, they wink at crime in order to preserve the illusion of public order. Hospitals do it. How sick you have to be to get into a hospital depends on how many beds they have empty at the time.

Cutting out information, or even shutting up, is the strategy of choice for preserving the status quo. Business leaders frequently protect their status by deliberately cutting sales which would require a threatening expansion. The American automobile industry did it. Until European competition forced their hand, American car makers limited production to high-margin big cars, ignoring the substantial demand for smaller cars that would have exposed them to risk for lesser return.

And as we have seen, the Wall Street establishment deliberately restricted advertising and trading hours to keep business down to the volume members of the exchanges could handle with existing facilities. In overloaded New York City, Con Edison has cut out its advertising department and the New York Telephone Company has cut down promotion and the introduction of new services. At one point the chairman of the New York State Public Service Commission begged the public to help by cutting down on phone calls.

Cutting out talk saves marriages and friendships. Husbands retreat behind newspapers after dinner to avoid embarrassing questions, just as Presidents leave Washington on weekends when peace activists converge demanding dialogue. The tactic works. Wives stop trying to get through. Demonstrators become discouraged and give up.

Cut has been the remedy of choice ever since the ancient Greeks told each other about Procrustes, the legendary robber who made all comers conform to the size of his bed by lopping off their limbs. It works, but it exacts a fearsome price.

Shrink, share, queue, move, and cut. The makeshifts save the system, but they also allow it to grow badly out of scale. The better they work in staving off disaster, the more trouble they pile up for the future.

• *Makeshift Creates Monstrosity*

An instructive way to see where saving the system can lead is to look at systems that have been preserved at all costs. Two contemporary social systems illustrate what happens when religious and cultural barriers prevent the increase of information, and thus make it impossible for the societies to change as they grow. One system has created Calcutta, the other the Hutterite colonies of North America.

The spectacle of Calcutta shows what can happen when

city-dwellers do not go through the process of urbanization that so many Americans think is at the root of many contemporary breakdowns. It is worth a brief look.

Calcutta is a great big, overgrown Indian village. It is actually less densely populated, on the record, than New York. It has seven million people in 400 square miles, compared with New York's eight million people in 365 square miles. Its special horror is that all these people are spread out, thickly, in low buildings without sanitation. Sixty percent of the population are single men who often sleep in the street in order to send money back to their families in the country, where the birth rate is much higher.

The trouble is the *failure* of the newcomers who come from the country to adapt to urban ways. Because they are restricted by the caste system, and because there have never been enough jobs to go around, the newcomers try to live the way they have always lived in their home villages. Stench, suffering, and early death are the price newcomers to Calcutta pay for clinging to traditional, personal, and community values that newcomers to American cities eagerly shed in an effort to "better" themselves.

To western eyes, Calcutta is as monstrous as an idiot child grown big without growing up.

The Hutterites are monstrous in a different way. They have found it necessary to restrict rigidly the size of their communities to preserve the primitive communism of their faith. Their success in retaining some of the old-fashioned virtues of rural life makes them an interesting anachronism.

The Hutterites are a German religious sect, like the Amish and the Mennonites. They now live in isolated colonies in the North Central part of the United States and in Canada, where they have attained what demographers believe to be the highest rate of population growth on record. They have done it by adopting modern technology while rejecting the acquisitive, materialistic values that usually go with it. Modern medicine and modern farming techniques make it possible for them to rear, in their simple way of life, almost as many children as is biologically possible, and they are encouraged to do so by the strict, Puritan organization of their communities.

In a Hutterite community, everything is public property, including family quarters, which can be entered without knocking. Husbands and wives eat together alone only on their wedding day. Normally, everyone eats in mess halls. All modern diversions are banned. Children are educated by special teachers and are not sent away to college. Perhaps because of their geographical isolation, the Hutterites have been remarkably successful in holding their young people. Since 1918, only two percent have left the colonies.

The big problem facing the Hutterites is their birth rate. Between 1950 and 1965, they doubled their numbers. Although there are probably fewer than 50,000 of them, and they are spread out in some of the most sparsely settled farming areas of the United States, they suffer from overpopulation within their own communities. They have discovered that their communistic system, which depends on voluntary and personal cooperation, works only when the community is limited to 100 persons, with about 15 working-age males. When the population builds up, the hog man and the carpenter have to take on assistants. "Brotherly cooperation" has to be supplemented by rules and direct orders. Cliques form.

Instead of grudgingly accepting the evils of bureaucracy and industrialization, the Hutterites take stern measures to preserve the good old ways at all costs. In order to avoid specializing tasks or establishing new services, the elders may retire the hog man and the carpenter at 45 to make way for younger men. When the community nears 150 people, the elders begin to look for new land on which to found a new colony.

Like our European forbears, the Hutterites have solved the crisis of abundance by migration. Their solution re-creates the national experience of the United States under controlled conditions that fascinate social scientists. The Hutterites would rather move than change, and their experience is a reminder that this country was settled by people who moved away from the problems of population growth to a place where they would not have to endure the discomfort of thinking big.

Chapter XII

How To Think Big

The bigger systems that large numbers require are, by definition, systems that make it possible to handle more information. When we asked how big the population of the world could get, we found that the numbers would depend on wealth. We also found that the fastest way to increase wealth is to increase the flow of information, and that the limit on wealth is the amount of information that can be processed by the sum total of the world's human heads.

Information flow is the key and the limit, and ultimately we have to come to grips with the capacity of the human nervous system, and what we can do to make better use of it as a communications channel.

A sober look at human capacity offers considerable grounds for hope. The easiest way to get more information and knowledge flowing around the planet is to put more through the heads of the large majority of people who are handling considerably less than the average American high school senior.

210

But there are even more exciting vistas. Not even the geniuses are thinking as well as they could. The striking thing about the human brain is not that its capacity is limited, as everyone complains, but that its capacity expands and contracts with use, like a muscle. And new knowledge about the human mind raises new hope for increasing its capacity.

• *Information Theory*

It all began with the computer, which ironically enough, was developed during World War II to speed the calculations involved in the aiming of big guns. The computer has created a new set of terms, including a word that can serve as a common denominator for information of any kind. This is the "bit." Technically defined, a bit is the smallest quantity of information which distinguishes between two equally probable outcomes, such as heads or tails when a coin is tossed. The concept of the bit as a measurable unit focused attention on the basic nature of information, and in 1949, Claude Shannon of the Bell Laboratories published a fundamental information theory that has since been broadly applied to many fields.

The Shannon theory is a mathematical formula governing the flow of messages through any communications channel, but most typically through telephone wires. Engineers warn that the formula measures only the quantity of information and not its meaning. But quantity is what people mean when they say "too much." Shannon defined the channel capacity of any communications medium—wire, pipe, road, radio wave—in terms of the bits per second which it can convey.

Social scientists have pointed out that the human nervous system can be regarded as a communications channel. Theoretically, of course, any impression received by any of the five senses can be reduced to bits and counted. Messages may originate in a person, a place, a thing, or in symbols—anything to which a human being responds. A dirty sock on the bedroom floor invites the viewer to wash it. The sight of an acquaintance on the street invites a greeting. Institutions such as libraries or the stock exchange can also be regarded as communications channels in the sense that they receive information and handle or process it in some way.

Human beings can be considered as communication channels, but they do not have the capacity of telephone wires, which can carry *thousands* of bits per second, or of computers, which can be designed to carry *millions* of bits per second. A human being is pushing his capacity if he can read a mere 50 bits per second of words, play 22 bits of piano music a second, or press a key on signal at the rate of six bits per second.

There are other differences. A computer has a virtually limitless memory. It doesn't care how much information it has to store, and since it is not confined by a skull, it can be built bigger to hold more. By contrast, the poor brain is pathetically limited. You forget telephone numbers you don't use every day, and your span of attention is so short that you have to hurry to dial a number you have looked up in the telephone book before you forget it.

"Man is a miserable component in a communications system," writes George Miller, Professor of Psychology at Harvard. "He has a narrow band width, a high noise level, is expensive to maintain, and sleeps eight hours out of every 24."

During the 1950s, Richard L. Meier, now at the University of California, and James G. Miller, now provost of Cleveland State University, were both at the University of

Michigan. Both were interested in seeing whether the information theory could explain the abnormal behavior of individuals and social institutions. If the human nervous system is a communications channel, like a wire or a pipe, then it must have a channel capacity that can be expressed in bits per second, and it should respond to "information input overload" in some of the same ways.

Meier assumed that the effective channel capacity of a person was the rate at which he could read, and he put the upper limit, for an attentive, fast reader, at 3000 non-redundant bits per minute. Assuming 10 bits per word, Meier's attentive, fast reader would be pushing his capacity when he was absorbing 300 words of prose a minute. (The virtue of the bit in estimating reading rates is that it provides a way to evaluate the difficulty of the material. There are more bits in each word chosen by a writer who uses a large vocabulary than one who confines himself to predictable baby talk, because the surprise value of a signal adds to the information that the signal conveys.)

• *Overloading the Brain*

James G. Miller compared the flow of information through cells, organs, individuals, groups, and social institutions. He noticed that an increase of information initially leads to faster responses, whether the inputs are electric shocks to the sciatic nerve of a frog, dictation to a typist, or letters to answer. Up to a certain point, the speed-up is all to the good. You know how it is when you have a flurry of phone calls. You dispatch them faster, and because you're more alert, you do it more effectively. Busy people make faster decisions, and since they make more of them, they often make wiser decisions than those who ponder overlong.

But what happens when the channel is overloaded?

James G. Miller, a psychologist by training, explored the hypothesis that nervous breakdown might, after all, be a literal picture of mental illness.

He describes what happens when any communication channel, including the human nervous system, tries to handle more bits per second than its capacity. "Finally, as the input rate speeds up even faster, the output falls drastically, sometimes to zero. The system is overloaded and can no longer transmit information." If pianists force themselves to play faster and faster, they lag behind the printed score, make mistakes, leave out notes, and eventually stop exhausted.

James G. Miller identified strategies for dealing with information input overload and started checking to see how many of them applied not only to cells, human beings, organs, and animals, but also to human social systems. His list is easiest to understand in terms of how people respond to overwork:

> *Omission* (don't bother to call back when you're busy).
> *Error* (don't type the letter over to correct a mistake).
> *Queuing* (let phone calls pile up and answer the important ones first).
> *Filtering* (have your secretary throw the junk mail out).
> *Approximation* (guess about the spelling of a word instead of taking time to look it up).
> *Multiple channels* (get someone to answer some of the mail).
> *Escape.*

Some of these strategies sound so much like common neurotic patterns (denial, defense, avoidance, withdrawal, escape) that he suggested mental illness might result from a defect in the nervous system which lowered the capacity of the patients to handle information.

Most people assume that communication breakdown is

the result of schizophrenia. James G. Miller thought that it could be the cause. "It's like a glass house closing in" he quotes a schizophrenic patient as telling her analyst. "You can hear the confusion on the outside. It happens when someone goes on and won't shut up. It doesn't even register. It's just a lot of noise. They don't even seem to be talking to me after awhile."

In the 1960s Meier thought that many hard-pressed professionals were already processing information at capacity and the ranks of the hard pressed were growing. Like James G. Miller, he suspected that information overload could damage people. "When the 'messages' come rolling in at a constantly increasing tempo, the distractions accumulate and interruptions become more and more frequent. Things get out of sequence. All the relevant readings are not scanned before the answers must be given. Mistakes are made which need to be rectified. Disorder and confusion begin to appear. The situation goes from bad to worse. The feeling of guilt that was aroused initially is supplanted by a desire to cut all connections with society, to escape, or to admit being 'beat' by the pressure. We have coined a scientific term for this desperate condition—*information input overload.*" Meier speculated that overload could produce nervous breakdown in people.

However suggestive, the analogy between wires and people is not exact. At first it looks as if the wires have it over the nervous system. But on closer examination, it seems as if the human race is going to be saved by what looks like its limitations.

When you comprehend how much a human being can put through his head, you discover that it is not a nice, neat engineer's figure in bits per second, but "it all depends on the circumstances." And as you examine those circumstances, you conclude that even Professor Meier's overloaded professionals are not taking advantage of all the strategies for processing information available to human beings.

• *The Elastic Human Channel*

Since the computer, there has been new interest among psychologists in how and why the channel capacity of the human nervous system varies. There are uniquely human techniques for dealing with overload, and they are worth examining in detail.

Take, for instance, the human attention span. At first blush, it looks pathetically limited. The phone company has discovered, pragmatically, that seven numbers is about as many as you can hold in your mind to dial. When an exchange runs out of numbers, they don't add a digit. They start a new seven-number exchange. There is sound psychology behind this practice.

In a charming scientific paper of 1956 entitled "The Magical Number Seven, Plus or Minus Two," George Miller tells how he was "persecuted by an integer." For years he brooded about the strange coincidence that the number of loudnesses people can normally distinguish, the dots they can enumerate at a glance, or random numbers they can remember, cluster around seven, which happens also to be the number of pitches in the musical scale, the days of the week, primary colors, and the degrees intuitively chosen for many different kinds of rating measurements.

Subsequent studies confirm George Miller's hunch that the number seven, plus or minus a few, keeps turning up because it is the number of different things that you can hold in your mind at once. The bottleneck of human transmission is the space that holds the seven things. Short-term memory, quick-access memory, span of attention, central processing capacity use the same mental facility. You can't remember the phone number you've looked up if your attention is distracted.

You run up against the bottleneck all the time. You can, for instance, knit and talk at once without strain, but if you get interested in what you are saying you drop a stitch. You realize that you have just so much attention. When you try to put one more item into it, something gets pushed out. You make a mistake, or forget something, or the items clamoring for attention have to wait to get in, so you slow down. It's your instinctive protection against overload.

As a receiver of bits, the human nervous system is no slouch. Theoretically, at least, a human being can take in thousands or even millions of bits per second. It's making sense of them that takes time, and experiments testing how many things you can do at once show that this interpretation of "central processing" interferes with short-term memory and span of attention. Motor responses aren't as speedy as sensory reception, but the "hand is quicker than the eye" when the hand is doing something practised that takes minimal central processing, and the eye is perceiving something unexpected. "Thought" is not instantaneous. It takes time.

But the brain is not only slow, it is carefully selective as well. Jerome Bruner, Professor of Psychology at Harvard sums up a world of experimental data in a pithy sentence: "Perception acts sometimes as a welcoming committee, and sometimes as a screening committee." Your computer fits inside your head because your nervous system is ingenious in paying attention to what matters most at the time.

Think of attention as the flashlight you deploy to sample the dark woods of the literally millions of bits your sense organs are capable of relaying to your brain every second. You may be able to pay attention to little more than seven things at a time, but there is virtually no limit to what kinds of things these seven may be. They may be numbers, notches on a stick, letters, words, or great abstract ideas. You may be able to distinguish only seven pitches, but you can tune yourself to distinguish seven high pitches or seven low pitches.

You shift the whole range up or down to catch something you hope or fear. You gear for soft sounds to catch the cry of the baby at night, and blunt your discrimination of differences in loudness in the morning to keep from being deafened by the jackhammers outside the window. You narrow the pupils of your eyes so that you are not blinded by the noonday sun, but widen them to catch the dawn's first light. You widen them to distinguish details that concern you: the pupils of men's eyes widen when they are shown pictures of nude women; the eyes of women widen even more when they are shown pictures of nude men.

• *To See Is To Choose*

The characteristic of the human information channel that is going to save us is that it can say "no" to a bit. If you feed impulses at 23-second intervals to a machine that is programmed to a 24-second cycle, the machine stutters nonsense. Feed a human with more bits than he has been handling and he skips some, makes mistakes but flounders on. He lets bits pile up until he can handle them, guesses, and sets priorities. The strategies for handling overload which Meier and Miller list are built into the human nervous system. They protect attention and direct it to the clues most needed for survival.

How do you decide what to admit to the precious space which may be able to hold only seven items plus or minus two? According to Bruner, on the basis of categories already set up in your mind. The new school of "cognitive psychology" he heads makes "perceiving" sound very much like "thinking," hence the name "cognitive."

The cognitive theory of perception explains things that weren't apparent when we thought of the brain as a telephone switchboard connecting incoming sensations with outgoing orders on a one-to-one basis. It explains, for instance, why a baby has to learn to see: until his mind is stocked with categories, he can't organize or make sense of the chaos of sights and sounds that bathe him. Well-informed people read faster and learn more because they have more and better categories for identifying incoming bits of information. An X-ray technician sees more information in the photograph of your chest than you do.

Tricks of perception are usually cited to warn that you can't believe your eyes and may be rudely shocked by the reality of your environment. The reverse is closer to the truth. The illusions are evidence of the ways in which you deploy your attention to what matters most at the moment. If your senses are crazy, they are crazy like a fox.

As you scan the woods of potential inputs, you "see" only the clues that help you find your path. You tune out the birds to zero in on the crackle that sounds like a human tread. Familiar, routine stimuli don't get a tumble. You "get used to" regular noises that do not demand action. Even more dramatic is your ability to ignore odors, which are not as relevant to modern man as they were to his animal forbears. If executives can be defined as people who habitually rule out trivia, then your senses are past masters at the art of "managing by exception." Only the unusual or the threatening gains admittance.

If you look at a wall of books, you don't stop to see if one of them is a safe in disguise. If it looks like a book, you call it a book and don't clutter your mind with it. If an experimenter springs a red Ace of Spades, you see it as black. Bruner calls this "minimization of surprise."

You tune yourself to perceive what you need to perceive. The mother may be the only one to hear the baby cry. You alone pick out your name in the babble of cocktail party conversation across the room. Your tuning changes with your need. If you are hungry you notice more restaurants while you're driving through the city, and if it is getting dark, you may also mistake the drugstore for a grocery store. Bruner calls this tuning the "maximization of attention."

This, then, is the human nervous system. Unlike inanimate wires and channels, it is equipped with so many strategies for dealing with input overload that it is hard to say just how many bits it can monitor. The limit recedes as it is approached in much the same way that the limits on world population and U.S. GNP recede. Very few people are handling their capacity for bits per second, and the more they handle, the more their capacity grows.

Think what your life would be like if you could sustain, even for an hour a day, the mental activity you have been able to attain at your peak. There are several ways to hit this stride more often.

Consider first the potential for increasing the flow by thinking better. Smart people pack an incredible amount of information into brains no bigger than everyone else's. How do they manage it? The way some people manage to go to Europe with only one suitcase. They take only what they need and they pack it neatly.

Symbols increase the data a brain can handle. If, as George Miller pointed out, the mind can only cope with seven things at a time, it is like a purse that holds only seven coins. You can fill your purse with pennies, or you can fill it with silver dollars and have much more money. If you look at books, you can see only seven at a time: call them a library and you have made room for six other libraries, or six other entirely different concepts or things. The acronym UNNRA fills one place in your mind, not five. The Christian cross is a symbol that stands for thousands of words. A mathematical formula recodes experience even more compactly.

- **Bigger Chunks**

Watch a demon speed-reader pick up a new nonfiction book. First he looks at the table of contents to see how the author has attacked the subject. Then he flips to the index to attack the material from his own point of view by looking up items that interest him. In five minutes of jumping around he may know whether he wants to read the book in whole or in part, and more important, what he can expect to get out of it. A half hour and he may have what he needs from it. And because he has reorganized it in terms of his own mental filing system, he will retain more of it than the slow reader who reads from beginning to end.

Reorganizing material is the secret of the controversial Evelyn Wood method of speed reading which has had top demonstrators gulping books at the rate of 20,000 words a minute.

Active readers get more out of books. Educators advise that whatever time you have to spend on a book, you will learn more by spending half the time reading and half the time thinking about what you have read. Other experiments show the quickest way to improve comprehension of what you read is to ask yourself a question about the material, or speak to someone about it every half hour.

The Crowding Syndrome

The act of reading involves three quite different processes. First, your optic nerve registers the printed words. Next, the words are assembled into phrases or groups. Finally the meaning of these groupings is "understood" by a mysterious process of comparison with material already stored in long-term, permanent memory.

The bottleneck is stage two, in which words recognized by the relatively speedy eye pile up in short-term memory awaiting assembly into spans the mind can interpret. This stage takes up the space that George Miller likens to a purse of seven coins. Fast readers "chunk" many words into each coin of meaning, but reading specialists say that the best chunkers can handle only 500 words a minute.

Higher speeds involve the uncharted third step of "understanding," and some reading specialists don't call this reading at all. The demon reader who takes in thousands of words a minute seems to abstract, guess, or generalize the author's thought on the basis of clues gleaned from a sample of the words his eye catches as he skims the print. He depends on what he knows, and the more he knows, the more he learns.

Every word that is read is a code, and language is a way of coding information so that more can be handled. Higher levels of abstraction extend the number of bits that can be "grasped" at once. Coding saves time. A filing code enables a clerk to put a letter in the right pigeon hole without reading all of it. Since "making sense" or coding of sense impressions limits human information-processing capacity, the better your coding, the more bits you can process.

Codes can help in several different ways. Information can be recoded to convey more data per symbol, as when a color is used to add another meaning to the word on a sign. Codes can be specially designed to reduce ambiguity: symbols are adopted for traffic signs that cannot easily be mistaken for something else. Finally, coding makes it possible to acquire habitual responses that save time and attention: a red light stimulates a driver to put on the brake "without thinking."

A good code is unambiguous. You can tell right away whether a signal fits. If you get a lot of signals that you can't classify, you suspect that there is something wrong with the code. You revise your file headings.

You do the same thing when you have trouble "making sense" out of the blizzard of signals that come at you so fast that you feel you are "losing your mind" (meaning, of course, your categories). You change the code or recode to a higher level of abstraction that handles rich quarters instead of pennies. The process is acutely uncomfortable, but when it's over, you "see things in a new way"—a way that processes more bits of information per second and makes more sense out of the blizzard than before. Changing the pigeon holes in your mind takes time, but it is the most productive use that you can make of mind space.

Dramatic improvements can be made in the way information is presented to the human communications channel. Engineers do a better job of designing knobs and dials to the capacity of factory workers than educators do in packaging information to the operating characteristics of the human brain. Printed material could be designed to challenge readers after every half-hour of reading time by introducing questions or by changing the typography. In future, much more information will have to be "chunked" at the source in digests, abstracts, and eventually in computer memory banks from which it can be retrieved only when, as, and if needed.

• *Sharper Choices*

People will have to learn to ignore the information that they don't need to know. To cope with irrelevance, it is necessary to set up sharper priorities. It isn't necessary to read all of the letters in the mail or go to every party. Sherlock Holmes wouldn't let Dr. Watson tell him about the Copernican theory of the solar system because he couldn't see how it could help him solve crimes. A friend of mine sold an invention to General Electric without bothering to find out how the thing worked. She knew the inventor and she knew where to go with his idea. Most of the time, small mistakes don't matter. Often a lot of energy can be saved by procrastinating. Many jobs simply don't have to be done. What most people need is not a better memory, but a more selective forgettery.

Anyone can get more through his head by taking steps to eliminate disturbing noise. It cuts channel capacity by taking up space that could carry messages. Experiments have shown that moderate noise doesn't interfere with simple tasks that don't use up all your attention, and it may reduce errors by keeping you alert. But noise does interfere with a combination of simple tasks that don't take up your attention when everything is quiet; and it does interfere with complex tasks of thinking that use the brain's central processing capacity. Especially when it is ambiguous or unpredictable, noise adds one more thing to the purse of attention than that space can hold. And noise interferes with transmission as well as reception: you have to simplify your thoughts to be heard in a noisy room, so you are more likely to be misunderstood.

The need for choice rises faster even than the volume of information. As we have seen, each addition to knowledge costs more. This means that while information-rich societies are richer, they must spend more of their wealth on information processing. This in turn creates more urgency for deciding which bits are worth the higher price. Some are, some aren't. A businessman weighs the value of information every time he decides whether a fact is worth a long-distance phone call.

A world of few choices is a world of either-or. If there is only one job you can get, you have to take your chances with it. There's no point even in calculating your chances of succeeding at it. But when you have to choose between two, you find yourself weighing odds. Your internal dialogue might go like this: Sure, I could do Job A, but it is certain to be a bore and unlikely to lead to promotion; but I might fall flat on my face in Job B, and while it is more likely to be interesting, there's more competition there for promotion so my chances of getting ahead, even if I do succeed, are less. All these are calculations of probability and given enough data they could be expressed in mathematical terms.

Increasing quantities of relevant data overload primarily because they compound the number of responses or decisions possible. Mathematics can be a powerful aid, and has, in fact led to the development of a whole new way of solving problems.

• *The Systems Approach*

The systems approach is a way to solve problems that involve more factors than even the most experienced man can hold in his head at one time. All the factors are identified and reduced to numbers so that their relationships can be expressed in a mathematical formula or a mechanical model. When this is done, it is possible to state with accuracy what changing one factor will do to all the rest.

Take, for instance, the problem of figuring out whether

you can make more money by raising the price of a can of soup. Raising the price will take in more cents per can, but you will sell fewer cans. If you know just how many fewer cans you will sell, you can figure out whether or how much to raise the price with paper or pencil. But if you don't know what a price rise will do, you have to think of all the factors that will influence people to accept or reject a price change. Some of the factors might be the competition of other brands of soup, the amount of money families have to spend on food, the popularity of soup as a food compared with other foods. A complete list would include many other factors for most of which there are no data or no basis for measuring their influence. At this point, most "practical" people simply give up. You can't know all those things, the practical businessman says, so you have to go on the basis of your experience or your "hunch."

The systems approach doesn't let it go at that. It requires you not only to identify everything that could possibly influence the outcome in question, but to make some assumption about how much weight to assign it. This, too, simply makes explicit and measurable in cold numbers the kinds of estimates that experienced observers make in their heads, often without realizing what they are doing.

Once all the factors are identified and their relationships assumed, the systems analyst can make a formula from which he can predict what will happen, say, to sales of soup if the price is raised one cent or two cents or three cents. Sometimes the relationships are expressed mechanically in a model of the problem. An hour glass is a model of passing time which registers elapsed time mechanically in the level of sand in the lower vessel. A thermometer is a model of temperature rise that is expressed mechanically by the expansion of the mercury or alcohol in a marked glass tube.

The systems approach has been used for predicting

what will happen to prices, wages, sales, and the GNP if taxes are raised or lowered. It has been used to decide whether we are better off spending defense dollars on airplanes or missiles. Businessmen use the systems approach to decide where to build warehouses, how much to manufacture, whether to market a new product. It comes in handy, too, in smaller decisions, such as how to route home delivery of fuel oil to keep all the customers tanks full with the fewest possible trips in all kinds of weather. Or what size tankers to build to move crude oil from Saudi Arabia to the United States. Or whether labor costs and transport considered, it's better to assemble automobiles near the market or near the plants that make the parts.

The systems approach is unparalleled in allocating something scarce, such as money or time, when most of the factors in the problem are well known. When it is applied to social problems, such as the management of crime, it is useful primarily because it requires policy makers to think through what they are trying to accomplish, and to list all the factors that may influence the goal they have defined.

In order to decide the best size for a primary grade class, for instance, you might have to know what you want the children to learn and how you want the children to behave, as well as the numbers of children and teachers, the size of existing classroom space, and the cost (and time) required to build more or different space.

The systems approach is insurance against piecemeal thinking that has produced airports designed for more passengers than the highways can carry to town, or factories located where there isn't enough housing to accommodate the labor they need. Simon Ramo, the founder of TRW, Inc., an aerospace research organization, warns that the systems approach is the only way to manage control of natural resources, mass transit, pollution, education, public health, and other services which he calls "civil systems" because they don't lend themselves to private enterprise, seat-of-the-pants policymaking.

The trouble with the systems approach is that it can't give you a better answer than your question. It won't help solve the social problem of crime, for example, until we have better data on what makes people commit crimes, although the attempt may help us find out. Intuition or insight can allow for gaps in data, but in order to program a problem, you have to be able to state it precisely, you have to know all the factors that affect the outcome and how they act on each other, and you have to express all these factors and relations in numbers, even if it means assigning an arbitrary dollars-and-cents value to something as intangible as the pleasure you get from a scenic view. Finally what comes out is not the one right answer, but more often a series of alternatives. The systems approach is an extension of the brain in that it enables man to solve bigger and more complex problems, just as the microscope is an extension of the eye that enables it to see smaller.

As individuals, we can get more bits through the bottleneck of attention by sharper choices (cut the trivia!) and bigger chunks (look at the woods instead of the trees!). Media transmitting information can recode the information to higher levels of abstraction for bigger "chunks," engineer it to reduce the attention-clogging ambiguity of poorly designed road signs, and package it to the characteristics of the human receivers. Mathematical techniques can help policy makers apply masses of data to social and political decisions that are too complex for the wisest naked brain.

Brains can think better, and they are doing it. A rising flow of information is forcing the elastic human channel to use all its strategies for increasing capacity. Even the hated computers are making human brains work better. When they take over the mind-numbing detail, they leave humans nothing but the mind-expanding decision-making.

Before the computers, executives could spend all day long rifling through paperwork to catch errors. Now they sit at clean desks—or in deskless offices—and address themselves to imponderables. Before the computer age, prestige went to the engineering-oriented managers who had to calculate the profitability of alternative products in their heads. Now that machines grind out these detailed figures, the engineering types are less valuable than those who can sense which product will sell.

Politicians used to talk with hundreds of citizens in order to spot trends. Now computers enable poll takers to do this sampling more accurately and quickly, and politicians are forced to think more seriously about what ought to be done. Moral issues loom larger in management thinking these days in part at least because managers and policy makers are relieved of the grubby, accounting-type details that formerly took up all their time.

Now that it is possible for one person to handle more data than a single human head has ever been able to encompass before, it has become possible to organize work in many different ways.

Chapter **XIII**

Toward Human Scale

Smarter thinking increases the flow of information that creates wealth by improving the function of the human nervous system. But the best way to increase information is to find out under what circumstances people can handle the most information, and to organize human institutions accordingly. The hope for mankind is that we can learn how to expand and sustain human capacity.

● *Human-Sized Work Loads*

Unlike wires and pipes, living channels lose capacity when too little is put into them. Sensory deprivation stunts the development of both animals and humans. The highest fatal accident rates are not in the populous states where traffic is heavy, but in states such as Utah and Arizona, where straight, untraveled highways demand so little response that drivers literally go to sleep.

It is probable that more American workers suffer from

monotony or underload, than from the overloads that worry the people who complain of "too much" talk. Industrial engineers prescribe background music, light noise, or conversation to maintain the vigilance of workers who have to monitor routine controls. At the other end of the scale, you aren't tired out by a busy day during which you have had to absorb continual talk, if you feel that something has been accomplished, while you can find it extremely wearing to spend ten minutes fruitlessly searching for a pair of scissors. These common experiences suggest that we should study the conditions under which people think better and bigger and then deliberately use them.

We know something about these conditions. Doctors, lawyers, editors, and other professional information processors have not only stretched their capacity by using it, but they rise to emergencies during which they handle bits per second at a rate which frequently surprises them. Why can't they maintain this capacity? Does the effort literally fatigue their brains or "nerves," or is the relapse due to something else that is happening, some obstacle that could be remedied so that the bursts of speed could be maintained without discomfort?

The place to begin is to go back and take a closer look at the notion that human beings burn out or blow a fuse when overloaded with bits per second, like wires overloaded with amperes. Maybe it's not the work, but the worry.

Even those theorists who bewail the quantity of information imply that something other than numbers is involved. When Toffler defines his concept "future shock" as "response to overstimulation" he also says it occurs "when an individual is *forced* to operate above his adaptive range." James G. Miller, who has documented "information input overload," in his monumental monograph *Living Systems*, sees "little clear-cut evidence that excessive information inputs can cause structural pathology" but a system may "respond pathologically to excessive rates or *threatening meanings* of information inputs, showing nonadaptive adjustments, panic, confusion, or useless emotional behavior.

The italics are added. The operative terms in these statements are *forced, threat,* and *meaning.*

• *Self-Pacing Expands Capacity*

Stress notoriously limits a person's capacity to deal with information, and in spite of loose talk about "nervous breakdown" due to "overwork," worry has more to do with the meaning of the information presented than its quantity. This becomes clear in analyzing the source of the stresses on executives, air-traffic controllers, and airline pilots, all of whom are regarded as stressed because they are required to respond to as much information as the human nervous system can take.

We have become familiar with the picture of harrassed executives overloaded into heart attack, ulcer, and nervous breakdown. In Europe, high-blood pressure is called "the manager's disease." The facts don't substantiate this image. In 1968, a Cornell University study of 270,000 men in the Bell Telephone system found that the higher a man rose in his job, the less likely he was to get coronary disease. About the same time, the myth of the executive ulcer was dispatched by Sidney Cobb in the course of a massive study of work and health at the Institute for Social Research at the University of Michigan. Cobb found that foremen had the most ulcers and executives the fewest.

The Michigan team found that the higher a man's status on the job, the better his health and they were able to prove that his rank was cause, not effect. Health deteriorated after demotion and improved after promotion, in spite of the fact that the promoted men were older at the time of their promotions. The other factor that damaged health was conflicting demands, but this stress was less acute for men who enjoyed good relations with their co-workers. The difficulty of the work and the quantity of demands did not make a difference.

Executives may be able to do more than their subordinates with less damage to their health because they are freer to work at their own pace. Stress of any kind is easier to bear if you can control it. Experiments show that people are much less bothered by unpredictable noises when they believe that they can stop them by pressing a button. It's not the speed of the assembly line that makes it tiring, but the fact that assembly-line workers have to dance to its tune.

The two aviation jobs, that of air traffic controller and pilot, force physically fit and highly trained men to respond to a heavy flow of information under exceptional constraints. Yet the two jobs differ widely in their impact on morale and health:

> Air traffic controllers are undeniably overloaded with demands close to the limit of their nervous system. They claim that their health is impaired by the "bloodrushers" or near misses that occur when aircraft they are guiding threaten to collide, and careful studies made under the auspices of the Federal Aviation Administration bear them out. Stress-related diseases—coronary artery disease, coronary thrombosis, hypertension, and peptic ulcers afflict four times as many air traffic controllers as Air Force men of similar age.

> On the other hand, Earl T. Carter, a former flight surgeon, says that monotony and boredom are making professional airline pilots sick. Pilots have to be intelligent, but modern flight regulations leave them little actual decision-making. Such things as direction, air speed, altitude, and traffic-separation maneuvers are supplied from outside the plane.

Controllers and pilots have to process information at rates outside their control, but the controllers are said to get sick because they are forced to process too much information, the airline pilots because they are forced to process too little. Eventually, perhaps, both jobs will be done automatically by machines which do not wear themselves out rising to emergencies and human work will be organized so that each worker can proceed at his own pace.

Self-pacing is proving its worth on many fronts. Authoritarian management practices that are characteristic of railroads and automobile manufacturers are less productive than new organizational devices which give more personal freedom even to factory operatives.

Many factories have abolished time clocks with no loss of productivity. Educators say children learn more arithmetic and spelling if they can go to a computer and practice these tough subjects when the urge is on them. The information is available when, as, and if needed, instead of at the convenience of human information keepers such as teachers. The teachers can then concentrate on the truly "human" work of motivating students by developing a personal relationship with them.

• *Participation Expands Capacity*

Dialogue is the most effective form of human communication because it passes over a two-way channel with a human being on either end. In normal conversation, the listener can receive bits of information faster than the speaker can produce them. This gives the listener time to think about what the speaker is saying, and he responds because an answer is expected.

Teachers have long known that students learn more when they can talk back, but dialogue is so costly and threatening that few schools are organized to take advantage of it. The deprivation is felt more keenly than formerly because more learning now comes from the one-way communications of media.

Books, broadcasts, lectures, and particularly television, destroy two-way communications. Children whose first exposure to fiction comes from the same box that reports the war in Vietnam may have difficulty grasping the difference between fact and make-believe. When ghetto children get to school and hear the teacher speaking in the same accent as the television people, they don't understand that the teacher is speaking directly to them and expects an answer.

Speakers on television can't be sure that the message is getting through, or that anyone is listening at all, or how many listeners have tuned in late and missed part of the message, so they have to keep on reiterating the main points and simplifying them to reach the inattentive and the stupid. The effort is self-defeating, because it encourages even less attention on the part of the listeners. Talk without feedback becomes unreal, but people don't turn it off. In most homes, the boxes rumble on, unattended and apparently unheard.

But not really, and there's the rub. The snatches of music, the blurry figures moving in their shadow world, the barely intelligible talk engage some part of the consciousness and force the listener to march unwilling to their distant drum. And though the reluctant listener may not realize it, he resents the compulsion for the same reason that assembly line workers resent keeping time with their machines.

Both the assembly line and the information boxes create a well of anger. Anyone who recalls the sullen fury on which the organizers of automobile workers were able to capitalize in the union movement of the 1930s can see this same anger welling up again. It is akin to the primitive anger of babies whose hands are held when they want to wave them.

In explaining the anger of Women's Liberation, Margaret Mead once suggested that women were angry because they are isolated at home, without human adult companionship all day. Bad enough. But the standard American home is not a vacuum all day long. It is filled with wheedling, thundering, and infuriatingly smooth voices that keep talking and talking and never let the incarcerated woman answer back.

The anger of the young puzzles their elders. More influential than their parents were at their age, the young say they are helpless. Freer sexually and personally than the young have ever been, they complain that the "system" oppresses them. The thing they say most often is that nobody listens. That's why they have to scream, they say. Yet the young have been given more serious attention by school administrators, psychologists, sociologists, parents, and media than the young have ever been accorded before. Their protests have been publicized more seriously, their views more sincerely invited. Their visibility magnifies and creates dissent, as we have said. But there is more to it. Inarticulate cries, bombs, and violent gestures inundated the scene in the late 1960s with a suddenness matched only by the rapid saturation of American homes with television some fifteen years earlier, when these angry young people were babies learning to talk.

For the television-bred, so much of life comes from the boxes that dialogue and response no longer seem attainable in the ordinary course of daily living, but have to be achieved by special programs: nudity, touch therapy, sensitivity training, body language, and one-to-one welfare work with underprivileged individuals rather than participation in movements directed to legislative reform.

We may be on our way toward solving this particular problem. Until recently communications advances have increased the one-way channels at the expense of the opportunities for dialogue. But computers are now programmed to respond to students who are learning a language, or solving mathematical problems. These new machines supply far more individual attention and elicit more back-talk than the most luxurious schools can provide.

Even more exciting is the prospect of home-based computer terminals and cable services that will let the television audience talk back. Professional colleagues based in different places could get together by closed-circuit television without leaving their desks. Students could query authorities at a distance, and with little disruption of schedules.

• *Emotional Support Expands Capacity*

Threat cuts capacity. Dialogue and the approval of people close to you, create and expand capacity from the cradle itself. Babies learn to talk when they succeed in transmitting a word to their mothers and their mothers respond to it. Success reduces the baby's frustration and encourages him to try again. The same process continues to nourish wealth-creating communications all through life.

The most supportive approval comes from the immediate family, but less of life is lived at home than in earlier times and more of it will inevitably be lived in work and play groups formed around specific programs. These ad hoc groups are easier to join and to leave than a blood-related family, and they can be deliberately structured by policy makers.

● *New Groupings*

Until recently, cities and work groups have been designed on the basis of material necessity of some kind. Large groups of workers all doing the same thing under strict supervision (no talking!) were necessary when ships had to be unloaded by hand labor and ditches dug by armies of men with shovels. Cities grew big because factories had to locate near coal or waterpower.

Now electric power that transmits energy cheaply has already spread factories to smaller communities, and soon it may be possible for many workers not to leave home at all. The new two-way computers and information machines of the future will enable many professional and executive workers to operate from their own living rooms. Video phones will handle face-to-face conferences, facsimile transmission of documents will save filing, and computer storage and retrieval will make it possible to handle information anywhere a terminal can be installed.

● *The Right Size*

The new ways of working may not improve life immediately. One of the discomforts of new inventions is that they constantly disrupt the scale of human groups. People are subjected to the distortions of a fun-house mirror. Some of the groups on which they rely are suddenly blown up to be too big, while new responsibilities and broader communications make others too small.

No nation will ever be big enough to deal with the communications satellites or to prevent, single-handedly, pollution of the oceans. Cities are too small to finance their own urban renewal or cope with the illegal sale of addictive drugs. The largest corporations are too small to abolish poverty by any policy within their power. The traditional family, on the other hand, is too small a unit to provide the full emotional support it could supply when less information was circulated and individuals were not tempted to take on many different roles. *The New York Times* is too big to read every day, but too small to live up to its historic promise to cover "All the News That's Fit to Print."

These and other institutions are out of scale. They need to be restructured to different sizes. Some work can be done most efficiently in big groups, other tasks should be broken down so that smaller units can handle them. It takes trial and error to find the best grouping for each function. Some business organizations oscillate between centralizing everything at the head office, and then breaking the functions up to allow small groups of men in the field to make the decisions.

Now that work groups can be big or little, a criterion is needed to determine the right size. The principle that talk makes wealth provides an unexpected guideline. If an organization is most efficient when it promotes the highest flow of information relevant to its purpose, then a class, firm, hospital, factory, or even a ski club ought to be the size that makes *for the most talk by the greatest number.*

Every organization or system starts out with a group of people exchanging information for a common purpose. As the organization gets bigger, there frequently is less and less communication instead of more and more. When this happens, the organization becomes a monster, literally too big to function.

Calcutta is monstrous because it is too big for village organization. Many other groupings are monstrous in the same way. People feel lost in the big universities or big companies when these institutions have simply added more students or workers without changing inside. Newcomers to the city are lonely because they don't know how to find friends among people sharing their special interests. They expect to find friends down the block, the way neighbors are friends in the country. Someone has to tell them that there's a hobby club at the YMCA or a night course where they will find people who like to talk about literature. Both interest groupings—the hobby club or the night course in the novel—have the makings of friendship groups.

The remedy for "alienation" or loneliness is to structure big organizations so that the activities are carried on in groups of a size that makes for the highest flow of communications. It is surprisingly easy to find that "right size."

• Primary Groups

All through human history, and if the ethologists are correct, even before the ancestors of man could fairly be called human, creatures such as ourselves have lived in small, closely knit groups. They are called "primary groups" because they are the basic building blocks of all societies.

The modern family consisting of mother, father, and children is only a special and historically recent case. Primary groups may be extended families, like the farm families of our grandparents, work units, play units, fighting units, the neighborhood kids, or quasi-official associations of people such as the self-selected residential units at Vassar College which Mary McCarthy celebrated in her novel *The Group*.

A group has to have more than three or four, but it breaks down when there is more than 20. The ideal number is, as an old New England adage prescribed for a dinner party: "more than the graces [3] but fewer than the muses [9]." Investigators of small group dynamics find that members are happiest in groups of from five to seven, which seems to be as many as can be considered as individuals at one time.

Bigger groups, the sociologists find, break down into cliques and suppress some members. Observations on British school children show that the children spend more time fighting and also less time interacting as the group is increased beyond six. Other evidence comes from studies of family size and achievement which generally show that children from small families outperform children from large families even when the occupation of the father is the same. Still other studies show that there are fewer expressions of affection among larger families with more than two children. Only children, once pitied, are more apt to succeed occupationally than children with brothers and sisters.

People divide themselves into primary groups whenever they can. When they come together in big agglomerations, such as the army, a college dormitory, a huge factory or office building employing thousands, they break into small primary "hanging groups," "gangs," "outfits," "cliques," and "buddy groups." Good leaders intuitively respect these informal groups and keep a weather eye on soldiers, students, or employees who don't "belong" to one. Social research confirms their worry: loners who don't "belong" are much more apt to fall physically or mentally ill and commit suicide.

A primary group is always a face-to-face group that gets together daily or frequently. Group members know a great deal about the past experience and the personalities of other group members. Charles Horton Cooley, the sociologist who may have been the first to coin the term "primary group" back in 1909, thought that the essential was "a certain intimacy and fusion of personalities." Since then we have learned that primary groups provide individuals with their identity, or sense of themselves; their emotional security;

and their opinions. They are the real police force holding society together. What Thomas Jefferson glorified as "a decent respect to the opinions of mankind" turns out to be a concern for what your daily associates think of you.

Most people have the feeling that big cities do not provide the surveillance of a primary group. The suspicion is well-founded. In 1968 two psychologists conducted an interesting experiment. They had college students act out a murder on a crowded street and observed that the likelihood of any one coming to the aid of the supposed victim declined directly with the increase in the number of witnesses. When a lot of people were present each thought the other would be the good Samaritan. When the passers-by were few, they felt more like a small group which extends mutual aid to its members.

In another city street experiment, Dr. Philip G. Zimbardo, Professor of Psychology at the Palo Alto Institution in California, left a car unattended in the Bronx for three days and counted 23 attacks on it, while a similar car left on the street in Palo Alto, a small middle-class city, was untouched for weeks. It was not, of course, the *size* of New York City which encouraged the vandals in New York, but the lack of any network of neighbors in the Bronx to watch over what boys in the street were doing.

In the past, small groups were formed among people living close enough to each other to see and talk with each other easily. Women who used a common well formed a group. Children had to play with the kids who lived on their block. Constantinos A. Doxiadis, the Greek city planner, points out that high-rise apartments and automobile commuting break up many traditional small groups. For affluent professional men, the change may simply mean a wider circle of friends and membership in a larger number of interest groups by phone calls and short plane trips.

The ease with which the rich keep up with each other across thousands of miles of space makes it clear that friendship groups spring up among people who see each other every day simply because physical closeness makes communications cheap and easy. For human beings, at least, there is no territorial imperative involved. It's just that talk is cheaper at close quarters.

It is particularly important for women and children to live where they can meet people easily because they are less mobile than men, and have less money to communicate at a distance. Several studies show that living patterns which isolate women can literally make them ill. One British study found that women living in flats had more psychosomatic ailments than women living in houses where they had easier access to neighbors, and a recent U.S. Public Health Service study finds more psychosomatic illness among housewives than working wives. They confirm the hunch that what public health analysts call the "housewife syndrome," is what women themselves call being "sick of home," where home means isolation for long hours of the day.

Anything that disrupts communication breaks up a primary group. Children and employees subjected to rigid discipline may feel that their school or plant is "too big" because they aren't allowed to talk with each other enough to make friends.

Disruption of primary group loyalties, the "uprooting" of country people when they move to the city is the key to the celebrated evils of urbanization, but we now know that they can be avoided. Rural people in Africa are urbanizing —and at a frightening rate. They create overwhelming problems in cities such as Durban, South Africa. But they do not suffer from alienation. When Africans get to town from the bush they simply locate the shacks inhabited by kinsmen who came ahead of them and move into a ready-made family, a solution possible in cultures which pay more attention to kinship ties of obligation than to personality differences. European immigrants to America also settled near their compatriots who helped to orient them. But for most American farm boys, the city held no welcoming primary group, hence its evil reputation.

• *Keeping Morale High*

American individualism has made it easy for our big organizations to ignore the importance of primary groups in getting work done and maintaining morale. Before World War II, for instance, the Army thought of soldiers as interchangeable parts, to be moved around from one unit to another at the convenience of staff planners. The Army now respects the integrity of fighting units by replacing entire units so the men can stay together. The policy was the result of deliberate sociological investigation.

One of the mysteries of World War II was the surprising resistance of the German army, the Wehrmacht, in the last months of the war. Neither merciless bombing nor persuasive propaganda seemed to stop them from making a last-ditch stand. To find out the secret of their morale, psychological warfare units interviewed former German soldiers and studied German records. Their conclusion was shockingly simple: the German Army held together because it encouraged and protected fighting units. According to Edward A. Shils and Morris Janowitz, sociologists who were studying psychological warfare, fanatic attachment to Hitler or Nazism had nothing to do with it. In their classic report, "Cohesion and Disintegration in the Wehrmacht in World War II," Shils and Janowitz say that Allied propaganda failed to demoralize German soldiers. Only a few individuals, they concluded, are influenced by abstract messages from the world beyond their immediate associates.

Advertising and public relations specialists took note. During the 1950s, Paul Lazarfeld of Columbia's Bureau of Applied Social Research investigated how Americans form their opinions and reported that new ideas spread in two steps: first to the leaders who keep informed through newspapers or their professional press, and then through them to the people they see every day. His investigation scotched the old idea that there was such a thing as a "mass mind" which could be swayed by direct radio or newspaper propaganda. People really changed their minds through the web of word-of-mouth, which spread out from primary groups. The influence of advertising had been exaggerated because it was mediated through group leaders who could and very frequently did ignore the blatant appeals.

The saving grace is that human beings can and do form primary groups around almost any circumstance that brings people together. It doesn't have to be blood relationship or geography, as it has been in the past. It can be the most accidental propinquity, such as having a last name beginning with the same letter when gym lockers are assigned in a residential college. The play groups of children which make so much difference in their growing up are always the result of the accident that their parents chose to live on the same street. Work groups, friendship groups, hobby groups are similarly accidental.

Once a group jells, belonging to the group becomes more important or at least as important as the "function" which precipitated it, even if that function is as critical as keeping the family farm or a family business going. And we really know more than we realize about what does make them jell and how they really do work. Novelists told us long before sociologists invented the word "primary group," and they may well be our most reliable source of information on how some people succeed in remaining human through changes which overwhelm other people.

• *Group Support*

If we applied what we know about how people relate in small primary groups we would not have to move people back to rural villages or break up big corporations or eliminate half the people in the United States in order to preserve human scale. As a modest starter, we might pay a little more official attention to the small groups which spring up spontaneously inside of big organizations now. Most work is actually done in small groups.

For many big-company specialists such as public relations advisors or patent lawyers, the problem is the other way around. They often suffer because they have no work group. Well-managed big corporations try to help them by encouraging them to maintain membership in professional associations, and they may sometimes create associations for them by retaining outside legal and public relations consultants.

Recognition of the problem instantly suggests solutions. Individuals are not stuck for life with the "families" in which they find themselves. They can move to other groups or create entirely new kinds of groups to meet their needs. A densely populated, highly-specialized society provides opportunities for common ground on a wide variety of bases impossible in the rural societies it is now fashionable to admire.

Take, for instance, the kind of social support offered to women in childbirth. In farm communities, women could count on the support of their neighbors when their babies were born. These were women they had known all their lives, and at the birth of whose babies they themselves might assist. A city woman whose baby is born in a hospital gets support from a group of an entirely different kind. She becomes fast, if temporary friends with the other women in the maternity ward who have just gone through the same experience. This relationship may compensate in immediate relevance and sharing for the historic security of the neighborhood group. If administrators recognized the importance of the maternity-ward group, they could rearrange beds and schedules to make it easier for the women to communicate. Hospital friendships may last only as long as the common experience, but they may be more supportive than visits from healthy kinfolk, however solicitous.

Institutions can be designed for the varying needs of different kinds of people to be apart and together for various purposes. As I write this, I look over my typewriter into an uninhabited pine forest in New Hampshire. But when the dinner bell of the MacDowell Colony sounds, I will join a dozen workers—writers, artists, composers—who have become a temporary primary group supporting each other in the lonely business of their respective crafts. When Edward Alexander MacDowell composed his music in these woods before World War I, so-called "creative" people had more trouble finding sympathetic emotional support than they now do. The colony his wife founded is an example of the kind of social invention by which human beings can save themselves from the loneliness associated with city life.

Small colleague-groups are essential to the arts and the sciences. Simon Kuznets, the national-income economist, once suggested that big countries had an advantage over small ones because they were more apt to produce geniuses. But geniuses do not appear like seven-foot basketball players, strictly on the numbers. Derek J. de Solla Price, the historian of science, has counted the really eminent men of science at different periods of history and discovered that scientists do not increase directly with the population but by compound interest as the number of encounters between people do.

Creative achievement depends dramatically on association with others who can support and stimulate new ideas. The Greek playwrights and philosophers were close enough in time and space for first-hand contact. So were the great French dramatists and philosophers gathered by Louis XIV at the Court of Versailles. So were the great German musicians beginning with Bach. And so, more recently, were the European scientists Fermi, Einstein, Planck, and Bohr, whose intellectual community led to a radically new view of the physical universe with practical consequences as momentous as the atom bomb and nuclear power. De Solla Price discerns "invisible colleges" of scientists in the same field who keep in touch with each others' work. Margaret Mead has analyzed the structure of "cluster groups" of intellectual workers who reinforce and stimulate each other, and she has suggested that administrators of universities and foundations could take practical steps to preserve and encourage them.

• Breaking Up the Behemoths

University administrators are beginning to decentralize activity so that meaningful small groups can form. The great state university systems are now so huge and the disciplines so ramified, that problem-oriented new groupings with names such as "Center" or "Institute" are springing up to assemble specialists in different fields who can, as the jargon puts it, "cross-fertilize" each other. In higher education, some of the most exciting educational experiments of the

1970s will be the formation of small liberal-arts colleges of different sizes and types so that college students will be able to choose from colleges with big campuses, small campuses, or cluster campuses, like those at Pomona, or pursue independent study in formally organized colleges which have no campus at all. If only because these organizations are flexible, they should provide havens for the development of informal, primary interest groups of the kind which Margaret Mead says foster genius.

Industrial operations can be restructured to respect the social needs of the work force. One way is to decentralize authority so that the primary working group feels it controls its own "show." Autonomy that builds group solidarity is not impossible even when sophisticated technology centralizes decisions formerly made by the men on the ground. Like the automobile which moves people away from their primary groups, technological advances may break up small work groups which have been the basis of the morale of a work force. Management consultants are beginning to pay much closer attention to this danger. At Arthur D. Little, Inc., for instance, a sociologist formerly with the manpower staff of the Navy has studied a computer-directed continuous flow process for making steel to see how the work group can be held together.

In addition to decentralizing decision-making some industry is decentralizing geographically. Although the population was more concentrated in metropolitan areas in 1970 than in 1960, the *increase* in concentration was lower in the 1960s than it was in the 1950s. This largely reflects the growth of work that can be done anywhere, a growth which computerization could greatly accelerate during the 1970s.

IBM, the perpetrator of the computer, is a pacesetter in the decentralization that computer operations permit. IBM is sensitive to the problem of groupings and some of its specialists point out that computers can free industry from geographical constrictions so that work can be done wherever people want to live.

• *Designs for People*

The technology exists to organize work on a human scale. What is needed is the imagination to see the potential and the will to consider the satisfaction of workers with their work as respectfully as we have hitherto had to consider their productivity.

Architects are beginning to study small groups so that they can design buildings around them. This is the message of Constantinos A. Doxiadis, the Greek student of "settlements" who has clients all over the world. Many planners are paying more attention to traffic patterns that cut people off from each other, as roadways cut children from their schools and playgrounds, or women from grocery stores they reach on foot. They are beginning to design residence units in clusters around courtyards so that people have informal access to each other. They are using the artist's bag of tricks to create the illusion of intimacy, such as color coding a long office or hotel into sections for easier recognition. Technology provides new ways to divide space to the needs of a particular group at a particular time. Holographic devices can project beams of light to look like walls and high-frequency sound waves can be used with them to shut out sound.

Orthodox sociologists may object that a primary group can't be formed and broken as quickly as some of these solutions require. Navy manpower studies have found that a service unit has to live and work together for six months before it develops real group spirit. Geographic proximity and generalized relationships across the board on a day-to-day basis are part of the orthodox definition of a primary group. Opinion is divided as to whether you can belong to two separate ones at the same time. Yet some people can and do learn to make and break intimacies which support them at various stages of their lives. People who are well integrated into one neighborhood are more apt to make friends quickly in a new one. Skill in interpersonal relations is learned. It may even be culturally transmitted as a specific value.

The spectacle of American mobility is appalling to the Japanese because in Japan white collar and professional workers stay with one firm all of their lives. When I visited Nakane Chie, the Professor of Anthropology at Tokyo University who has been called the "Margaret Mead of Japan," she wanted to know how it was that Americans could stand moving from one job to another and one part of the country to another.

I'm not sure what the answer is, but I told her that it must have something to do with the way we bring up children. We want them to do well in their studies, as the Japanese do, of course. But we put much more emphasis on how well the children get along "with the other kids at school," and we support organizations such as Little League Baseball and the Boy Scouts because they provide situations which give children practice in "getting along."

Living in groups can be learned. Making and breaking groups can be learned. The future belongs to those who can find emotional support by using the potential of a rich, urban society to form associations that satisfy the "territorial" and social needs they may have inherited from our animal past.

Chapter XIV

How To Think New

We are now at one of those uncomfortable periods of history when patching up the old systems won't stop the breakdowns. Instead of trying to coax more capacity out of the old pipes and wires, we've got to throw them out and make new ones. Instead of overworking the existing doctors and librarians, we've got to find better ways to deliver the new volume of health care and information.

Bigger-capacity pipes and wires and more doctors and librarians won't do. We're at the point of growth where increases in traffic mean that we have to think big and we have to think new. We need entirely new systems.

A system is any set of things, people or concepts arranged to do a specific thing such as teach children, cure patients, govern cities, settle disputes, or distribute groceries, messages, or electric power. By definition, a system is designed with some level of traffic in mind.

Up to a certain level of traffic, an overloaded system can simply be built bigger.

If you want to sell more grocery items in a supermarket, you can extend the aisles and build the building bigger. If you want to put more shoppers through it, you have to build the parking lot bigger. But there comes a time when the aisles inside and the lot outside are so big that shoppers who need only a few items find that it is not worthwhile to park or walk the distances required. The supermarket loses business, and the bigger it gets, the more business it loses. Soon, someone will build another supermarket and the growth process will be repeated. But eventually all the existing supermarkets will become too unwieldy, and there will be no room for new ones. Groceries will have to be distributed in a radically new way. New systems are already being projected. In some, shoppers will visit a show room where a home economist will supply information on food items and the shopper will make a grocery list which the store will fill and deliver from a warehouse. In other systems, the shopper will choose from items displayed by cable television on her home screen.

● *New Systems for Old*

This may sound visionary, but we have had to throw out old systems and build radically new ones many times before. Only the oldest Americans now alive remember the days, before World War I, when lower Manhattan was a thicket of poles and wires. The financial district, with its narrow streets was a hazard for horse and man. The dirt, the smell, and the accidents were worse than they are today, to put the case gently. Every new phone that was connected, every new establishment that required gas or electric light added to the jumble. Only when it became literally impossible to add more was the money spent to put the wires underground.

The history of the international monetary system is another case in point. The current crisis is the latest in a series of breakdowns for a system that has repeatedly reached overload and repeatedly been redesigned. When international trade was small, debtor nations could pay their debts by shipping gold to their creditors abroad, but as trade increased, it became burdensome to ship the metal itself. Banking systems developed so that the gold could be earmarked for the account of the creditor nation no matter where it was. This worked well all through the nineteenth century and into the twentieth century as well.

Now the system of settling international balances is again overloaded. Since World War II, international trade has become so large that there is not enough metallic gold in existence to settle the balances in gold even in theory. Balances have been settled in dollars which until 1971 were redeemable in gold. In 1971 an imbalance in trade which made the United States a debtor overwhelmed this precarious system. Bankers and international traders are agreed that the new volume requires a new, higher-encounter system for settling these balances. As in all the other new systems required to handle higher volume, the restructure is viewed suspiciously by those whose power may be affected. In the case of the international monetary system, the United States may have the most to lose.

Actually, the problem itself has become too large for any one country to cope with. Electric power, air travel regulations, copyright, the assignment of broadcast bands, are a few of the other arrangements which can no longer be handled by national governments, but it will probably take a crisis or dramatic breakdown to internationalize any one of them because of the entrenched interests that now make the rules.

In order to design a new system, you have to stop

making shift with what you have and think big about what you have to do. Instead of complaining that you can't feed four billion people on this planet, you have to turn the problem around and say: We're soon going to have four billion people, what's the best way to feed them? There comes a time when patience and ingenuity are counterproductive. What's needed is imagination to think about new ways of handling large numbers of people, things, and thoughts.

There are no lack of suggestions. Power blackouts could be averted, the specialists say, if the power grid were nationwide and eventually planet-wide. What's needed is the global view.

The throng of men shouting at each other on the stock exchange must be replaced by computers which automatically weigh bids against askeds to register an instantaneous price, and ways must be found to keep the records of stock ownership in computers instead of entrusting them to pieces of paper that can be lost or stolen.

These and other new systems could handle the volume, but none of them is being seriously considered by those who have the power to install them. The reason is simple. All of them threaten the power or prestige of someone in a position to veto them.

• *The Power Structure*

A national or international power grid threatens the existing arrangement under which private power companies help each other out in power shortages. It is ignored because it leads logically to public power, a development bitterly fought by the electric power industry ever since the Tennessee Valley Authority of the New Deal demonstrated what public power could do.

A totally computerized stock exchange would eliminate

many of the specialists now employed in Wall Street and threaten the livelihood of stockbrokers.

The paper industry is threatened by proposals to protect the environment and conserve natural resources by simpler packaging, or putting a tax on disposable items such as paper milk containers to encourage reusable bottles.

Recycling wastepaper could solve the worst of the trash problem, but rather than absorb the cost of recycling, paper manufacturers support anti-litter campaigns that keep the problem out of sight at no expense to the industry.

Air and water could be restored if polluters were identified and required to pay for the damage they do, but this equitable move is not made because it threatens the existing distinction between public and private responsibility.

Cable television could provide a selective communication system that would rescue the captive audience from the blizzard of unwanted images which snows it, but advertisers and broadcasters who now control commercial television and sell access to that captive audience will not support anything that threatens their monopoly.

Public transportation or electric minicars could solve the traffic jams of our metropolitan areas and increase personal mobility, but automobile manufacturers and highway builders have the money and political influence to keep us convinced we prefer driving ourselves around in private cars.

Doctors focus public attention on the "doctor-patient relationship" as if this luxurious arrangement for maintaining their unchecked authority was the only way patients could be treated.

Teachers deprecate computer-assisted instruction, informal educational methods, and correspondence courses which could greatly extend the spread of knowledge by liberating learners from the classroom authority of the teacher.

And so it goes. No one who exercises power is willing to let go of it without protest. Politicians, diplomats, scientists, lawyers, professors, generals, psychiatrists, policemen defend their authority in much the same way. All of them are convinced that their power is essential to the survival of civilization.

• *The American Way*

An even more formidable obstacle to the new, higher-capacity systems is the peculiar culture of America. It is hard to imagine *any* system for handling more people, things, or ideas that would not collide with one or more of the principles we cherish as "the American way." Our establishment is, after all, descended from pioneers who exploited one farm after another for quick gains and solved social and political problems by moving away from them.

We do not like to be fenced in. Our fundamental law promises each and every one of us an "inalienable right" to "life, liberty, and the pursuit of happiness." We believe that every man is or ought to be the sole master of his fate. He ought to better himself, rise as high as he can (while never forgetting, of course, that he is just as good as the next man, but no better).

Deep down in our bones, we don't think a city is a fit place to live. A man ought to have his own house and lot, and his home should be his castle. A man has a right to do whatever he pleases with his own property. That government is best which governs least. These are the pieties of our culture.

It is not impossible to think of ways of handling more

people, things, and encounters, but they don't sound "practical." What we really mean is that they violate some "truths" we hold to be self-evident.

Logical solutions are rejected as "unthinkable."

Why? Plans for higher-encounter systems founder on three "unthinkables":

1. They involve restriction of some private right regarded as inalienable, such as the right to drive your own car or dispose of your property as you see fit.

2. They involve making the rich pay for the poor by having the government provide many services that are now private enterprises. This is the real objection to all the reforms that are dismissed as fine in theory but too costly to be practical. Among them are plausible suggestions that mass transportation in cities is of benefit to the whole community and so should be totally tax supported and free to the riders, and that health, education, and welfare services are so important to the whole society that they must all be offered to those who need them at public expense.

3. They involve public control of decisions now wielded by private and often secret cliques. Publicly supported health care systems and open admissions for higher education are objectionable not only for their costs, but also because they threaten the privileges of doctors and college faculties.

In order to cope with an abundance of people, things, and ideas, we are all of us going to have to learn to be more precise in defining goals less urgent than physical survival and in discriminating between alternatives of equal urgency. We need practice in answering new questions:

What exactly is it that we want? Take "abolishing poverty." Do we want to increase the consumption of the lowest-income group of the population to the level of the highest-income group? Or do we merely want to narrow the gap in consumption between the highest and the lowest? And what is consumption? Food only, or food and square-footage of housing space?

It is tempting to roar, "Everyone knows what poverty is. Stop nit-picking and start doing something about it!" But do *what?* Now that the poor are a minority of the population it becomes practical to inquire why some people are poor, but the reasons are not clear enough to frame a practical program for abolishing poverty.

We lack even the yardsticks to think constructively about poverty. We'll have to find a better measure of economic achievement than the GNP, or at least others to consider with it. Statistical technicians have all sorts of suggestions for companion yardsticks. Social scientists are designing "social indicators" that will measure changes in sensitive indexes of well-being such as infant mortality, or social goals that seem desirable, such as a higher rate of black employment. At the National Bureau of Economic Research, statisticians are trying to measure "dis-products" such as noise and nuisance.

Is it worth it? We know better how to put up with hardship than to choose among luxuries. If jobs are scarce, the benefit of the one you have is worth what it costs you in freedom, self-expression, or even self-respect. You don't have to think about keeping it. Comes along another job—or two or three alternatives—and you have to think hard about what it is you want in addition to a paycheck. And the more choices confronting you, the less attention each is worth. For instance, it is probably not worth the time it takes to choose among all the differing models of similar automobiles and breakfast foods offered to consumers. By contrast, many of the underpublicized alternatives among which we must choose are of critical importance.

Although most power-industry spokesmen insist that all systems can be made reasonably compatible with environmental interests, the more thoughtful of the executives admit that the public is going to have to make hard choices. "Should every business be weighed by whether it can restore fresh air and water and livable earth as fast as it destroys them?" asks Donald C. Cook, president of American Electric Power, Inc., a company serving the Midwest and near South. "Would you throw on the scales the social value of the product—as, for instance, medical supplies?" In March 1970, hard-pressed Con Edison took a full page ad in *The New York Times* to plead for a broader view of the environmental dilemma. "Can we allow unlimited use of automobiles with unlimited horsepower? Non-returnable bottles and cans? Unessential paper and plastic wrappings for groceries and other articles?"

Trade-offs will have to be made, but we have yet to develop the governmental system for making them. None of the regulatory agencies in a position to veto new power plants is charged with the responsibility for balancing environmental and esthetic considerations against need, reliability, and relation to other new power projects, and costs.

Conservative economists like Milton Friedman, a frequent Nixon adviser, suggest that the poor, if they were given a say, might prefer cheaper cars to cleaner air. Reducing smoke pollution from factory chimneys will raise the price of chemicals and paper, and so in turn the price of food as it is presently preserved and packaged. Whole-grained flour grown without chemical fertilizer and distributed without polluting packaging in cracker barrels for baking at home might be healthier and "better" than the soft breads in the supermarket, but it would be interesting to see how many soft-bread customers could be induced to bake their own whole-wheat loaves by giving "good" bread equal advertising time and space. Bakery companies say that the public prefers soft bread and maybe they do.

Politicians are not eager to raise such issues. Identifying all the social and environmental factors will open a Pandora's box of conflicting interests that will be harder to reconcile than those now coming to the surface. The protest movements mounted by the blacks, the poor, the young, and women have given us a taste of what full political consciousness can mean. When a new highway was planned to relieve Washington's evening rush hour, black activists protested that "white men were building highways through black men's bedrooms" in order to get home faster.

Once you start classifying people by their interests, it is easy to see how supposedly neutral practices can discriminate. When young people become conscious of themselves as a separate group, they may cite unemployment figures by age to show that unemployment is not only higher for teen-agers, but rising faster than for older workers. And only since women's liberation has it become apparent that women are discouraged from applying for a job if it is listed under "Help Wanted, Male."

Identifying and charging polluters will create instant-pressure groups which might make the country really ungovernable on the basis of its existing political institutions. Fishermen who want clean rivers would battle authors who want cheap paper, which is obtainable only if paper mills are permitted to continue to dump their wastes in rivers. Householders who have invested in electric heat would fight conservationists blocking a badly needed new nuclear power plant.

Living with conflicts like these is going to require

"willingness on the part of all to settle for less than everything they want," according to social scientist Howard S. Becker of Northwestern University. In his belief, this "culture of civility" is the political style of San Francisco and the reason why this city is everybody's favorite.

Many people will have to make unaccustomed choices, and choosing is hard work. Until recently, only those few who had actually enjoyed the right to "life, liberty and the pursuit of happiness" realized that these rights are not absolute. Now that a substantial sector of the population is demanding them, it is possible to see that there are limits on how much of each everyone can have at once.

• A New Bill of Rights

Some rights now regarded as absolute will have to go. Among them might be:

1. *The absolute right to life.* As population mounts, it may not be possible for every woman to have as many children as she wishes, or for every fetus conceived to be born. There are many observers who now believe that the unrestricted right to bear children may expose the planet to intolerable risks of overpopulation.

Dubious, also, is the absolute right to live as long as medical technology can keep you breathing. The right to life could be absolute when medicine was ineffective. Prohibitively expensive methods of prolonging life now exist, but they cannot physically be offered to all. Eventually, medical resources will have to be deployed on a cost-benefit basis. A model might be the battlefield principle of "triage," under which limited medical resources are deployed in war. The wounded are classified into three groups: those who will get well or who will die anyway are treated only after all of those who could be saved by medical attention.

262

2. *The right to consume as much as you can buy.* It is obvious that you no longer have the right to throw your gum wrappers in the gutter, burn soft coal in New York City, water your lawn in a drought, or kill ostriches to wear their feathers in your hat, but we may soon have to ration such intrinsically limited commodities as apartment space in Manhattan.

3. *The right to build your house to your pleasure.* The more people there are, the more rules there will have to be to insure that one house does not obstruct the view or otherwise interfere with its neighbors. There will also have to be laws protecting natural resources and wildlife wherever they may occur.

4. *The right to own a gun.* There will be a growing list of products prohibited to private ownership. The private production of commercial goods and services will inevitably be restricted by the expansion of publicly controlled activities.

5. *The right to privacy.* Population density and particularly the flow of information may make it impossible to catch airplane highjackers, credit-card embezzlers, or bomb plotters without violating rules of privacy established in a simpler technology. The rising potential for crime in the rising information-flow will require a new trade-off between the power of the police and the presumption of innocence. Criminals have never in the past been in a position to do as much damage.

6. *The right of access to all public places.* Traffic rules have prohibited parking on public streets and severely limited where you may go with your car, or, for that matter, on foot. Museums, the galleries of Congress, hospital waiting-rooms, and courtrooms cannot accommodate all the people who may wish to exercise their "right" to visit them, and safety may require that this right be rationed. In future, the

terms of access to various places will have to be defined and articulated more explicitly than at present.

Some rights won't be practical in the abundant world of the future, but others will take their place. By the year 2000 we may be able to insure everyone on earth some privileges now available only to a few.

A new Bill of Rights might include:

1. *The right to food, clothing, shelter, medical care and physical subsistence regardless of contribution for all those legally born into the world.* A minimum income is now practical because the poor in the United States are a smaller proportion of the total population than they ever have been. It is economic because a minimum income allowance may be cheaper than existing welfare provisions.

2. *The right to choose the contribution you are willing to make.* This will become important when everyone has a right to subsistence whether he chooses to work or not. The ground of conscientious objection is being expanded: you can now refuse to serve in a war you personally regard as immoral. The minimum income to which all have a right can be set low enough to motivate substantial numbers of people to do work they don't like, but wages may no longer channel workers to work as effectively as in the past. The concept of conscientious objection to civilian work is bound to emerge, and with it the right to turn down a morally repugnant job.

3. *The right to pay attention only to messages of your own choosing.* Freedom of the ears is now a more important civil right than freedom of speech, but it can't be an absolute right. Just as you cannot be allowed to cry "fire!" in a crowded theater, so you can never have the absolute right to ignore a red light when you are driving. It is clear, of course, that you have the right to tune out the President of

the United States when he preempts your favorite program, but then you should have the reciprocal right of access to all the programs which could be made available to you. The right of access to information and the right to put information on the publicly available networks will be clarified and articulated in the coming battle for cable television.

4. *The right to a private sex life of one's own choosing.* No one seriously now maintains that you have no right to sex unless you are willing to get married and rear children, but sex is far from free. Divorce courts, welfare authorities, credit investigators, character witnesses, prospective employers, and even the neighbors pry into the bedroom behavior of other people and penalize them if it is irregular. Married women are still deprived of public identity as individuals, sexual behavior is still prescribed from the outside by law, custom, and social coercion, and sexual partners are still presumed to have property rights in each other's affections.

5. *The right to choose and change a style of living.* The logic of abundance, particularly abundant information, requires that individuals choose whether they want to live alone, with partners of the same or opposite sex, or in permanent or temporary groups. And because individuals will be expected to grow, no one else may logically have the right to prevent a person from changing his life style or his living companions. The right to seek new living arrangements will become as absolute as the right to change jobs.

These are some of the new concepts that could accommodate more people, things, and ideas. They sound far out. They sound as if they required basic changes in human nature. But they are not at all impossible. "Human nature" is not immutable. It has changed before. A good case can be made for the optimistic view that human nature can change to save itself in the future as well.

● *The Model of Space*

The space program is often deplored as the obstacle to funding the bigger systems required here below on earth. Money spent on space, say the critics, would clean up Lake Erie.

The charge is sheer polemic. If the space program were abandoned the money would not be spent cleaning up Lake Erie because lack of money is not the reason why we won't clean up Lake Erie. The reason we don't do it is politics. Millions of people are dumping things into Lake Erie. Life is going to be more expensive and/or more uncomfortable for all of them in some respect if they are forced to stop. People identify with the interest they have in dumping, not with the vague, general interest they have in clean water.

By comparison, the moon is clean as a whistle. It is a fairer field for experiment than the American continent when Columbus discovered it. There were Indians in the New World, but there is nobody on the moon. Nobody has it staked out. No vested interests prevent the engineers from trying new things or things that will work.

There's nobody on the moon, but by a miracle of luck, it isn't dull. On the contrary, it inspires the kind of urgency that moves many people to climb mountains. The moon is the long-awaited "moral equivalent of war." Like war, it compels cooperation toward a simple, clear-cut goal, and like victory in a war, the goal is unmistakable and dramatic. You either get there on the appointed day, or you do not. No environmental cleanup can possibly compete in drama with the moonwalk.

Far from "wasting" money that should be spent on other things, the space program has been a model of everything we will have to do to build the new, higher-capacity systems we will need to take care of more people, things, and data here below on earth.

The purely technological spin-offs of the space program have been exaggerated to justify space budgets. If history is any guide, these outcomes will take longer, but will go farther than the most ebullient forecasters now imagine. In order to get a man to the moon, the engineers have had to invent new ways to miniaturize, encapsulate, and recycle—operations obviously useful in increasing the capacity of any system.

To the space program we owe our weather and communications satellites. "Via satellite" is a familiar line on over-the-ocean television scenes but these programs are only five percent of the communication handled by the eight satellites always in orbit 22,300 miles aloft. The rest is private voice, picture, or computer data handled just as if by wire.

Weather satellites detect and follow hurricanes with a speed and precision never possible in the past. Hurricane Beulah in 1967 and Hurricane Carla in 1961 proved their value. Satellites warned of both in time to evacuate some 350,000 people from the target areas on the Gulf Coast. While damage ran into many millions, only 54 persons died in Beulah and even fewer in Carla. These satellites also find fish and water supplies.

Some 2500 spin-off benefits from the space program have been listed. These include materials stronger and lighter than ever before, tiny fuel cells and batteries, tiny cameras, dehydrated food, freeze-dried coffee, a sight switch that can be controlled by eye movement, and a great array of tiny instruments that can enable a single doctor or nurse to monitor the heart beat and other body functions of many seriously ill patients.

The Crowding Syndrome

Putting a man in a capsule has forced us to think of human metabolism and communication in terms of wires, tubes, and pipe applied directly to the body instead of to a room that simulates the natural environment. The concept can be as liberating as the notion that an airplane does not have to fly like a bird. Future hospital beds could be capsules which monitored and cared for patients automatically, with savings in space and nursing time. Wires and pipes hooked directly to the body's systems extend the range of personal services. A language student can go into a cubicle whenever he feels like practicing and put on earphones that connect him with a faraway teacher to the exclusion of distractions physically present. Wires recording heartbeat, temperature, and other diagnostic data can link patients with medical specialists in another city.

The recycling demonstration may be the most influential lesson of space. To get a man on the moon, engineers had to find ways to recycle human wastes into potable water and breathable air. Even if none of the technology required for the feat was applicable to any earthly situation, there is hardly a human being alive today who does not know that recycling is possible. The analogy for earthly pollution is inescapable. If wastes can be recycled for one man in a space capsule, then why not the wastes polluting the air, water, and land of spaceship earth?

Putting a man on the moon required mobilizing an unprecedented number of things and data to a very specific end. Ways had to be found for large numbers of people to interact more intimately than ever before. More important than the gadgetry, or the consumer products such as the "Space Sticks" we put in our children's lunch boxes, is the workout in new man-machine relations and new man-man relations. Thanks to television, everyone got a chance to see

268

the rows of alert men, each watching his own console, who were working together like cogs in a mammoth brain.

The space program could have been planned only by the systems approach. It developed a corps of systems engineers who in 1972 were being turned loose by cutbacks in the space program to bring their skills to other problems. It also gave thousands of specialists practice in a new kind of work organization, the only kind, as a matter of fact, that could possibly mobilize as much specialized skill on a sharply defined goal. That organization is the small, leaderless, task force of specialists assembled to solve a specific problem.

A task force is democratic and consensual rather than authoritarian. Each member of the small force has an area of knowledge in which his judgment is undisputed. In order to solve the problem, the members of the task force have to do more talking with each other than an ordinary committee or corps of specialists reporting to a coordinator. Encouraged originally because it improved morale, the task force turned out to be so productive that crash programs in government, industry, and research, are now routinely broken down into small bits that can be assigned to a task force small enough for general participation.

Buzz sessions, discussion groups, training groups, seminars, interdisciplinary and joint committees involving people of different statuses, have become popular ways of improving decisions by increasing the interaction between individuals who would be "lost in the shuffle" of a big, impersonal, machine-like organization. The small, democratic group has become the unit of choice for education, research, and therapy.

Astronauts undoubtedly have as much to do as air controllers, and they have to do it under more severe constraints than the pilots, but so far they have come through space flights without damage to their health.

The comparison between controllers and astronauts isn't entirely fair, but there are interesting trade-offs. The consequences of error are dire for both, but the controllers endanger others, the astronauts themselves. Astronauts aren't subjected to the grind of years of stress on end, but the dangers they face are less well known.

The astronauts have several important advantages. They are more rigidly selected and trained. Their occupational status is higher. They are buoyed up by the thrill of exploring the unknown. But what the astronauts themselves credit for their morale, and with a fervency that suggests more than public relations piety, is the teamwork of the whole operation, the backup they get from ground support, and the concern and admiration of everyone on earth. If prestige and "good relations with co-workers" fight stress, then it is hard to imagine any men who have enjoyed more of these powerful protections.

There may not be much of anything for a man to do when he gets to the moon, but a great many people had to learn to think new to do it. Space has pioneered mechanical, social, and emotional ways of getting more information mobilized on a single objective. It has expanded the human information processing capacity. If wealth depends on the capacity to process information, the space program may well have paid for itself.

Chapter XV

The Case
for Optimism

If a visitor from outer space was taken on a global tour of our planet and was told there had been a world war 25 years ago, he might easily conclude the Japanese had won. The financial district of Tokyo is spanking new. The people are prosperous and cheerful. The Japanese Gross National Product is rising faster than ours, or for that matter, than that of our Allies in the war, the now-shabby British.

Japan—and Germany—have recovered so phenomenally partly because of our financial aid, but also because our bombs made rebuilding necessary. There are moments when it is tempting to wonder whether blacks in Harlem— or at least those who survived—wouldn't be better off if the place was fire-bombed to the ground by an enemy as generous with rehabilitation funds as we were after World War II. In 1972 our old enemies have the new systems, while we struggle along under the handicaps of the old.

Unconditional surrender liberated the Japanese from a

burden greater than the cost of maintaining a defense establishment. It liberated them from a system which could never have developed mass consumption. They lost everything—their buildings, their military ambitions, their pride, and the limitations imposed by these outgrown mental and physical furnishings. People do not willingly relinquish their limitations. On the contrary, they shed them only when forced—and most often at the point of a gun.

The upsetting record of history is that nations have been forced into progress. While individual leaders are easily deposed, the power structure which they operate doesn't change unless it is violently overthrown by war or revolution. Even minor innovations which shift the locus of power in a society are seldom adopted in peacetime. War has also been responsible for social and scientific changes.

The obscene truth is that the medical advances growing out of military medicine may well have saved more lives than have been lost on the battlefield. Most of the inventions, concepts, and amenities that make life really worthwhile were widely adopted only when someone discovered that they could solve a military problem. My husband and I once thought of doing a small book on the subject, but editors quite properly were horrified at the very idea. Still the evidence is clear. Here are just a few examples.

The ambulance was invented by Napoleon's Surgeon-General, Baron Dominique Jean Larrey, to bring the hospital to the battlefield. The horse-drawn vehicle of mercy has given way to the motorized version, and sometimes to the helicopter, and now ambulances of all kinds rush aid to the ill and injured around the world.

Practical blood transfusion and the idea of blood banks were born in World War I and popularized by World War II. Blood transfusions have saved millions of lives—and do so at the rate of half a million a year in the United States alone. Some babies are even transfused before they are born.

Plastic surgery techniques which were devised to reconstruct the war-maimed are now available to correct misfortunes like harelip, and tolerant surgeons will operate to remove the markings of age and even to improve upon nature as far as our faces, noses, and breasts are concerned. They learned their craft on the battlefield.

Penicillin was first observed by the late Sir Alexander Fleming in 1928. But there was not enough of this delicate wonder drug to treat patients until the pressures of World War II brought British-American cooperation and the outlay of millions of dollars. Spurred by the success of penicillin, the pharmaceutical industry found broader spectrum antibiotics effective against as many as a hundred diseases, for some of which there had been no previous remedy.

Our huge food-processing industry, with all of its advantages for the producer and consumer, can be traced to a prize of 12,000 francs offered by the embattled French government in 1795 for a new way to preserve food for its fighting men. Nicholas Appert, a Parisian candymaker, won it in 1809 with the idea of canning.

Radar was first developed in World War II for the detection of enemy aircraft and ships. It is now a routine tool for weather forecasting and navigation and a highly valuable safety device for the prevention of collisions in the air and on the water.

Out of World War II also came atomic power, the beginnings of the computer, advances in aptitude testing and training, the government corporation for the financing of war production, pay-as-you-go income taxes, and the wide use of Gross National Product as a statistical device.

But why do we have to wait for a shooting war? Why

can't we mobilize for something worthwhile, like wiping out poverty or cleaning up our polluted waters? The reproach is so familiar that the difference has to be clarified again.

In a conventional war, the objective is simple and concrete. The enemy is out there and he will get us if we don't get him, but poverty, or the scum on a lake are familiar and rather dull evils a lot of us have survived for a long time. Solving them would cost some people a great deal. The "Huns," the "Japs," or even Godless Communists are a clear and present danger, overriding individual conflicts of interest. A "war" against poverty, on the other hand, is socially divisive, and so is a campaign to clean up Lake Erie. In order to "win" these campaigns, some of us are going to have to give something up to others of us, and no one can clearly predict who will lose the most.

War unleashes human potential. Under the influence of a single, clear, urgent, and nationwide goal, individuals are lifted out of their apathy. People perform as well as they know how. They are freed to use everything they know, to think logically instead of mythically. Take, for instance, the mythic weakness and timidity of women. During wars, women discover that they can operate machinery and shoot guns. When peace returns, they are mythically incapacitated again.

Wars always redistribute power more widely. Woman suffrage in virtually every country dates from World War I or World War II. Deficit spending in the United States and Britain in wartime improved the share of the common people at the expense of the rich. The mechanics of raising, training, feeding, and caring for armies have upgraded the underprivileged. After World War I, the Veterans Administration pioneered direct medical service to veterans. After World War II, the G.I. Bill of Rights offered higher education to all veterans and was considered one of the most progressive and beneficial laws ever enacted by any nation.

● Breakdown and Restructure

Wars are not the only disasters that have precipitated breakdowns, leading to constructive restructures. An instructive case is the potato famine in Ireland, one of the great natural catastrophes of all time.

The facts are undisputed. The Irish multiplied extravagantly after the potato was introduced from the New World to an all-time peak population of more than eight million in 1841. Four years later, the potato blight struck. Millions starved to death who could have been saved. The English could have saved the Irish, but relief measures dissolved in politics and red tape.

Still, Ireland survived, and so did the Irish. They responded to the catastrophe in two constructive ways. The first thing they did was to turn their heads around on having babies. In the absence of contraceptive devices of any kind, or even any rationale for birth control, the Irish cut their birth rate from one of the highest in the world to one of the lowest. The result is that Ireland has fewer people in 1971 than it had 130 years earlier. Heaven only knows how they do it, but the rumor is that they are good Catholics and simply abstain from the kind of sex that results in pregnancy.

The more celebrated response was emigration. Those who could manage it crammed themselves into immigrant ships and went to the United States. Instead of going into farming—the scene of the Irish disaster—they stayed in the cities, where they did not reproduce themselves at the high rate they attained when they were living on potatoes. On

275

the contrary, their birth rate in America has been lower than that of Americans in general.

The story of the Irish disaster sounds surprisingly similar to the reports of what happened in 1970 when a half million Pakistanis died in a tidal wave that inundated the rich delta of the Ganges River. Indian authorities hesitated to permit relief supplies to pass from West Pakistan across their country to the stricken East Pakistanis. Medical expeditions from Europe found little work when they finally got to the scene, because the only survivors were adults in good enough health to find shelter when the waters rose.

Will the flood victims of Bangladesh do as well as the Irish? Probably not. If history repeats itself in the Ganges Valley, as it has a way of doing, the dead will soon be replaced by farmers pushing into the fertile delta areas, there to await another decimating flood.

The Indians have telephones. Their governing bureaucracy knows all the organizational techniques for disaster relief that the world has developed. But they aren't moved to use what they know in the way that Americans will act, if and when the San Andreas fault adjusts itself, as the geologists warn it will, and causes a big earthquake that will displace millions of Californians from their homes.

Why? The answer lies deep in the difference between the two cultures, and no one has a convincing explanation. But this much seems clear: in the West we are able to deal constructively with change because of whatever it is in Western culture that made it possible for us to industrialize. Unfashionable as it is to say so out loud, the fact is that the Africans and the Asians and the Indians, East and West, did not invent the scientific method and they did not apply it to solving the practical problems of everyday life. The technology that we developed is less of a threat to us than it is to them because it was our own handiwork. We have always found it easier to see alternative ways of doing things. Our systems constrain us but not absolutely. We don't always think big enough, but we do see glimmers of light around the blinkers.

In India, it is overload, breakdown, reload, and so back to the beginning again. East Indian history takes the circular path that figures in some oriental cosmologies. With us breakdown clears the ground for something new.

Overload. Breakdown. Restructure. We have made a habit of it. During most of history, populations have been self-limiting. Take a walled city. It could not grow bigger than the population that could be supported by food grown in the surrounding area. Waste disposal did not become a problem because disease promptly cut back the population to the number who could survive in a community which dumped its wastes in the streets. Sewage was recognized as a cause of disease long before the concept of public responsibility for sewage disposal, and there are many places in the world where private behavior has not changed. In 1854 when John Snow recognized the cholera deaths attributable to the Broad Street pump in London, he started people thinking of new ways to distribute water and dispose of sewage, so that many more people could live close together in safety. The new systems inside the city, and new governmental and agricultural systems outside enabled cities to grow out of their walls and expand.

The West has always responded constructively to the overload of numbers. Steam power concentrated the population of England in cities and created the first modern urban crisis. The pressure of the old slums stimulated the development of railroads and trolley lines that permitted workers to live at a distance from their work. Electric power that can be transmitted long distances cheaply made it possible to move some operations out of town. The dial telephone overcame the limitations imposed by manual exchanges. Computers rescued the Social Security system from the limitations imposed by paper handling. Something new has always come along to keep a small breakdown from becoming a large catastrophe.

The biggest and best studied general breakdown is the breakdown of the Roman Empire. It is instructive for us because it eventually led to restructures of many political, economic, and intellectual systems which persist in the West today. Scholars don't agree about what caused the breakdown, but they do know that the existing arrangements became incapable of supporting a growing population. As the cities grew they needed more food, but slave labor and heavy taxation on farm produce made agriculture unpopular. Laws were passed to keep people tilling the soil, but to no avail. The Romans did not bring new land under cultivation to feed more people. On the contrary, land may have actually gone out of cultivation, and some scholars argue that oppressive taxes made the farmers so poor that they simply could not reproduce themselves. In any event, more and more people became dependent for their food on relatively fewer and fewer until the top-heavy economy broke into simpler, local subsistence economies of the Middle Ages.

Could anything have saved the Roman Empire as an economic and political unit? Agriculture based on money for wages and crops might have increased the food supply by unleashing the ingenuity and incentive of farmers. The income tax might have helped by shifting the burden of government off the backs of the poorest. Neither remedy was within the conceptual grasp of the intellectuals of antiquity. Instead of thinking big, the old Romans bewailed the decline of the old agrarian virtues in phrases still used by modern conservatives.

The Case for Optimism

Breakdown is not the only avenue for the development of new concepts. When the world was younger, there were more opportunities to build without running up against already existing systems and interests.

Farming for cash instead of by custom started the United States on the road to wealth. It was possible only because no one owned the land already, just as space is an opportunity for new concepts because there's no one out there.

By World War I, American farmers had raised production enough to feed the Allies, but when the war was over there were too many farmers raising too much. The system of cash-crop agriculture was overloaded. Conservatives tried to save it by Government subsidies to keep the price of crops above their market value.

In the end the farmers were not saved by laws or pegged-crop prices. They saved themselves by going to town, where they helped build an industrial economy that could support bigger numbers than agriculture alone could ever have maintained.

Now it's the industrial economy itself that is overloaded with more workers than it can gainfully employ. The excess workers congregate in the center of big cities, a "hard-core unemployed." Like the Roman Senators of old, contemporary conservatives deplore the decline of morality, some prescribe larges doses of law and order, and suggest cutting down on the numbers of "excess people." Others, no less conservative, blame poor housing, and propose rebuilding the ghettoes.

Jay Forrester, Professor of Management at M.I.T., points out that housing projects in the ghetto make the ghetto bigger and more intractable by attracting the poor to live where there are no jobs, instead of pushing them out to find new work elsewhere. Like the bread and circuses of the last days of ancient Rome, palliatives may simply make an unbalanced system not only worse, but harder to abandon.

Forrester's example is intended to sell sophisticated long range planning by the systems approach, but to conservatives it is an argument for doing nothing. If what Forrester says is true, ghetto dwellers are better off if they are driven out of their homes by the economic law of supply and demand for their labor. The reasoning fascinates conservatives, like Chicago economist Milton Friedman, but so many interests are involved that it is hard to stand by and let market forces disrupt thousands of lives. In the end, property-minded conservatives join with humanitarians in stopgaps intended to save the immediate situation, at least briefly.

Restructure might be cheaper and easier if the overloads were permitted to break the system down completely, before half measures allow the problems to grow to monstrous size. This is what happens in a war.

Apathy and "taxpayers revolts" may accomplish the same thing in peace time. Bond issue failures, for example, permit many overstrained public institutions to fall of their own weight, one at a time, instead of waiting for the worldwide apocalypse projected by those who worry about too many and too much.

• *The Art of Breaking Down*

Luckily, we are now rich enough to afford the risk of little breakdowns. The United States of the 1970s is less fragile, more flexible, and much more diverse than the Czarist regime of 1918, pre-Castro Cuba, or the France of Louis XVI, when they were on the brink of total breakdown. We already have so many alternate ways of doing things that we may be able to take our breakdowns one after another, or even concurrently, without tearing everything down at once. We may be able to mend our overloaded institutions the way engineers replace railroad bridges without delaying a single train.

Take New York City. The real phenomenon of New York City is not that everything in the city breaks down, but that nothing ever breaks down completely. New York survives catastrophes that bring smaller and simpler communities to their knees. It is like those Liberty ships that were unsinkable because they were built in watertight compartments, so that a direct hit couldn't flood the entire hold. In New York the subways may go out, but enough people struggle to work by bus, by taxi, by bicycle, private car, helicopter, train, and boat to keep the city working.

The garbage piles up, but we learn to package it in plastic bags and eventually the trucks come back and carry it away. The sewage goes down the drain pipes somehow even though the city engineers themselves are said not to know where all the pipes go. When the newspapers strike, readers discover the radio news and the neighborhood newspapers, and many of them discover that they've been clogging their attention with a lot of daily data they can do without. When the taxis strike, many people discover the subways and the buses.

New York City is complex as well as big. When the linotypers go out, the material can be printed by offset. There's always a store or a restaurant open when the one you depend on is closed, a typist you can summon by phone when the one you expected can't come. What most people remember about the blackout of 1965 was the magnificent and ingenious ways the unlighted city made shift. Equally encouraging, over the long run, has been the response. We haven't redesigned the power system so that it couldn't happen again, but we've already begun to think big about power. With a little bit of luck, we'll make it in time to avoid a bigger and more damaging breakdown. We're better off, not worse off, that it happened as early as it did.

Maybe we ought to let the City of Newark go bankrupt so that the Federal government would have to bail it out. Maybe it would hasten welfare reform to allow New York City to run out of money, just as the big postal strike of 1970 speeded reorganization of the postal system along lines that made it easier to adopt methods appropriate to contemporary mail volume. A real breakdown of the New York City subway system could be instructive. It would demonstrate to all the citizens just how much a subway system is worth and who profits by it. A fare high enough to make the subways pay for themselves would make it easy for everyone to see that mass transit benefits so many people that it probably ought to be financed directly by taxation rather than through the fare box.

Our locally responsible school system is made to order for instructive little breakdowns. Nothing convinces taxpayers to vote bond issues like a school shutdown that leaves youngsters roaming the streets for a few months. The way for bigger and broader-gauge education might be paved if some local school board went the whole way and actually declared its independence of state control, and faced the whole task of setting up its own rules and its own funding from scratch; or if groups of parents challenged the school law and established the right to rear their children without sending them to school.

We are learning the art of breakdown and restructure, the way athletes and ballet dancers learn the art of falling down in ways that make it easy to regain a new balance. We are really better at it than we give ourselves credit for, and much better at it than many other nations, more resilient even, perhaps, than the British who make a fetish out of their ability to "muddle through."

Some of the most constructive breakdowns are never recognized as such. One is the quiet abandonment of the notion that colleges have the responsibility of parents for the behavior of resident minors. The fact is, of course, that mass higher education could not function *in loco parentis* without unbearable regimentation.

Another is the speedy adoption of the notion that there ought to be an income floor under every American family regardless of whether anyone in the family can or will earn. In 1972 the controversy over welfare reform was not whether there ought to be a floor on income, but where the floor should be.

New systems sometimes generate a lot of talk, but often they are silent.

Take housing. It's obviously a disaster area of the economy. We need many times more new housing units than we can find credit to finance. Labor unions and local building ordinances block the technology which could build the housing that is needed at prices that the improperly housed can afford. But what is happening? Without much fanfare, we are rehousing ourselves in mobile homes that aren't subject to the crippling restrictions on conventional home building. No one is particularly proud of the proliferation of mobile-home communities. We snub them and even pretend they are not there. But the mobile-home system makes sense so it survives.

Take shopping. Conventional trips to the store are breaking down. Most affluent, active consumers don't have the time to "go shopping" and frequently there isn't a place for them to park. So what happens? Householders do more and more of their shopping from mail-order houses or by phone. Consumers, especially women, don't like to admit that they save time by ordering the children's clothes from Sears Roebuck instead of fighting the downtown traffic, but the trend shows up when you look at the retail sales figures broken down by type of outlet.

Or take a system as close as home, the family system that gives grandmother a "right" to live with her grown children. Having grandmother in the home is less comfortable than formerly because family doesn't mean as much. We now rely on outside associations for some of the companionship and emotional support we used to get at home. So grandmother goes to live in a retirement village where she makes new friends with people in her own circumstances.

• *Changing "Human Nature"*

Many well-informed people think we're going to have that big breakdown. They claim "human nature" can't change, or that enough human beings can't change fast and far enough to keep us afloat.

These are the constitutionally faint of heart. Many of them are the same people who in the years after Hiroshima were saying that national sovereignty was rooted in "human nature," so we couldn't give it up fast enough to learn to live on the planet with the atomic bomb. Back in the 1950s, even Margaret Mead, an observer who is perennially hopeful, thought the human race had a fifty-fifty chance of extinguishing itself.

We could have dropped the bomb as if it were a conventional weapon and wiped ourselves out, but policymakers everywhere were able to see that the winner of an atomic war would suffer as much as the loser, and no bomb was dropped in anger. In 1972 no one really worries about atomic holocaust, and those who still believe that military power is a practical instrument of national policy are everywhere on the defensive—even when they advocate using force short of atomic bombing.

The fact is that human nature is not unchangeable. We are changing it all the time. And while change is not comfortable for everyone, and exacts a high casualty rate of individual neurosis, it has not killed us off wholesale the way anthropologists say culture shock killed off fragile, simple primitive societies when their premises were shattered by missionaries. On the contrary, a surprising number of contemporary adults have learned to function successfully in ways quite different from those of their own parents.

One of our assets is the very communications speed-up that causes so much discomfort. More information is forcing people to think bigger, to take more people, things, and data into account, to challenge parochial, low-encounter ways. People who skipped the headlines about the Pakistani floods couldn't quite escape the pictures briefly flashed on the television screen, of the victims running after helicopters to catch food packages. The image wasn't as disturbing as scenes of the Vietnam front, in which the actor could have been a relative or friend, but it kept a global perspective in the viewer's mind.

Finally, we are approaching Thomas Jefferson's dream of an educated citizenry. Half our college-age young people are going to school, which means that they are getting practice in dealing with abstractions. Abstraction makes change easier, if it is not, in fact, essential to it. You have to be able to state what you believe before you can free yourself from it. That's why revolutions are so talky. Up to now most people have been prisoners of their upbringing. Their thinking was programmed almost as rigidly as the behavior of ants and bees. Now many more are equipped to change because they are being taught to speak for themselves.

We are developing enough tolerance for ambiguous

authority and conflicting, competing ways of doing things to provide growing space for the new systems before the old ones collapse with a resounding crash.

A significant minority—hopefully a critical mass—have learned the survival art of "turning their heads around."

The blackout of the Northeastern United States in 1965 came as a shock to young Americans who imagined that the establishment had everything under control. It dramatized the blind spots of technology limiting American prosperity. In this age of breakdowns that it inaugurated, it is easy to cry doom.

Now, in the 1970s, America and the planet as a whole seem to be living from crisis to crisis. Observers daily doubt that the human race or the United States can long survive. Yet even as we complain, we do survive, as New Yorkers survived the blackout—with a little bit of luck, and by the skin of our teeth, the way the human race has been doing now for the past million years.

Notes

Chapter I

Breakdown!

One affected enterprise that overcame the difficulties of the great blackout of November 9, 1965, was *The New York Times*. Its staff prepared copy by candlelight in its West 43rd Street building, trucked this under the Hudson River to New Jersey, and published a 10-page morning *Times* on the presses of the *Newark News*. The *Times* coverage of the blackout was published a few days later by the New American Library as a Signet Book, *The Night the Lights Went Out*. The Federal Power Commission report on the power failure was released December 6, 1965.

The overloads of garbage, air travel, phone service, schools, hospitals, and the stockmarket were well reported all through the last half of the 1960s and can be verified from *The New York Times* index, in the Chronology of the *World Almanac*, and *Time* Magazine feature stories, summarized in the magazine's annual index, which supplied many of the anecdotes of the impact of the overloads on individuals. Much of it is available from *The New York Times* in a convenient reprint of a series of articles entitled "The Changing City" appearing in June 1969. Reprints of excellent accounts of these overloads in *Time*, *Life*, *Fortune*, and *Business Week* are available through *Time* and *Business Week* index and reprint services.

Harder to find, but well worth reading are *New York* magazine reports, especially "Are We Ready for Jumbo?" by William E. Burrows, and "The Garbage Apocalypse," by Paul Wilkes, both of March 10, 1969, and "The Parking Hassle: A System to Beat the System" by Barry Tarshis, March 17, 1969. The rise in crime is documented in the Uniform Crime Reports issued by The Federal Bureau of Investigation every year, and its causes are explored in the Final Report of the National Commission on the Causes and Prevention of Violence, entitled "To Establish Justice, To Insure Domestic Tranquility," December 1969, and a June 1969 Report to the Commission entitled "Violence in America: Historical and Comparative Perspectives." Patrick Daniel Moynihan cited the tripling of the fire rate in New York City as an index of social disorganization in his famous memorandum to the President on the status of Negroes of March 1, 1970, which advised "benign neglect" of them.

The connection between the Mafia and the downfall of Hayden Stone was suggested in a *New York Times* article of August 1, 1969, "Heir to Genovese Held in Stock Theft." For an analysis of how it could happen, see "The Unbelievable Last Months of Hayden Stone" by C. J. Loomis in *Fortune*, January 1971.

Many public and private officials patiently explained specific overloads. In 1969, Floyd D. Hall, chairman of Eastern Airlines told me that of 9000 airports in the United States, only seven were overloaded. The trouble, he said, was that "everyone wanted to be in the same place at once." Dr. Ira L. Sommers, Director of Research Laboratories, National Canners Association in Washington told me about the problem of DDT in cannery wastes which formerly were fed to cattle.

The story about the rich man recruited to population

control because of his yacht problem comes from Frederick S. Jaffe of Planned Parenthood-World Population.

Chapter II

Too Many People

Basic data for world population comes from the United Nations Demographic Yearbook. Discussion of population problems of every kind can be found in the references cited in the bibliography, *A Sourcebook on Population*, of November, 1969, issued by the Population Reference Bureau, Inc., 1755 Massachusetts Avenue, N.W., Washington, D.C., 20036. The quickest way to find out about current issues is to get on their mailing list.

The ominous rise in population is not a new worry. For historical projections see the classic work, *Population*, by William Petersen, 2nd edition, New York: Macmillan Co., 1969.

Kingsley Davis, Professor of Sociology at the University of California at Berkeley summarizes the J-curve of rising population in an article in the *Annals of Political and Social Science*, of January 1945: "Viewed in long-run perspective, the growth of the earth's population has been like a long, thin powder fuse that burns slowly and haltingly until it finally reaches the charge and then explodes." Examples of what this can mean are assembled in Garrett Hardin's anthology, *Population, Evolution, and Birth Control, a Collage of Controversial Ideas*. W. H. Freeman and Co., San Francisco, 1964; Louise B. Young, ed., *Population in Perspective*, Oxford University Press, New York, 1968; and Paul R. Ehrlich, *The Population Bomb*, Ballantine Books, New York, 1968.

The Crowding Syndrome

Szent-Györgyi's prophecy of cannibalism was made in testimony before the Senate Government Operations subcommittee of 1966 headed by Senator Ernest Gruening of Alaska.

N. J. Berrill's warning that the total biomass possible is limited by the amount of phosphorus was reported by William Braden in *The Chicago Sun-Times* of November 19, 1967. The summary charge against overpopulation quoted from Lincoln and Alice Day was made by them before the Subcommittee on the Effects of Population Growth on Natural Resources of the House Committee on Government Operations, headed by Henry Reuss of Wisconsin, on September 15, 1969. The Reuss hearings are a mine of speculation and information.

The population of India started to soar in the 1920s, after World War I. Gunnar Myrdal summarizes the trend on page 1394 of Volume II of his three-volume monograph, *Asian Drama*, Pantheon, New York, 1968: "Through the 50 years 1871–1921, the total population increase amounted to no more than 20 percent, owing to the heavy toll of life taken by the famines in the 1870s and at the end of the century and by the influenza epidemic in 1918–1919. By contrast, in the thirty years from 1921 to 1951 the increase was no less than 43 percent. In this period there was no major demographic catastrophe. . . . In the following single decennium, from 1951 to 1961, the rate of growth was over 21 percent."

Kenneth Boulding's "utterly dismal theorem" is presented in his book, *The Image*, University of Michigan Press, Ann Arbor, 1956.

The official U.S. and U.N. policy statements are set forth in issues of the *Population Bulletin*, a monthly review of the Population Reference Bureau.

The debate between advocates of compulsory and voluntary population control is documented in the appendix to the Reuss Committee hearings. Planned Parenthood-World Population was split internally over the issue. Techniques for bringing down the birth rate are listed and evaluated in "Beyond Family Planning" by Bernard Berelson, president of the Population Council, 245 Park Avenue, New York, N.Y. 10017 and available from that organization.

Garrett Hardin issued his call for celebrating 1976 with a "pregnant pause" at a meeting of the John Muir Institute at Aspen in September 1969.

Science magazine editorials and articles did much to promote the case of the compulsory birth control party.

For involuntary birth control suggestions, see Melvin M. Ketchel, "Fertility Control Agents As A Possible Solution to the World Population Problem," *Perspectives in Biology and Medicine*, Vol. 11, No. 4, Summer 1968. Richard Schreiber told me about his contagious virus personally. Others with plans are Dr. Walter Howard, a biology professor at the University of California at Davis, and Dr. Donald Aitken, a professor of astrophysics at Stanford University.

Economists suggest economic incentives to smaller families; some of the most imaginative are those proposed by Joseph J. Spengler in "Population Problem: In Search of A Solution," *Science*, December 5, 1969. The sociologists, notably Judith Blake Davis, think in terms of changing the role of women along feminist lines.

The conflict of values on size is dramatic in comparing the various estimates of the ideal size of a city. Politicians and monumental architects like Le Corbusier want big cities. Cultural advantages require a city of 300,000 according to a World Health Organization study. Big cities are better for starting a new business, says Jane Jacobs. Several professional city planners and the designers of new towns favor 250,000 for efficient municipal services. Amenities—ease of living, light, air, space, quiet, and accessibility—seem to be most available in cities of 50,000.

The rationale for Sweden's pronatalist policy is set forth in Gunnar Myrdal's *Population: A Problem for Democracy,* Harvard University Press, Cambridge, 1940. It makes quaint reading now, when neither Myrdal nor anyone else seriously worries about what used to be called "race suicide."

A good account of population policies of the past is in William Peterson's text, *Population,* Macmillan, London, 1969.

The study of Vermont town meetings was made by St. Michael's College students and reported in *The Burlington Free Press* of March 13, 1969.

Richard M. Bowers wrote me on April 29, 1970, that "encouraging suicide" would be more effective than compulsory sterilization in attaining his new goal: "100 million Americans by the year 2000." He enclosed a detailed program.

For population infinity, see "Doomsday: Friday, 13 November, A.D. 2026," by Heinz von Foerster, Patricia M. Mora, Lawrence W. Amiot, *Science,* November 4, 1960.

Most of the estimates of maximum world population were in the Reuss Committee hearings, but Calhoun's is from a 1970 interview with Tom Tiede of the Newspaper Enterprise Association. For Kahn's estimate, see page 151 of *The Year 2000,* by Herman Kahn and Anthony J. Wiener, Macmillan, New York, 1967, which is a fascinating look at the future. This and other studies of the food-population problem of underdeveloped nations report the statistics which show that there has been a slight increase in food production (and also Gross National Product) per capita in all of them.

Jean Mayer, the Harvard specialist in nutrition, told the Reuss Committee that environment, not food would be the limit to population. Specialists in foreign agriculture say that the problem will not be raising food, but providing work for the millions of Asiatic farmers who will have to be displaced from the land in order to introduce efficient, machine-operated methods capable of growing enough food for all.

Preston Cloud's estimate of future power from breeder reactors is in the Reuss Committee hearings.

Estimates of biological limitations to population are made in a *Scientific American* special issue of September 1970 on the Biosphere. See especially Siegfried Singer, "Human Energy Production as a Process in the Biosphere."

Calculations of the melting of the polar icecap were made by my son-in-law, Dr. John Paul Barach, Associate Professor of Physics at Vanderbilt University.

Density of cities is from World Health Organization release for World Health Day, April 7, 1966.

Though old, a thoughtful analysis of Hong Kong's density is "Implications of Density in Hong Kong" by Robert C. Schmitt, in *The Journal of the American Institute of Planners*, August 1963.

Steubenville's shame was reported by *The Wall Street Journal* of August 7, 1970.

Chapter III

Living With Numbers

Browsing in *The Statistical Abstract of the United States* turns up all sorts of declining rates that refer to rising numbers of human beings. In spite of a vaccine, more cases of measles are reported than formerly, for instance.

Fifty and even 100-car crashes are common, hurting

more people than when traffic was lighter; a railroad accident in India kills off scores because trains are so crowded. A friend of mine who grew up on the Palos Verde peninsula, south of Los Angeles, says that there was always some oil washed up, but bathers were too few to bother about it.

Emotions, morals, and Women's Lib demands for male responsibility for contraception have exaggerated the side effects of the pill. For statistics on side effects see the Nelson committee investigation of the pill in Congress during 1970 and a series of reports in *Medical World News*. Dr. Edwin B. Astwood, Boston endocrinologist, reports that the pill is "one of the safest and most effective drugs ever developed for any purpose." It is conceded to be much safer than the pregnancy it prevents. The Food and Drug Administration estimated in 1969 that the pill caused 3 deaths in 100,000 users (*New York Times Magazine*, July 20, 1969, p. 34), far less, per dose, than most drugs. The anti-pill people retort that risk is not justified because the pill is not a drug curing a disease. You can lay off sex and be 100 percent safe.

Fifty-six thousand were killed in automobile accidents in 1969, more than the American casualties of nine years of war in Vietnam.

The actual numbers and percentages of people unemployed during the Depression, and during the 1970–1971 recession are as follows:

	LABOR FORCE	NUMBER UNEMPLOYED	% UNEMPLOYED
1930	45 million	4.3 million	8.7%
1970	80 million	4.1 million	4.9%
10/71	80 million	4.7 million	5.4%

The poor are defined, redefined, counted, and studied by age, sex, family status, and location in the Current Population Reports, Series P-60 of the Bureau of the Census. The number of poor Negro families headed by females was 683,000 in 1959 and 837,000 in 1970.

The Austrian sociologist George Simmel has pointed out that a millionaire makes a bigger splash in a city of 10,000 middle-class people than as one of 50 millionaires in a city of 500,000. Large numbers make for classifications of skill as well as prestige. Where traffic is heavy, poor drivers are a bigger danger. It may soon be necessary to classify drivers' licenses, and issue limited licenses for the young and elderly that bar them from thruways. The economics of corporate size have been scrutinized anew in connection with the merger wave of the late 1960s, few of which promised operating advantages. See "Numbers—Or Most Giants Are Happy Giants," *Forbes*, May 15, 1970.

For comparison between Tokyo and New York, I am indebted to Tokue Shibata, Professor of Urban Sociology at Tokyo Metropolitan University. Tokyo statistics are available in *Tokyo Municipal News*, a monthly journal of the Tokyo municipal government. The Tokyo yearbook is in English. I am indebted to International House in Tokyo and especially to M. Kato there for access to many Japanese officials and students who helped me gather material for my *New York* article, "What New York Can Learn from The World's Biggest City" March 16, 1970.

William Peterson discusses the many consequences of age distribution in *Population, op. cit.*

The crime figures are from the Federal Bureau of Investigation Uniform Crime Reports. The impact of changing age distribution on crime is from *Toward A Social Report*, U.S. Department of Health, Education and Welfare, 1969, p. 61.

Characteristics of newcomers are summarized under the heading "Migration," in Bernard Berelson and Gary A.

Steiner, *Human Behavior*, Harcourt Brace & World, Inc. New York, 1964.

Chapter IV

Too Crowded

Life's chilling picture is in the January 9, 1970, issue illustrating "The Problem of People Pollution."

Department store elevator waiting time forecast is made by Joseph Timan, president of Horizon Land Corp. in Tucson.

For another horror scenario of the crowded future see also Harry Karns in November 24, 1968, *Detroit News*. Much of the speculation was inspired by the working papers of the Commission on the Year 2000, published in the Summer 1967 issue of *Daedalus*. For renting a room for privacy, see Harry Kalven, Jr.'s, contribution, "The Problem of Privacy in the Year 2000."

Classic urban studies documenting the decline of social pathology with distance from the center of cities are summarized in Ralph Thomlinson, *Urban Structure: The Social and Spatial Character of Cities*, Random House, N.Y. 1969.

For Ashley Montagu's views, see collection of essays entitled *Man and Aggression* which he edited, Oxford University Press, New York, 1970.

Best account of impact of poor housing on people is in Alvin L. Schorr, *Slums and Social Insecurity*, Social Security Administration, Division of Research and Statistics, Washington, 1966.

Louis Wirth was one of the founders of urban sociology and did much of his fieldwork in the "back of the yards" where depressed stockyard workers lived in Chicago. His

"Urbanism As A Way of Life," July, 1938, *The American Journal of Sociology* is a landmark document. The quotation is from the abstract preceding the article.

A good quick historical review of U.S. population distribution policy is in *Toward Balanced Growth: Quantity with Quality*, the report of the National Goals Research Staff prepared under the direction of Daniel P. Moynihan and issued, with his usual concern for drama, on July 4, 1970. His term "policy-responsive" is quoted by Lawrence A. Mayer in "New Questions about the U.S. Population," *Fortune*, February 1971, a good summary of the 1970 Census findings.

For Nixon administration proposals to send people back to the country, see Report of the Task Force on Rural Development of March 10, 1970. The funding for plans for glamorous "new cities" to be built from scratch has since been withdrawn. Private consortiums built Columbia, Maryland, and Reston, Virginia, but the recession of 1969–1970 slowed private interest in this long-term investment.

Stewart Udall was quoted in *The New York Times* of January 16, 1970, as telling a forum at the New School for Social Research that "we have passed the optimum population level in this country." He then went on to say that 100 million people, or almost half the present population would be about the right number.

John A. Baker, U.S. Assistant Secretary of Agriculture in 1969, has many suggestions for the "rural alternative."

Herman Miller, author of *Rich Man, Poor Man*, Thomas Y. Crowell Company, New York, 1971, a lucid analysis of Census statistics, has pointed out that most of the increase in the population of the metropolitan areas was natural increase, and only one-fourth was net immigration.

The migration from the rural regions to the central city has about ended. For the long-term decline in central city densities, see Thomlinson, *op. cit.,* pp. 83–86, and Hans Blumenfeld in *Scientific American* issue on cities of September 1965. For New York, see Benjamin Chinitz in the same issue.

The Census has issued a handy booklet "Metropolitan Area Statistics" summarizing key figures by SMSAs from the Census of 1970.

The decline in Watts and Hough is reported by Dennis H. Wrong, Professor of Sociology at New York University, in "Portrait of A Decade," *New York Times Magazine,* August 2, 1970.

The New York Times Almanac for 1971 has a section "Representative American Cities" which gives a wealth of information on scores of cities so that they can be compared on such things as density, morbidity, infant mortality, educational attainment of adult population, personal income, and many other social indicators. It makes fascinating reading for anyone interested in the personality of cities.

In November 1971, the mayor's office in Newark reported that the projected college would be built on the site in the ghetto in spite of community opposition.

Campbell Gibson, Population Studies, Bureau of the Census agrees that it is quite likely that the final census tract reports, when published, will show a decline in the density in Harlem as in other ghettoes for which they now have statistics.

A good analysis of why the thin-out hurts the central cities has been made by John D. Kasarda of the University of North Carolina at the American Sociological Association meeting in 1970.

Blacks claim they are systematically undercounted in the Census because black males are most likely to be out when the census man calls, and the count is politically sensitive because it is the basis of state and Federal aid as well as representation in state legislatures and the House of Representatives. Extra care was taken with Harlem in 1970. For a scholarly report on the undercount problem, see Jacob S. Siegel, "Completeness of Coverage of the Nonwhite Population in the 1960 Census and Current Estimates, and some Implications," available from the Census Bureau on request.

The FBI reported that serious crime increased only 3 percent in the larger cities compared with 10 percent in suburban areas in the first of 1971, though there was still more crime in the central cities than in the suburbs. An ugly development in the fall of 1971 has been the effort of suburbanites to keep housing projects out of their neighborhoods. See roundup of Zoning Laws in *The New York Times* of October 10, 1971.

The New York Journal of Commerce, where I was the Burlap and Bag Editor in the Textile Department during World War II was the only place where many of the more esoteric commodity markets ever broke into print.

Chinitz estimates are in *Scientific American* issue on cities, September 1965. The population of metropolitan New York was 11,410,000 in 1970, and the farm population of the country was down to 10 million. "Bos-Wash," "Chi-Pitts," "San-San," and "Ja-Mi" are terms coined by Herman Kahn, director of the Hudson Institute and well-known student of the future.

Chapter V

Not Enough Elbowroom

Edward T. Hall, *The Hidden Dimension*, Doubleday, New York, 1966, is a fascinating book that will open your eyes to the way you move toward or away from people.

The Crowding Syndrome

William C. Loring, Jr.'s findings are reported in his "Housing Characteristics and Social Disorganization," *Social Problems*, January 3, 1956. Since then, American sociologists haven't seriously studied housing space. Rural housing is often more crowded than urban, and housing that replaces slums often has less space, but more facilities and better construction. Best summary is in Schorr, *Slums and Social Insecurity* cited in notes to Chapter 2.

Two more recent attempts to relate space have been equally inconclusive. One is a French study directed by Paul Henry Chombart de Lauwe, *Famille et Habitation*, Centre National de la Recherche Scientifique, Paris, 1960. The other is by Halliman H. Winsborough, "The Social Consequences of High Population Density," *Law and Contemporary Problems*, Winter 1966.

The importance of the neighborhood to working-class families is documented by Marc Fried and Peggy Gleicher in "The Territorial Sense in the Working Class," *Journal of the American Instiute of Planners*, XXVII, No. 4 (November 1961), pp. 305–15.

Robert Sommer summarizes the shelter experiments and other evidence on space in "Man's Proximate Environment," *Journal of Social Issues*, October, 1966.

Bruno Bettelheim, the psychiatrist, gives a perceptive first-hand report of life in a Nazi prison camp in a paper innocuously titled "Individual and Mass Behaviour in Extreme Situations," *Journal of Abnormal & Social Psychology*, October, 1943.

The survival of the slaves through the Middle Passage is described by Albert D. Biderman, Margot Louria, and Joan Bacchus, in *Historical Incidents of Extreme Overcrowding*, Washington, Bureau of Social Science Research, 1966.

Noel Barber, *The Black Hole of Calcutta*, Houghton Mifflin, Boston, 1966 is a recent account of this classic horror.

Sidney Stewart recounts the sickening American prisoner-of-war episode in *Give Us This Day*, Norton, New York, 1957.

According to a New York City housing census reported in *The New York Times* of March 11, 1971, there was an average of 2.6 persons in each rental unit in 1970, down from 3.5 in 1960. There were similar declines in the occupancy of owned dwellings. Manhattan lost 3.4 percent of its housing units between 1960 and 1970, and 15.5 percent of its white and 4.3 percent of its black population. It adds up to fewer people and a little more houseroom. The City Planning Commission finds that rising need for space is the main reason why manufacturing jobs are leaving Manhattan. They estimate that floor-area requirements for each worker are growing by one percent a year.

According to *Toward a Social Report*, U.S. Department of Health, Education, and Welfare, Washington, 1969, 16 percent of the nation's housing was "overcrowded" by more than one person per room in 1950, while in 1960 only 12 percent was overcrowded by this standard, and the housing built since 1960 should have continued the improvement. In 1966, the Tile Council of America, a trade association, reported that new tract houses averaged three times the 850 square feet of the 1947 models and that the one-bathroom house was "nearly extinct."

In 1969, Columbia University started converting double rooms in their dormitories to singles.

The woman whose husband had no place to hang his pants is quoted in Schorr, *op. cit.*, p. 13.

Edward T. Hall told the Subcommittee on Urban Affairs

of the Joint Economic Committee that trees made Washington seem less crowded, when he testified in hearings on Urban America in September 1967. Many of the principles cited come from the new discipline of spacing he calls "proxemics," or rules of closeness between people.

Robert Sommer reports the debate on windowless schools in "Man's Proximate Environment."

The 18-inch elbow-to-elbow spacing of operators at boards is one of the reasons the phone company gives for limiting the job to women. They've argued that close contact with men would bother the girls. But Paul Ehrlich and Jonathan Freedman report experiments that show women bear up under crowding better than men and tensions are less in mixed-sex crowds.

For the freedom of Samoan children to escape under the wall mats of the huts, and many other insights on human spacing, see Gerhard Rosenberg, *op. cit.*

Robert Sommer describes the territorial behavior of academics in his delightful spoof, *Expertland*, Doubleday, Garden City, 1963.

Chapter VI

The Animal Analogy

Vero Copner Wynne-Edwards's article, "Self-Regulating Systems in Populations of Animals," based on a Dec. 26, 1964, lecture at the Montreal meeting of the American Association for the Advancement of Science, appeared in *Science*, Vol. 147, pp. 1543–8, March 26, 1965. He has been Regius Professor of Natural History, Marischal College, University of Aberdeen, Aberdeen, Scotland, since 1946.

Edward S. Deevey summarized World War II rodent

research and also reviewed the history of observations of the lemmings in a highly readable article, "The Hare and the Haruspex: A Cautionary Tale," *The Yale Review*, Vol. 49, pp. 161–79, December 1959. He recalled that in an 1862 migration, lemmings actually invaded what is now the University of Oslo, apparently begging to be investigated, but that the Norwegian savants were busy and "scorned the impertinent intrusion."

Lemming observations in Alaska by Dr. Frank A. Pitelka and Dr. William B. Quay of the University of California at Berkeley and Dr. David A. Mullen of the University of San Francisco were reported by Walter Sullivan in *The New York Times*, May 7, 1969. More recently, Ola and Emily d'Aulaire report Scandinavian scientists as believing overtaxed adrenal glands responsible for demise of the lemmings. Their report in *Viikkosanomat*, a Finnish publication, was condensed in *Reader's Digest*, August, 1970, titled "The Lesson of the Lemmings."

John J. Christian was head of the animal laboratories of the Naval Medical Research Institute at Bethesda, Maryland, and as such, in Deevey's words, "commander of the Navy's rodents." In 1961, he updated his gland observations in "Phenomena Associated With Population Density" published in the Proceedings of the National Academy of Science for that year, pp. 428–449. He was then associated with the Penrose Research Laboratory, Zoological Society of Philadelphia, and the Department of Pathology, University of Pennsylvania.

Dr. John B. Calhoun, a research psychologist for the National Institute of Mental Health, coined the phrase "pathological togetherness" which his friends predict will outlive his rats. He authored "The Role of Space in Animal Sociology," *Journal of Social Issues*, Vol. 22, No. 4, 1966.

On March 29, 1971, the *Washington Post* published a lengthy account by Tom Huth of Dr. Calhoun's famous Maryland rat colony.

The fact that animals and men are similar in many respects makes possible much medical research. Dr. Maurice Lane Tainter, for 26 years research director for Sterling Drug., Inc., once explained: "Differences are very small in the functions of the organs of the common laboratory animals, such as mice, rats, rabbits, cats, dogs, and monkeys, from those of man. These animals have the same type of circulation and the same respiratory organs. . . . When they move, their muscles contract under the control of impulses sent from a central nervous system similar to that of the human in all essential particulars. . . ." This appeared in a chapter by Dr. Tainter in *Drug Research and Development*, edited by Austin Smith and Arthur D. Herrick, Revere Publishing Co., New York, 1948.

If a new drug defeats a disease in an animal, and men and animals share many diseases, it ordinarily requires only a simple weight-ratio calculation to determine the proper dosage for human beings. Still there is a vast gap between animals and men and nearly all experts on animals quickly concede this.

The 1970 Claude Bernard Science Journalism Award given by the National Society for Medical Research in the magazine field went to Morton Hunt for an article, "Man and Beast," taking issue with Lorenz, Ardrey, and Morris. It appeared in *Playboy*, July, 1970.

"Man does have an aggressive instinct," summarized Hunt, "but it is not naturally or inevitably directed to killing his own kind. He is a beast and perhaps at times the cruelest beast of all—but sometimes he is also the kindest beast of all. He is not all good and not perfectible, but he is not all bad and not wholly unchangeable or unimprovable. That is the only basis on which one can have hope for him; but it is enough."

Chapter VII

Too Rich

The best authority on the environment are the two reports of the Council on Environmental Quality set up under the National Environmental Policy Act of 1969, both entitled *Environmental Quality*. The first was transmitted to the Congress in August 1970, the second in August 1971, and they are available from the Government Printing Office. The voluminous activist literature is ably anthologized in *The Environmental Handbook* prepared for the first National Environmental Teach-in April 22, 1970, edited by Garrett de Bell, Ballantine Books, New York.

Tokue Shibata, Professor of Urban Sociology at Tokyo Metropolitan University, told me about the unexpected emergence of Japan's sewage disposal problem when I was in Tokyo in 1969. René Dubos, the microbiologist, who was for years a professor at Rockefeller University is the best authority on the growth of resistance to antibiotics. For a sample of recent medical thinking, see "The Threat Still Smoulders: New Trends in Hospital Infections," by Leighton E. Cluff, M.D. in *Medical Opinion*, May 1971.

It doesn't seem that way, but according to the summary in the *Pocket Data Book* 1971 issued by the U.S. Bureau of the Census, U.S. Government Printing Office, the average weekly earnings for nonfarm private workers kept pace with prices from 1965 to 1970. In 1970, home ownership costs were 28.5 percent higher than in 1967; medical care was up 21 percent, meals away from home, 19 percent. Between 1965 and 1970, tuition and required fees per full-time resident degree-credit student in all private colleges rose from $1,088 to $1,830, a substantial wallop to anyone's budget. For a handy, accessible overview of health care costs, see *Time*, June 7, 1971, "Health Care: Supply, Demand and Politics."

John Kenneth Galbraith explains why cleaning up the cities can't substitute for defense outlays in his chapter on the regulation of aggregate demand in *The New Industrial State*, Houghton Mifflin, Boston, 1967.

Americans concerned about the destruction of great works of art in Venice are invited to contribute to the Venice Committee of the International Fund for Monuments, Inc., 15 Gramercy Park, New York, N.Y. 10003.

According to Wayne H. Davis, in "Indian equivalents," the population of the United States is "at least four billion," *New Republic*, January 10, 1970. For paper consumption as an indicator of business cycle, see "Paper and Board Consumption Patterns and Development Trends in the OECD Countries," by Arne Sundelin, Nasbypark, Sweden, November 1, 1969, available from the American Paper Institute in New York City.

Mishan's paper, "The Spillover Enemy," is in the December 1969 issue of *Encounter*. He has become the "in" economist for American liberals to quote. His 1969 book, *Twenty-One Popular Economic Fallacies* was published by the Penguin Press, Baltimore, Md.

Cheaper by the Dozen, Thomas Y. Crowell Co., New York, 1949, is the story of how Lillian Gilbreth brought up 12 children while founding the profession of management science. It was written by her son, Frank Gilbreth, Jr.

For the theory of networks, see "Network Analysis," by Howard Frank and Ivan T. Frisch, *Scientific American*, July 1970. For the service industries, their definition, growth, productivity, and future, see Victor R. Fuchs, *The Service Economy*, National Bureau of Economic Research, New York 1968, distributed by the Columbia University Press. The disheartening lack of improvement in Manhattan transportation during the past half century, is illustrated in "The Managementality Gap," by Robert K. Mueller, in *Science Journal*, November 1968. Estimates of how the cost of municipal services per citizen rises with the size of the municipality are given in the *National Civic Review* of November 1968.

The summary generalizations about the differences between the rich and the poor are not without some exceptions, but enough evidence can be marshaled to make them suggestive. Herman P. Miller's *Rich Man, Poor Man*, Thomas Y. Crowell Co., New York, 1971, has fascinating statistics on individuals. W.W. Rostow's *The Stages of Economic Growth*, The University Press, Cambridge, 1960, has insights on what wealth means to nations, and those who have to deal with business firms soon acquire rules of thumb about the behaviour of rich and poor enterprises. The answer to F. Scott Fitzgerald's celebrated question is that the rich are *not* like us. Whether nation, firm, or individual, money makes many differences.

Chapter VIII

Too Much Talk

The word "speed-up" is documented by Ben H. Bagdikian in his fascinating book of 1971, *The Information Machines*, Harper & Row, New York.

The toilet-door study was cited by Vernon Williams, Harry Canon, and James Harding of the University of

Nebraska in their article "Learning in Residence Halls Revisited," in *The Journal of College Student Personnel*, September 1968, pp. 330–331.

In 1967 the number of "non-published" or private numbers in the Bell Telephone System was 4,620,000; in 1968 the count had risen to 5,215,000 and in 1969 the total was 5,766,000. This 1969 figure equaled 10.5 percent of the telephones associated with basic service in the Bell System.

I made a study on how company presidents deal with their voluminous mail and discovered that they have many devices for making short shrift of it. The study was entitled "The Communications Explosion in the President's Office," September-October, 1969, and is available from the Presidents Association of the American Management Association, New York City.

The intellectuals fighting unwanted mail were Van R. Potter, see letter to *Science Magazine*, November 21, 1969; and Roger C. Staples, see *Time* Magazine, September 19, 1969, p. 24.

Alvin Toffler has graphically documented the speed of change in *Future Shock*, Random House, New York, 1970.

Sheer information is, of course, just as helpful to the underworld as it is to anyone else. A television commercial invites the audience to "come and get" a bargain, giving the address of the store, and a thief takes the invitation all too literally. My husband, Tom Mahoney, was inordinately flattered when a copy of his book, *The Story of Jewelry*, was found in the room of a master jewel thief who had succeeded in lifting some celebrated ice from the American Museum of Natural History.

For the transistor radio and Middle East politics, see Henry M. Boettinger in his "Big Gap in Economic Theory," *Harvard Business Review*, July-August, 1967, p. 56.

On speed reading, see Lawrence Galton's article in

The New York Times Magazine, August 27, 1961, entitled "2,000 W.P.M.—But Is It Reading?"

Chapter IX

The Arithmetic of Growth

The blackout year was a watershed. Consumer prices rose less than 1.5 percent per year during 1960–1965, but 4.3 percent a year between 1965 and 1970, *Pocket Data Book USA* 1971, p. 12. Stockmarket volume took off in 1965, too.

Houseroom and birth rate may be directly related. Ulla Olin, a demographer on the staff of the United Nations, points out that fertility is traditionally higher in rural areas than in cities. She thinks that the postwar baby boom was bigger in the United States than in her native Sweden because our growing families move to the suburbs where there is a room for children, while Swedish families are housed in apartments. Limited housing space sharply curbs the size of families in Japan and the Soviet Union. During the 1950s, Federally financed mortgage insurance made houseroom relatively cheaper than alternative uses of money which preclude babies. Perusal of birth rates and densities of states shows high birth rates in the wide open spaces.

There has been so much misunderstanding about the underdeveloped countries that it is worth citing the evidence that "overpopulation" is not so much the cause of poverty as it is the result of rising wealth. Richard A. Easterlin, a specialist in population studies now at the University of Pennsylvania, studied 37 developing nations and reports that: "the data for the period since 1957–1958, when population growth rates in most of these countries are among the highest ever experienced, show that per capita income has generally increased. Moreover, if India, where long-term estimates are available, is representative, it is likely that in a number of cases these rates of economic growth are noticeably higher than earlier in the century. Thus, accelerating population growth in recent years has not generally precluded positive per capita income growth, and has perhaps even been accompanied by accelerated income growth." His paper, "Effects of Population Growth on the Economic Development of Developing Countries," is in *The Annals of the American Academy of Political and Social Sciences,* January 1967.

For the "Peanut Principle" I am indebted to Donald O. Hebb, the psychologist of perception, who wrestles with the salted-peanut problem in his monograph *The Organization of Behavior: A Neuropsychological Theory,* John Wiley, New York, 1949. "A lack of food cannot be increased by eating something, and stomach contractions are stopped by chewing and swallowing," he says on page 200. "If, however, we consider hunger to be neither a particular condition of the body, nor a set of sensations from the stomach, but an organized neural activity that can be aroused (like any other conceptual process) in several ways, the puzzle disappears." He explains the counterproductive appetite for peanuts by treating hunger as an addiction. Dieters would agree!

The arithmetic of encounters is a consideration for traffic engineers. It is stated by Joseph J. Spengler in his article "Population, Housing, and Habitat," *op. cit.*

Emile Durkheim, the French sociologist, came close to the encounter theory of wealth. He pointed out that "dynamic" or "moral density" is what brings about division of labor, and population density is important because it facilitates social intercourse. See p. 262 of his "On the Division of Labor in Society," Macmillan, New York, 1933.

Notes

For the incredible efficiency of Manhattan in providing opportunities for face-to-face encounters, see Stanley Milgram, "The Experience of Living in Cities," *Science*, March 13, 1970.

Richard L. Meier, now Professor of Environmental Design at the University of California at Berkeley, has suggested that an estimate of the number of hours a day people spend in various activities, plus an estimate of the bits per minute received in each kind of activity could be used to measure the flow of information in a community. Reading is "information-rich" because it allows the individual to take in 1500 bits a minute; "observation of the environment" is information-poor because it may mean an input of only 10 bits a minute. In "The Metropolis As A Transaction-Minimizing System," *Daedalus*, Fall, 1968, he added up estimates of "social transactions" such as the number of checks and credit-card payments, purchases, trips, mail, shipments, newspapers read, and proposed using this flow as an accurate indicator of social and economic health.

Land values corroborate the notion that cities grow rich because they are places where people go to exchange information. Land in the Ginza, Tokyo, and on the waterfront at Hong Kong is more valuable per square foot than land in the business district of Manhattan.

We've just been through a lush period of economic growth. Gross National Product per capita was $1877, $2408, $2788, and $3520 in 1950, 1955, 1960 and 1965 respectively, according to the *Pocket Data Books* for 1969 and 1971.

In *Asian Drama*, Gunnar Myrdal points out that the Indians are relatively immobile by our standard of migration (p. 437) and that colonial rule kept Indians isolated from each other (p. 451). Ben H. Bagdikian's *The Information Machine*, Harper & Row, New York, 1971, is an invaluable source on the information speed-up. For my list of

311

innovations I am indebted to the monumental study prepared for the National Commission of Technology, Automàtion and Economic Progress by Lynn Frank, of 1965, entitled *An Investigation of the Rate of Development and Diffusion of Technology in our Modern Industrial Society*, pp. 37–69. For an interesting list of dates of inventions and dissemination of communications advances, see pp. 11–69. The change in price and volume of air travel, phone calls, and mailings are available to anyone willing to use a sharp pencil on the tables in the *Statistical Abstract of the United States*.

For the rising role of communications in the GNP, see Fritz Machlup, *The Production and Distribution of Knowledge in the United States*, Princeton University Press, Princeton, 1962.

For the library pinch, I'm indebted to information from Walter Curley, of Arthur D. Little Inc., and Edward M. Heiliger of Kent State University. See also Carl F. J. Overhage, "Science Libraries: Prospects and Problems," *Science*, February 17, 1967. The phenomenal growth of the lethal copy-machine is documented in *Business Week*, October 12, 1968. The wonders of computers are lovingly recorded in the business press.

The Monsanto Company's income tax return is cited by Robert K. Mueller, in "The Managementality Gap," *op. cit.*

The Wall Street speed-up is documented in statistics easily available from The New York Stock Exchange and the American Exchange in New York City. Officials of both helped educate me in the mysteries of the back office. In 1969 I talked with Tony Weichel of Goodbody & Company, one of the first brokerage houses to use computers on a large scale; Tony Miles of the Trade and Markets department of the Securities & Exchange Commission; Ted Hasin, vice president in charge of the Autonetics Division of North American Rockwell; Leon Kendall of the Association of Stock Exchange Firms, and others concerned with the improving and functioning of the exchanges. Two *Fortune* articles by Carol J. Loomis, "Big Board, Big Volume, Big Trouble," May 1968, and "They're Tearing Up Wall Street," August 1, 1969, tell the story. Finally, I am indebted to Faye Henle, author of *350 New Ways To Make Your Money Grow*, for checking facts on the Wall Street speed-up.

Chapter X

The Slowdown

The slowdown of the birth rate has been avidly studied by demographers and economists. The National Center for Health Statistics in Washington, D.C., has the latest statistics and studies, and anyone who wants to understand the demographic terms and techniques should get out William Peterson, *Population*, Macmillan, London, 1969. *Fortune* did a good, early job of predicting the slowdown in "Why the U.S. Population Isn't Exploding," April, 1967.

The drop in family size expectations is from a current population survey of the Census, Series P-20, No. 232, February 1972.

On smaller families, Margaret Mead has pointed out that in the world today, a higher ratio of adult-time per child is needed to rear children.

Leonard Silk, *The World of Economics*, McGraw-Hill, New York, 1969, is a good introduction to economic concepts for those who don't normally think in economic terms. He explained many things to me.

For the economics of time, see Gary S. Becker, "A Theory of the Allocation of Time," *The Economic Journal*,

September 1965, and a fascinating book by a Swedish economist, Staffan B. Linder, *The Harried Leisure Class*, Columbia Press, New York and London, 1970.

Victor R. Fuchs, *op. cit.*, has documented the increase in the service sector of the GNP. The most conscientious attempt to reconstruct the GNP of past times for a realistic comparison is "Production of Goods and Services: The Measurement of Economic Growth," by Arnold W. Sametz in *Indicators of Social Change: Concepts and Measurements*, edited by Eleanor B. Sheldon and Wilbert E. Moore, New York, Russell Sage Foundation, 1968.

The most perceptive report on the impact of growth on creative activity is Derek J. de Solla Price, *Little Science, Big Science*, Columbia University Press, New York and London, 1963. Writing at the height of the science boom, he explained why returns would diminish.

Peter F. Drucker lucidly rounds up the outlook for slower growth and its social consequences in "The Surprising Seventies: Why the Young Will Soon Find Themselves Concerned with Issues That They Don't Expect," *Harper's Magazine*, July 1971.

The decade which was to have created abundance for all, whimpered out in what was variously called a "pause," a "recedence," a "slope," an "episode," and finally, in the fall of 1971, a conceded "recession."

Chapter XI

Makeshifts: Shrink, Share, Queue, Move . . . and Cut

Applications of share and queue to crowded golf courses were described by Leslie Lieber in "How to Cure Golf's Creeping Paralysis," *This Week Magazine* May 11, 1969, also Richard D. James, "A Pitch for the Kids: New,

Short Golf Links Are for Youths Only," *Wall Street Journal,* April 19, 1969.

Queuing and the other strategies of dealing with overload were observed by Professor Richard L. Meier in a big university library. He discussed them in "Information Input Overload: Features of Growth in Communications-oriented Institutions," presented at the Colloquium on The Economics of Information, sponsored by the American Economic Association at the December 26, 1961, meeting of the American Association for the Advancement of Science.

For a general discussion of queuing and how to deal with it, see Martin A. Leibowitz, "Queues," *Scientific American,* August 1968. He traces queuing theory to A. K. Erlang who began to study telephone-service congestion for the Copenhagen Telephone Company in 1908.

The Army's change from serial to Social Security numbers was reported by *The New York Times,* July 2, 1969.

For accounts of Dove Data Device see *Library Journal,* November 1, 1966, p. 5352, and May 15, 1967, p. 1907. The University of Toronto Press on January 1, 1971 began to issue all of its books simultaneously in conventional form and microfiche. See Ian Montagnes, "Publishing The Pre-Shrunk," *Publishers' Weekly,* November 22, 1971.

Rubens's ability to deal with so much is recorded in Ruth S. Magurn's, *The Letters of Peter Paul Rubens,* Harvard University Press, Cambridge, Massachusetts, 1955.

For data on Calcutta, I am indebted to Nirmal Kumar Bose, a Calcutta-born anthropologist. See his "Calcutta: A Premature Metropolis," *Scientific American,* September, 1965.

Hutterite information is principally from S. C. Lee and Audrey Brattrud, "Marriage Under a Monastic Mode of Life: A Preliminary Report on the Hutterite Family in South Dakota," *Journal of Marriage and the Family,* XXIX, No. 3,

The Crowding Syndrome

August, 1967, pp. 512–20. The authors studied 25 Hutterite colonies.

Chapter XII

How To Think Big

Development of the electronic digital computer can be traced to research and development support provided by the United States Army Ordnance Corps during the wartime years of the early 1940s. Work under Ordnance Corps contracts proceeded at the University of Pennsylvania, the Institute for Advanced Study at Princeton, and the University of Illinois. Under the direction of Dr. John Mauchley and Dr. J. Presper Eckert, these efforts led to the Electronic Numerical Integrator and Computer (ENIAC), the world's first electronic digital computer.

Then came the Electronic Discrete Variable Automatic Computer (EDVAC); the Institute for Advanced Study Computer (IASC); and the Ordnance Variable Automatic Computer (ORDVAC). The early ENIAC and EDVAC were used to solve ballistic equations, prepare bombing and firing tables, solve fire-control problems, and a host of related military scientific tasks.

George A. Miller wrote about man's shortcomings as a communications channel in *The Psychology of Communication*, Penguin, Baltimore, 1967, p. 50. He joined the Rockefeller University faculty in 1968 as Professor of Experimental Psychology.

For the application of information theory to the behavior of individuals and social institutions, see James G. Miller, "Psychological Aspects of Communications Overloads," *International Psychiatry Clinics: Communication in Clinical Practice*, edited by R. W. Waggoner and D. J. Clark, Little,

Brown and Co., Boston, 1964, pp. 201–21. See also Richard L. Meier, "Living With the Coming Urban Technology," in *Man and The Modern City*, edited by Elizabeth Geen, Jeanne R. Lowe, and Kenneth Walker, University of Pittsburgh Press, Pittsburgh, 1963, pp. 59–70.

The qualities of the number seven are discussed by George A. Miller in "The Magical Number Seven, Plus or Minus Two: Some Limits on Our Capacity for Processing Information." *The Psychological Review*, March 1956, pp. 81–97.

For a summary of the recent thinking of Jerome Bruner and other psychologists, see Tom Alexander, "Psychologists Are Rediscovering the Mind," *Fortune*, November 1970. Another useful article is by D. E. Broadbent, "Information Processing in the Nervous System," *Science*, October 22, 1965, pp. 457–62.

Believe it or not, the pupils of eyes of female subjects widen an average of 20 percent in viewing nude males, while the pupils of male eyes widen only about 18 percent when viewing nude females, according to experiments reported by Eckhard H. Hess and James Polt, "Pupil Size as Related to Interest Value of Visual Stimuli," *Science*, 132, 1960, pp. 349–50.

Among the educators who urge that we spend as much time thinking as reading is Dr. James E. McClellan of Syracuse University.

Sherlock Holmes rebuffed Dr. Watson about the Copernican Theory in "A Study in Scarlet." See Sir Arthur Conan Doyle, *The Complete Sherlock Holmes*, Doubleday, Garden City, N.Y., 1938, p. 21.

"If there is background noise of any sort, such as traffic noise, ventilating systems, etc., it becomes more and more difficult to hear speech, music, etc., that we may wish to hear, enjoy or understand," writes Dr. Hallowell Davis,

Central Institute for the Deaf, St. Louis, Mo., in a personal communication. "We know very well just how much noise it takes to render speech unintelligible.

"It is a matter of the amount of acoustic energy at frequencies corresponding to the frequencies of human speech. When the speech and the noise are at about the same intensity, the listening is difficult and requires more and more effort. . . . The more closely the competing messages resemble the voice to which we wish to listen, the more difficult does the task become. Elderly people and people with 'nerve deafness' have particular difficulty in the situation."

See also D. E. Broadbent, "Effect of Noise on an 'Intellectual' Task," *The Journal of the Acoustical Society of America*, September, 1958, pp. 824–27, and David H. Boggs and J. Richard Simon, University of Iowa, "Differential Effect of Noise on Tasks of Varying Complexity," *Journal of Applied Psychology*, 52:2, April, 1968, pp. 148–53.

Chapter XIII

Toward Human Scale

Berelson and Steiner, *Human Behavior*, Harcourt, Brace & World, Inc., New York, 1964, is the quickest reference to the extensive literature on sensory deprivation, and in-dustrial-engineering studies of the influence of conversation and music in reducing boredom and the errors it causes.

The quote from James G. Miller comes from "Living Systems: Basic Concepts," *Behavioral Science*, July 1965, section 5.6, titled Pathology.

The Cornell study of executives in the Bell system was headed by Dr. Lawrence E. Hinkle, Jr., Head of the Division of Human Ecology of the Departments of Medicine and Psychiatry at Cornell University Medical College, New York, and reported at the American College of Physicians meeting in Boston on April 2, 1968. The Cobb study is reported in a roundup on stress in *Psychology Today*, September 1969.

The stress on air traffic controllers was an issue in their "sick out" of 1970 in New York. Federal Aviation Administration studies are summarized in Robert Lindsey, "On the Hottest Spot in Aviation," *New York Times Magazine*, September 14, 1969.

My daughter, Carol Barach, and I reported new findings on how babies learn to talk in *Woman's Day*, September 1969. Carol's study of her son helped confirm the importance of dialogue in learning.

The notion that the right size is the one that facilitates communication is a natural corollary of Meier's communications theory of urban growth set forth in an earlier chapter.

The concept of the primary group was defined by Charles Horton Cooley in his early textbook, *Social Organization*, New York, 1909. According to Cooley, primary groups are "those characterized by intimate face-to-face association and cooperation . . . the family, the play group of children, and the neighborhood of community group of elders," p. 24. Berelson and Steiner indicate major works on primary groups since. The study on British schoolchildren is reported in *Nature*, March 26, 1966.

Constantinos A. Doxiadis is an architect-planner and president of Doxiadis Associates, Athens, Greece, and Washington, D.C. His practice is international, and he is one of the truly charismatic architect-planner-utopians in the tradition of Frank Lloyd Wright. Kenzo Tange of Japan is another. All are sensitive to the influence of space on social institutions. For an introduction to the thinking of Doxiadis, see his "Ekistics, the Science of Human Settlements", *Science,* October 23, 1970.

The study of the Wehrmacht by Edward A. Shils and Morris Janowitz, is in *Public Opinion Quarterly,* Summer 1948.

In *Fortune,* November 1954, William H. Whyte, Jr., reported the emergence of neighborhood influence-groups in his persuasive article, "The Web of Word of Mouth." Whyte counted air-conditioner boxes visible from the air in Philadelphia row-houses to show how new products really get accepted.

Warren G. Bennis, president of the University of Cincinnati, has elaborated the concept of the ad hoc task force in organization planning. See his book *The Temporary Society,* with Philip E. Slater, Harper & Row, New York 1968.

Chapter XIV

How To Think New

James G. Miller, Lecturer, Department of Psychiatry and Behavioral Science, Johns Hopkins School of Medicine and editor of *Behavioral Science,* defines a system as "a set of interacting units with relationships among them." In his monograph, *Living Systems,* to be published by John Wiley & Sons in 1973, he discusses a general systems behavior theory at seven levels: "cell, organ, organism, group, organization, society, and supranational system." He identifies organizational similarities between these levels.

Dr. Herbert Brinberg, American Can Co. economist, predicts housewives will dial grocery orders to warehouses in

1987. Jim Bishop reported his prophecies in the *Detroit News* of June 16, 1967.

A hypothetical personal transit system that would provide the speed and privacy of the automobile with the advantages of rapid transit was described by William F. Hamilton II and Dana K. Nance in "Systems Analysis of Urban Transportation," *Scientific American*, July, 1969.

"It is historically true that in the American psychology, the city has always been a basically suspect institution," wrote Mayor John V. Lindsay of New York in "Why Americans Don't Like Cities," *New York*, March 23, 1970, and his book, *The City*, W.W. Norton & Co., Inc., New York, 1970. Criticism of cities from Thomas Jefferson to Frank Lloyd Wright is summarized by Morton and Lucia White in *The Intellectual Versus the City*, Harvard University Press, 1962, and Mentor Books, New York, 1964.

Initiated as part of an effort to appraise the social impact of outer space exploration, *Social Indicators*, edited by Raymond A. Bauer, the M.I.T. Press, Cambridge, Massachusetts, 1966, was hailed as "a major contribution to man's efforts to find out where he has been, where he is, and where he is going." That year President Johnson asked John W. Gardner, then Secretary of Health, Education, and Welfare, to seek better ways to chart social progress.

He set up a 43-member Panel on Social Indicators under the leadership of Mrs. Alice M. Rivlin, Assistant Secretary for Planning and Evaluation; Daniel Bell, Columbia University; and William Gorham, Urban Institute. In 1969, Mrs. Rivlin's office produced *Toward A Social Report*, a 100-page study of aspects of quality of life such as health and illness; social mobility; the physical environment; income and poverty; public order and safety; learning, science, and art; participation and alienation.

For the possible alternative choices of the poor and the public, I am indebted to Dr. Ronald H. Coase of the University of Chicago Law School, a disciple of Dr. Friedman.

The San Francisco way of life is admiringly analyzed by social scientists in *Culture and Civility in San Francisco*, edited by Howard S. Becker, Aldine Publishing Co., Chicago, 1971.

Of 50,000 Americans in need of a kidney transplant or a kidney machine in 1971, only 6700, or 14 percent, had them, according to Dr. Belding H. Scribner, *The New York Times*, October 24, 1971. Advent of organ transplants stirred interest in the ethical and medical problems of death. *On Death and Dying* by Dr. Elisabeth K. Ross, a noted Swiss-American psychiatrist, was published by Macmillan in 1969. HEW later published a 60-page *Selected Bibliography on Death and Dying* compiled by Joel J. Vernick, National Institute of Child Health and Human Development.

Carl Bakal dramatically described America's gun problem in *The Right to Bear Arms*, McGraw-Hill, New York, 1966.

NASA lists the 2500 spin-off benefits, some patented and available for licensing. An issue of the *UNESCO Courier*, March, 1970, was devoted to them. See also Lester David, "What We're Getting from Space Science," *American Legion Magazine*, May 1970, and Wernher von Braun, "How the Space Program Is Helping You," *Parade*, December 5, 1971, in the *Washington Post, Boston Globe, Chicago Sun-Times, Detroit Free Press* and other newspapers.

Chapter XV

The Case for Optimism

Napoleon considered Larrey the most virtuous man he had known and bequeathed him 100,000 francs. Larrey recorded his experiences in his four-volume *Mémoires de Médecine Militaire*, Paris, 1812–1817. An English translation by John C. Mercer, a Virginia medical student, was published as *Surgical Memoirs of the Campaigns of Russia, Germany and France*, Philadelphia, 1832. See also John E. Ransom, "Baron Larrey—Father of Ambulance Service," *Ciba Symposia*, February, 1947.

Blood transfusion is the best and sometimes the only treatment for serious injury and certain grave medical conditions. As of 1972 the American Association of Blood Banks estimated that 7,000,000 pints a year are required for surgery and therapy by U.S. hospitals. For war background see *Doctors at War*, edited by Morris Fishbein, Dutton, New York, 1945, and Brig. Gen. Douglas B. Kendrick, *Blood Program in World War II*, Office of Surgeon General, Washington, D.C., 1964.

For war development of penicillin see J. D. Ratcliff, *Yellow Magic*, Random House, New York, 1945, and Tom Mahoney, *The Merchants of Life*, Harper, New York, 1959, pp. 12–14, 237–245.

For war birth of radar and atom bomb, see Vannevar Bush, *Modern Arms and Free Men*, Simon and Schuster, New York, 1949; William L. Laurence, *Men and Atoms*, Simon and Schuster, New York, 1959, and many other works.

For service and gains of women see Caroline Bird, *Born Female*, David McKay, New York, 1968 and 1970, pp. 35–41.

Basic sources on the Irish famine are R. N. Salaman, *The History and Social Influence of the Potato*, University Press, Cambridge, 1949, and K. H. Connell, *The Population of Ireland, 1750–1845*, Clarendon Press, Oxford, 1950. It is also analyzed in Marston Bates, *The Prevalence of People*, Scribner's, New York, 1955. His chapter, "Role of War, Famine, and Disease in Controlling Population," is included in *Population in Perspective*, edited by Louise B. Young,

Oxford University Press, New York, 1968. Marston Bates is Professor of Zoology at the University of Michigan.

John Snow reported the Broad Street pump in a classic medical paper, "On the Mode of Communication of Cholera." It is in *Great Adventures in Medicine*, edited by Samuel Rapport and Helen Wright, Dial Press, New York, pp. 214–220.

Professor Jay Forrester of Massachusetts Institute of Technology, discussed ghetto housing in "Counterintuitive Behavior of Social Systems," *Technology Review*, January, 1971. "The United States," he wrote, "is running away from its long-term threats by trying to relieve social pressures as they arise. But if we persist in treating only the systems and not the causes, the result will be to increase the magnitude of the ultimate threat and reduce our capability to respond when we no longer have space to flee. . . . The greatest challenge now is how to handle the transition from growth into equilibrium." His graphs indicating the cuts he believes necessary in birth rate, pollution, food production, and other factors have been the subject of wide comment including David C. Anderson, "Mr. Forrester's Terrible Computer," *Wall Street Journal*, September 28, 1971.

Revolutions seem to bring about basic changes, but closer study discloses that they simply punctuate an evolution that has been going on for some time. They are an expression rather than a cause of break with the past. Revolutions lack the external compulsion that forces people to think new. Wars are a different story. Even when undertaken by dictators to perpetuate themselves, or by expansionist nationalists, they are an external discipline which impels individuals to put out extra effort.

Index

Index

DATE DUE

new book Aug 26-74	MAR 30 '81		
NOV 14 '74	APR 16 '83		
NOV 28 '74	NOV 3 '82		
DEC 12 '74	NOV 30 '95		
FEB 11 '75			
APR 30 '75			
JAN 14 '76			
JUL 14 '76			
NOV 16 '76			
APR 3 '77			
APR 18 '77 pd			
MAY 4 '77			
APR 4 '78			
APR 18			
APR 29 '78			
DEC 11 '79			
FEB 23 '81			
MAR 16 '81			PRINTED IN U.S.A.